Time It!

2nd Edition

Marg Melanson
Professor
Office Administration Division
Seneca College of Applied Arts and Technology
North York, Ontario

Copp Clark Pitman Ltd.
A Longman Company
Toronto

ISBN 0-7730-5210-0

Editing/Carol Ring, Sheila Fletcher
Design/Linda Hosso and Patti Brown
Cover/Steve MacEachern
Typesetting/Marg Melanson
Printing and binding/Quebecor Printing Inc.

Canadian Cataloguing in Publication Data
Melanson, Marg, date
Time it!

2nd ed.
Includes index.
ISBN 0-7730-5210-0

1. Typewriting – Problems, exercises, etc.
2. Electronic data processing – Keyboarding – Problems, exercises, etc. I. Ring, Carol. II. Fletcher, Sheila. III. Title.

Z49.M45 1992   652.3'07   C92-093684-9

Copp Clark Pitman Ltd.
2775 Matheson Blvd. East
Mississauga, Ontario
L4W 4P7

Printed and bound in Canada

11 12 DPC 05 04 03 02

Acknowledgments

Many thanks to the following authors and publishers who have given permission for the adaptation of their material in the pieces listed below. Special thanks to my sister Ann Thornton and editor Sheila Fletcher for their significant story contributions.

Badham, Michael
   HANK GOT CUT and HANK GOT EVEN Adapted from "Herbert" by Michael Badham, published in *The Country Side Magazine*, Winter 1991, Terra Cotta, Canada.

Baker, Sandy
   PARACHUTING THE FIRST TIME Adapted from "I can not think ...." by Sandy Baker, Toronto, Canada.

Banks, Joan Brix
   VINE GIANT Adapted from "The Mile-a-Minute Vine" by Joan Brix Banks from *Ranger Rick's Nature Magazine*, July 1980, Washington, U.S.A.

Berton, Pierre
   BILLY BISHOP Adapted from "Billy Bishop: The Lone Hawk" by Pierre Berton, *My Country*, used by permission of The Canadian Publishers, McClelland and Stewart Limited, Toronto, Canada.

Canadian Government
   HOME INSULATION Adapted from "Highlights from the History of Canadian Insulation" leaflet distributed by Energy, Mines and Resources Canada. Reproduced by permission of the Minister of Supply and Services Canada.

Churchill, Sir Winston
   IN THE WORDS OF SIR WINSTON Adapted from *A History of the English Speaking Peoples* by Sir Winston Churchill, used by permission of The Canadian Publishers, McClelland and Stewart Limited, Toronto, Canada.

Creative Landscaping
   LANDSCAPING Adapted from "Ideas in Landscaping" by Creative Landscaping published in *The Country Side Magazine*, Summer 1991, Terra Cotta, Canada.

Cunnington, Joan
   MARTHA SEEKS EMPLOYMENT and MARTHA'S JOB INTERVIEW Adapted from "You're Not Going to Believe This, But ..." by Joan Cunnington, Toronto, Canada.

Elliott, Marion
   OFFICE OF THE FUTURE Adapted from a report by Marion Elliott, Toronto, Canada.

Fletcher, Sheila
   BUSINESS CONFERENCES Adapted from "Business Conferences" by Sheila Fletcher, Hamilton, Canada.
   CAR IN THE FAMILY and CAR OF MY OWN Adapted from "My Love Affair" by Sheila Fletcher, Hamilton, Canada.
   LUMP IN MY THROAT Adapted from "A Life Turned Upside Down" by Sheila Fletcher, Hamilton, Canada.

NEW COUNTRY Adapted from "A New Land" by Sheila Fletcher, Hamilton, Canada.

PRINCESS PASSING Adapted from "The Day I Saw the Princess" by Sheila Fletcher, Hamilton, Canada.

ROYAL ENCOUNTER Adapted from "More Brushes with Royalty" by Sheila Fletcher, Hamilton, Canada.

Holliday, Jon
OPERA Adapted from "A Too Comic Opera" by Jon Holliday, *WineMine, A First Anthology*, edited by Anthony Hogg, published by Souvenir Press. By permission of Peter Dominic Publications, Harlow, England.

Kemp, Murdina
CHILDHOOD Adapted from "My childhood days ...." by Murdina Kemp, London, Canada.

EPPY Adapted from a story told by Murdina Kemp, London, Canada.

Kemp, Ryan
MAGLOR Adapted from the preface of an untitled book by Ryan Kemp, Toronto, Canada.

Kipness, Jean
ON TIME Adapted and reprinted from "Just In Time" by Jean Kipness, published in *World of Work*, with permission of Webster/McGraw-Hill, New York, U.S.A.

Kucharski, Joyce
NEW WORLD Adapted from "It Happened One Day" by Joyce Kucharski, Toronto, Canada.

Leacock, Stephen
HUMOUR Adapted from "Humour As I See It" by Stephen Leacock, *Leacock Roundabout*, used by permission of The Canadian Publishers, McClelland and Stewart Limited, Toronto, Canada.

MOTHER'S DAY Adapted from "How We Kept Mother's Day" by Stephen Leacock, *Leacock Roundabout*, used by permission of The Canadian Publishers, McClelland and Stewart Limited, Toronto, Canada.

SMITH'S HOTEL Adapted from "The Hostelry of Mr. Smith" by Stephen Leacock, *Sunshine Sketches of a Little Town*, used by permission of The Canadian Publishers, McClelland and Stewart Limited, Toronto, Canada.

SPRING Adapted from "First Call for Spring" by Stephen Leacock, *Leacock Roundabout*, used by permission of The Canadian Publishers, McClelland and Stewart Limited, Toronto, Canada.

Macdonald, John
NULLARBOR PLAIN Adapted from "I often thought ...." by John Macdonald, Melbourne, Australia.

McNulty, Velma
MOTHER'S LITTLE HELPER Adapted from "Mother's Little Helper" by Velma McNulty, Schomberg, Canada.

WHY ME? Adapted from "Why Me" by Velma McNulty, Schomberg, Canada.

Meschino, Dr. James P.
BACK TALK Adapted from "Talk Back" by Dr. James P. Meschino, published in *Ricky McMountain Buyer's Guide*, Jan./Feb. 1992. Toronto, Canada.

Money, Dr. Herbert
DISASTER Adapted from "The Ranrajirca Disaster" by Dr. Herbert Money and Mrs. Netta Money, Christchurch, New Zealand.

REVOLUTION Adapted from "My First Revolution" by Dr. Herbert Money, Christchurch, New Zealand.

Olsen, Selena
METAMORPHOSIS Adapted from an untitled story by Selena Olsen, Toronto, Canada.

Ontario Science Centre
ROBOTS Adapted from "Men of Steel?" from *Newscience*, October 1982, published by the Ontario Science Centre, Toronto, Canada.

Petersen, Susan
HOMEMAKER Adapted from a letter by Susan Petersen, published in *Homemakers Magazine*, October 1980, Toronto, Canada.

Ring, Dr. W. A.
INUIT ART Adapted from "Eskimo Art ...." by Dr. W. A. Ring, St. John's, Canada.

QUILTING Adapted from "Quilting ...." by Dr. W. A. Ring, St. John's, Canada.

Selick, Karen
YOUR WILL Adapted from "Planning Your Will" by Karen Selick, LL.B, published in The Canadian Money Saver, Volume 6, Number 7, Bath, Canada.

Soriano, Zilla
SKIING Adapted from "To Ski or Not to Ski" by Zilla Soriano, Toronto, Canada.

Tanner, Rosemary
SMALL TOWN LIFE Adapted from "Small Town Life" by Rosemary Tanner, published in *The Country Side Magazine*, Summer 1991, Terra Cotta, Canada.

Thompson, Tommy
OTHER SIDE OF THE WINDOW Adapted from "Message to Members" by Tommy Thompson, *Trellis*, January 1983, published by the Civic Garden Centre, Toronto, Canada.

Thornton, Ann
COUNTRY MOUSE Adapted from "The little country mouse ...." by Ann Thornton, London, Canada.

HOGS Adapted from "The hog ...." by Ann Thornton, London, Canada.

HOUSEHOLD SCIENCE Adapted from "The Family Studies classroom ...." by Ann Thornton, London, Canada.

LIGHTNING AND THUNDER Adapted from "Lightning is ...." by Ann Thornton, London, Canada.

MUSICAL TRAINING Adapted from "All Children ...." by Ann Thornton, London, Canada.

SALT Adapted from "The chemical compound ...." by Ann Thornton, London, Canada.

VIOLIN – FIRST STRING and VIOLIN – HISTORY AND CARE Adapted from "The Violin - Queen of Instruments" by Ann Thornton, London, Canada.

Vanstone, Kay
EXERCISE NEEDED and LETTER WRITING Adapted from *Develop Your English Skills* by Kay Vanstone, published by Copp Clark Pitman, Toronto, Canada.

Winter, Steve
INSURANCE VIDEO Adapted from "Insurance Video: Better Than a Written Inventory" by Steve Winter, published in the *Canadian Money Saver*, Volume 6, Number 7, Bath, Canada.

Worthington, Peter
HORNETS' NEST Adapted from "The Story of Peter and the Wasps" by Peter Worthington, published in *The Country Side Magazine*, Winter 1991, Terra Cotta, Canada.

Table of Contents

Preface

Ever since the first typewriter invaded the office, employers have been using keyboarding speed as the major measurement of keyboarding skills. Because employers demand adequate speeds from keyboard operators, timed testing of speed/accuracy achievements is of prime and increasing concern to educational institutions.

It has been shown that students perform best when using an abundance of varied and interesting materials. With the addition of thirty timed writings in this second edition, *Time It!* certainly provides this. As well, the first fifteen timed writings in each difficulty level are speed scored and paced so that they may also be used for speed/accuracy building.

Part 1 ▪ Warm-up Drills

Timings usually benefit from being preceded by a five- or ten-minute warm-up. It's important that the warm-up have specific purpose, rather than being aimless keying. The warm-up drills in *Time It!* provide a mini, self-monitored, skill-building program.

Part 1 comprises 83 warm-up drills. Each drill contains three lines: an easy line for speed, a variable line for building proficiency on a specific element, and a line of challenging difficulty for reinforcing accuracy.

The syllabic intensity (SI) of easy lines progresses in difficulty from 1.00 SI to 1.28 SI. The challenging lines progress from 1.55 SI to 1.90 SI.

All lines are 70 characters long.

Part 2 ▪ Timed Writings

Part 2 comprises 145 timed writings. The content of these writings covers a broad range of topics and stories that students will find interesting and often humorous.

Students are not expected to key the titles of the writings as they have not been included in the word counts. The format used for keying such elements as dashes and ellipses is that which is most compatible with the word wraparound feature found on most computerized equipment. Accents have been omitted from words of foreign derivation to avoid confusing students as to how to handle them.

Three difficulty levels are provided for as follows:

Easy Copy

There are 30 easy (1.20 SI – 1.30 SI) timed writings for use as timed tests. The first fifteen easy writings may also be used for building speed/accuracy, as they are speed scored and paced for each minute. Speeds start at 28 gross words per minute (gwpm) and increase four words with each timing up to 100 gwpm.

Average Copy

There are 85 average (1.35 SI – 1.45 SI) timed writings for use as timed tests. The first fifteen average writings may also be used for building speed/accuracy, as they are speed scored and paced for each minute. Speeds start at 28 gwpm and increase four words with each timing up to 100 gwpm.

Challenging Copy

There are 30 challenging (1.50 SI – 1.65 SI) timed writings for use as timed tests. The first fifteen challenging timed writings may also be used for building speed/accuracy, as they are speed scored and paced for each minute. Speeds start at 28 gwpm and increase four words with each timing up to 100 gwpm.

Keyboard Speed Record

A feature of this second edition is the inclusion of a student Keyboard Speed Record at the end of the book. This page may be photocopied for classroom use with this book.

Part 1 ▪ Warm-up Drills

Purpose The first line in each drill is an easy one to limber up the fingers and promote speed. The second line provides drill on a specific aspect of keyboarding. The third line is of challenging difficulty to reinforce accuracy.

Procedure
1 Type each line three times in succession as follows:

- at a slow, accurate rate;
- at a moderate, accurate rate;
- at a rapid, but accurate rate.

Single space same lines. Double space before beginning a new line.

2 When you have finished the whole drill, proofread and circle errors.

3 If you had **up to five errors, move on** to the next drill next time.

4 If you had **more than five errors, repeat** the same drill next time.

Drill 1

Easy	Most nights, he can park the car down the street in front of the shop.
Alphabetic	I just asked him to quote a very low price for a dozen boxes of rings.
Challenging	This patient has missed several weeks of school because of infections.

Drill 2

Easy	Peas can be sown in the garden just as soon as the soil can be worked.
Home Row	He asked Dad to adjust the shelf so his glass won't skid off and fall.
Challenging	We have no service charge for travellers' cheques or cash withdrawals.

Drill 3

Easy	As soon as Fran gets home, she will sew that button on your blue coat.
Third Row	It is true they wrote that the portly squire is quite worthy of power.
Challenging	Slow, gentle stretching of body muscles can reduce stress and fatigue.

Drill 4

Easy	This firm adds a service charge to all bills not paid by the due date.
Bottom Row	Can Vic and Bob give me the exact city, cove or zone which was bombed?
Challenging	His workload is kept at a level he can handle mentally and physically.

Drill 5

Easy	You will need a list of the accounts which are two or more months old.
Adjacent Keys	A pious porter has options to buy cashews and remnants above our cave.
Challenging	Poor flying conditions have brought about a delay in flight schedules.

Drill 6

Easy	If we were all heroes, then who would clap and cheer as we marched by?
First Fingers	I gave a jaunty young man the rights to buy the timber from the grove.
Challenging	Don't forget to include your full name, address, and telephone number.

Drill 7

Easy	Your cottage is close to a clear lake in which they can swim and fish.
Second Fingers	His sidekick, who seeks to accent diet, cried at my dock like a child.
Challenging	It's difficult, but he tackles everything he does like a true fighter.

1 | 2 | 3 | 4 | 5 | 6 | 7 | 8 | 9 | 10 | 11 | 12 | 13 | 14

Drill 8

Easy · I plan to build a high fence around the whole yard and paint it brown.

Third Fingers · We shall soon show those exiles who stole lassos from our saloon wall.

Challenging · Further research is needed to resolve the matter of a safety standard.

Drill 9

Easy · I found a deep sense of pride welling up in me as I read your account.

Fourth Fingers · Papa packed the prizes: a cape, a blazer, a parka, and aqua bandanas.

Challenging · It appears neither of us had understood the scope of this undertaking.

Drill 10

Easy · It is my job to open the store in the morning and lock it up at night.

Vertical Keys · Dick saw and gave Jim squeezed juice for my broiled pike and cold hen.

Challenging · A shareholder may appoint someone to attend and act on his/her behalf.

Drill 11

Easy · We prefer the picture of the boat scene done in tones of blue and red.

Left Hand · The haze made it hard to get a view of the steep descent to the river.

Challenging · Three agents offer discounts for homes with smoke detectors installed.

Drill 12

Easy · It seems the file has been misplaced but a search for it is under way.

Right Hand · Young Joanie may munch on my dill pickle and dunk it in jam and honey.

Challenging · The attitude of tenants has much improved over the last several years.

Drill 13

Easy · The very same day the old brick house came on the market, it was sold.

Opposite Hand Keys · Wow! How did Jeff move, load, and tuck eighty hefty bombs below deck?

Challenging · Notice the product's top quality and the attention paid to its detail.

Drill 14

Easy · The snow has settled in the trees and bushes and it is a lovely sight.

Short Words · We know it is a long way to go to get to bask and play in sun and sea.

Challenging · In a business, a good, efficient support staff makes a big difference.

Drill 15

Easy · The children liked the tale about a day in the life of a young prince.

Long Words · General knowledge of the specialized materials available is essential.

Challenging · Trade your time for equal time in another season, resort, or location.

Drill 16

Easy · Come into our store, see what we have to offer, and let's make a deal.

One-Hand Words · Jim can pull a million crates of poppy extract up my hill in a decade.

Challenging · Up until now, the education market has always been your prime concern.

Drill 17

Easy · As the key witness in the case, the girl must appear in court at noon.

Double Letters · Appeal to Ann to keep mall dressing rooms free of attire and commerce.

Challenging · At present, we have six operators handling the needs of twenty people.

1 | 2 | 3 | 4 | 5 | 6 | 7 | 8 | 9 | 10 | 11 | 12 | 13 | 14

Drill 18

Easy	The buzz of bees and flies is produced by the movement of their wings.
Numbers	In 1983 my restaurant had 46 beer mugs, 72 wine glasses and 50 plates.
Challenging	The company is planning a work incentive program to reverse the trend.

Drill 19

Easy	Our meetings are held at three on the first working day of each month.
Numbers/Symbols	Dunn & Park's rate for a 2-year, $4985 loan is 10% with $236 payments.
Challenging	Does their program stress that sound management practices be followed?

Drill 20

Easy	The best buys at that market this week are bacon and prime rib roasts.
Alphabetic	When the viper quit the stage, Jack made his exit in a blaze of glory.
Challenging	I believe this information will assist in the research he is planning.

Drill 21

Easy	This free booklet tells what you need to know to make a wise purchase.
Home Row	The lad sulked and fidgeted till she passed along a full jar of dills.
Challenging	Newport owns and operates an emerald mine which is in full production.

Drill 22

Easy	When the soft snow clings to its branches, the tree is a pretty sight.
Third Row	Try to equip the prow with square tips; then pursue that witty porter.
Challenging	Detailed figures on the extent of the problem are still not available.

Drill 23

Easy	He has written eight books, five of which are sold in three countries.
Bottom Row	Must the canny band combine a mix of nibs, combs, and bones in a maze?
Challenging	The accused was arrested in a factory where police seized his handgun.

Drill 24

Easy	One child was laughing so hard the tears were streaming down his face.
Adjacent Keys	Many say it is obvious the pretty buyer has a passion for sporty fads.
Challenging	The proposed system would result in a significant drop in basic costs.

Drill 25

Easy	The person was caught by police and charged with nine counts of theft.
First Fingers	Junior thought he may have fumbled the trigger of the gun from fright.
Challenging	To a great number of people, the telephone has now become a necessity.

Drill 26

Easy	The children can have fun, learn outdoor skills, and make new friends.
Second Fingers	I did accord rides to kind but derelict kids who decried the incident.
Challenging	Each day, his courage and cheerful determination are called into play.

Drill 27

Easy	At the end of the day, we just sit and relax and listen to soft music.
Third Fingers	We stood still. We saw loose owls swoosh down on a slow, swollen fox.
Challenging	We have birding tours, wilderness canoeing and many high arctic tours.

1 | 2 | 3 | 4 | 5 | 6 | 7 | 8 | 9 | 10 | 11 | 12 | 13 | 14

Drill 28

Easy · Thank you for the offer, but I am sorry I must refuse it at this time.

Fourth Fingers · The ape has quite a craze for papaya and apples; it also eats bananas.

Challenging · This committee asks that you support these candidates in the election.

Drill 29

Easy · Before I go to the store, give me a list of all the items you require.

Vertical Keys · Fran could swim, jump and kick, frolic, and dance to jazz in the loft.

Challenging · Study the final chapter to learn the machine's many advanced features.

Drill 30

Easy · A new light bulb is needed in the laundry room and in the dining room.

Left Hand · Ask a driver the real extent of the damage caused by the diesel crash.

Challenging · Doug can shovel the driveway before departing for his downtown office.

Drill 31

Easy · This may allow you the freedom to do the things you really want to do.

Right Hand · Many youths in the mob are myopic; they spoil to kick, maul and punch.

Challenging · We have herbal teas such as peppermint, rosehip, jasmine and camomile.

Drill 32

Easy · As soon as I receive the list of contacts, I can get the work started.

Opposite Hand Keys · The kiddies worked to sell the vine, lest it lose its opaque blossoms.

Challenging · You recommend that all new drivers complete a driver education course.

Drill 33

Easy · In fall, the bear curls up in his cozy den and sleeps the winter away.

Short Words · Put a new hat in a big box, tie it up and ship it by rail to the firm.

Challenging · Something must be done to reduce or eliminate the number of accidents.

Drill 34

Easy · We are closing up our shop and every piece in the store is half price.

Long Words · Contractors did tuckpointing immediately, especially around a chimney.

Challenging · Many apartment blocks and motels could be exempt from the requirement.

Drill 35

Easy · As it happened, I returned home just in time to help with the harvest.

One-Hand Words · Fred agreed plump Barbara has oomph; you got wax or ink on my sweater.

Challenging · Our easy maintenance programs are designed to fit your personal needs.

Drill 36

Easy · He earns his living on a farm growing crops and raising pigs and cows.

Double Letters · The poor press will oppose the bill but cannot scoff at the committee.

Challenging · They pay cash dollars for estate and antique jewellery, diamonds, etc.

Drill 37

Easy · This project may be the challenge I have been seeking for a long time.

Numbers · I had 497 orders, 285 bills, 103 enquiries, and 6 pieces of junk mail.

Challenging · Those exploring for or mining these metals dominate their market news.

1 | 2 | 3 | 4 | 5 | 6 | 7 | 8 | 9 | 10 | 11 | 12 | 13 | 14

Drill 38

Easy

Numbers/Symbols

Challenging

In the last hockey game, the star player got two goals and one assist.
He did sell 736 copies of Paul's "fun" article (4 pages) @ $2.89 each!
Brace yourself for this outstanding offer you cannot afford to resist.

Drill 39

Easy

Alphabetic

Challenging

If they wish to prevent a further loss, they must call him right away.
Judy explained my next great sequence of bleak events in the war zone.
Now really immerse yourself in the culture and traditions of Scotland.

Drill 40

Easy

Home Row

Challenging

More than one car insured with the same firm often means a lower rate.
She shuddered and hardly talked as she soaked the girl's jagged flesh.
These include a private residence, an office building and vacant land.

Drill 41

Easy

Third Row

Challenging

That club sends out a news bulletin each month to each of its members.
We wrote to enquire about the route, territory, and pay for that trip.
This public knows that huge government deficits make the dollar shaky.

Drill 42

Easy

Bottom Row

Challenging

A simple phone call could have saved a lot of time, effort, and money.
Can some men, a bobby, and a convict examine nozzles in the mauve box?
Develop a professional image right from the beginning of your new job.

Drill 43

Easy

Adjacent Keys

Challenging

The book will be one you will cherish and consult time and time again.
Appointment of mining lads to power threw a curve at the dubious talk.
We permit no assignments of our contracts without our written consent.

Drill 44

Easy

First Fingers

Challenging

We will give them the best service they have ever had for their money.
The fifty frogs may have fun jumping for bugs on your avenue at night.
At their next meeting, nominations for the committee will be received.

Drill 45

Easy

Second Fingers

Challenging

He must change the ribbon on the printer before he can print the text.
Derek, a medic at the accident, decided to keep the sick child hidden.
The changes are the result of a document submitted by this commission.

Drill 46

Easy

Third Fingers

Challenging

With blue skies and a very light breeze, the weather was just perfect.
All of those silly lasses still swoon as soon as Wilcox does his solo.
Try to save money through better management of your insurance dollars.

Drill 47

Easy

Fourth Fingers

Challenging

Please arrange for the carpets to be cleaned within the next few days.
Paul zipped up his parka; a palace scamp was piqued at Paul's apparel.
Your involvement was vital to bringing this to the public's attention.

1 | 2 | 3 | 4 | 5 | 6 | 7 | 8 | 9 | 10 | 11 | 12 | 13 | 14

Drill 48

Easy	She will assign a date by which you should have finished this section.
Vertical Keys	I like Janice to dole out hefty sums like five or six hundred dollars.
Challenging	Because only a limited number of seats are available, get tickets now.

Drill 49

Easy	The young hunter was trapped with no shelter or food, and little hope.
Left Hand	Several smart rovers reached over, grasped a square box, and squeezed.
Challenging	We highly recommend a purchase at the current price of eleven dollars.

Drill 50

Easy	We should serve praise as we do champagne - while it's still bubbling.
Right Hand	Appoint your pilot to the jury; smile at John's jokes; play his hunch.
Challenging	He owns his vacation home as a co-owner along with fellow timesharers.

Drill 51

Easy	In most cases, we would be able to save you a very large sum of money.
Opposite Hand Keys	In my movie, a lassie on a dock sells a bin of ebony wools in a jiffy.
Challenging	We are confident that your company has emerged in a stronger position.

Drill 52

Easy	We will need support crews that are well trained, fast, and efficient.
Short Words	He has hit the top of the list of sales each day for a year or so now.
Challenging	He reformatted the left margins to allow room for three-hole punching.

Drill 53

Easy	Could I call upon you for advice when I am ready to set up our centre?
Long Words	Explanations of the specific strategy initiated contagious excitement.
Challenging	Symbol of human courage and endurance, it tested both body and spirit.

Drill 54

Easy	A love of nature can be seen in the beauty and spirit of her subjects.
One-Hand Words	A million jolly beavers jump in the water to scare a puppy I gave you.
Challenging	We had several personnel changes over the year which may interest you.

Drill 55

Easy	Please notify me of any change in address so that I can keep in touch.
Double Letters	Commission Scott to carry coffee and wrapped cheese food to my office.
Challenging	Even a busy work schedule doesn't deter her from an effective workout.

Drill 56

Easy	He will edit the report and then give it to you to revise and reprint.
Numbers	The years 1057, 1462, and 1938 were the important ones in our history.
Challenging	Collecting plates as a hobby and for wall decoration is quite popular.

Drill 57

Easy	As you know, the opposite sides of a dice cube always add up to seven.
Numbers/Symbols	Pat's latest "steal" is a Soo & Lee's coat (style #30-754) for $62.98.
Challenging	They expect payment of the invoice within the time period agreed upon.

1 | 2 | 3 | 4 | 5 | 6 | 7 | 8 | 9 | 10 | 11 | 12 | 13 | 14

Drill 58

Easy

Alphabetic

Challenging

Barrels of water were hauled on a sled pulled by a horse or a tractor.
The big wet swamp froze quickly and proved just excellent for skating.
We can offer several good reasons for having an early inspection made.

Drill 59

Easy

Home Row

Challenging

I am sure there is not another actor who would be better for the part.
Jeff and a saleslady haggled over the deal for the sake of half a fig.
Get tickets now for this gigantic celebration and avoid the onslaught.

Drill 60

Easy

Third Row

Challenging

Please sign the attached form and return it to me as soon as possible.
Quit worrying about the pretty person who hurt her wrist at the party.
Read our collection of amazing events and be prepared to be astounded.

Drill 61

Easy

Bottom Row

Challenging

The town is booming with new life but retains a reverence for the old.
Can many of the brave men memorize such a complex accent for the exam?
A company expands its facilities to meet the demands for its products.

Drill 62

Easy

Adjacent Keys

Challenging

We still live up to the standards set by our founder thirty years ago.
Jokers were poised above a cave to address you at an opportune moment.
A magazine issue coming up will spotlight a number of success stories.

Drill 63

Easy

First Fingers

Challenging

We look to the past for patterns which we can project into the future.
Marvin bought them butter, many round buns, and a big jug of vermouth.
We give you thoughtful service, friendly attention, and happy results.

Drill 64

Easy

Second Fingers

Challenging

That park is open to campers from early spring until late in the fall.
I deceived an addict who likes dice, drinks cider, and dances on deck.
I have included numerous pictures, graphs, maps, charts, and diagrams.

Drill 65

Easy

Third Fingers

Challenging

Until the trout season opens, I will have to settle for bass or perch.
Leslie will swallow our story about losing his axle in a shallow pool.
Most classmates entered a profession, like medicine, law, or teaching.

Drill 66

Easy

Fourth Fingers

Challenging

They suspect the links in the chain will become weaker as we go along.
A lazy captain napped. Has Pat placed equal parts of pizza on plates?
Give the document a more professional look; justify all right margins.

Drill 67

Easy

Vertical Keys

Challenging

She saw the evil around her and grew to become the tale's moral force.
A judge decided my hubby licked Judd, wins the quiz and gets a collie.
Readers relive the drama and excitement of bygone peoples and empires.

1 | 2 | 3 | 4 | 5 | 6 | 7 | 8 | 9 | 10 | 11 | 12 | 13 | 14

Drill 68

Easy
One after another, the birds swooped down on the cat to scare it away.

Left Hand
The clever squire wants the darker flowers delivered a great distance.

Challenging
Remember to print your desktop published documents on a laser printer.

Drill 69

Easy
Please do not take any cart farther than the parking lot of our store.

Right Hand
No cloud in yon glorious sky may hunt or jolt your tough, gloomy ship.

Challenging
Handsome old houses help to preserve the atmosphere of this community.

Drill 70

Easy
I can tell you that my line is, in fact, much better and much cheaper.

Opposite Hand Keys
He lied or kidded that slow drinks ruin those trying to woo and marry.

Challenging
I am enclosing an order form and return envelope for your convenience.

Drill 71

Easy
I compete in games for the sake of sport and the honour of my country.

Short Words
I will pay the bill for the two pots he sent me just as soon as I can.

Challenging
For earliest colour indoors, depend on cuttings from flowering shrubs.

Drill 72

Easy
We were both happy and sad to be leaving the firm after so many years.

Long Words
Intelligent individuals reacted spontaneously to a proposed adventure.

Challenging
Donations were arranged on your behalf to seven, well-known charities.

Drill 73

Easy
Why not ask the four leaders what action should be taken in this case.

One-Hand Words
Look at my best pony, Pinky, in the fastest races in its great career.

Challenging
The local chapter receives strong support from the federal government.

Drill 74

Easy
Of course all of us know that a door cannot be a door when it is ajar.

Double Letters
Snooze or sleep better on a queen, rubber-filled mattress and bedding.

Challenging
Which products are receiving the most attention from potential buyers?

Drill 75

Easy
When you hear the tone, dial the last party to whom you wish to speak.

Numbers
Of 1286 who ran, 739 dropped out and only 547 crossed the finish line.

Challenging
You help in the development of this publication by providing feedback.

Drill 76

Easy
Bob will warm the food first, then put it on the table for the guests.

Numbers/Symbols
He said, "J & B Trust will lend you $2804 at just 8% for three years!"

Challenging
My report includes a table of contents, footnotes, and a bibliography.

Drill 77

Easy
You take the high road, I'll take the low road, and I'll arrive first.

Alphabetic
Do be very quick and just fax me the two copies on legal size by noon.

Challenging
Readers remain strong believers in the value of our excellent library.

1 | 2 | 3 | 4 | 5 | 6 | 7 | 8 | 9 | 10 | 11 | 12 | 13 | 14

Drill 78

Easy	In spring he pulls the weeds while I plant flowers in the garden beds.
Home Row	Jack had to dash to fill sacks with loads of gold and jade in a flash.
Challenging	Our companies retain the largest gas reserves of any resource company.

Drill 79

Easy	Joan held onto the live fish while I released the hook from its mouth.
Third Row	You were not quite equipped to power the port up to my top ferry rope.
Challenging	Take several minutes to examine our offer; you're under no obligation.

Drill 80

Easy	Watch my dog chase the tennis ball and return it to the waiting child.
Bottom Row	Anne can zoom in, Bev can mix the cubes, and Vic can curve every maze.
Challenging	All events listed were available to the public unless otherwise noted.

Drill 81

Easy	That product has sold well not only here but right across the country.
Adjacent Keys	We sought the realty guy in a new suit who was walking above the cove.
Challenging	The evening will begin with a reception in authentic island tradition.

Drill 82

Easy	Turn on your machine, put the disk into the drive, and close the door.
First Fingers	Fruit is very gritty, but put a bag through the muffler into my buggy.
Challenging	Telephone Bantam today and arrange an interview for a convenient time.

Drill 83

Easy	She liked best the story about the hen who thought the sky had fallen.
Second Fingers	Dick dieted and reduced, then caked the kid, deck, and dike with muck.
Challenging	We would appreciate permission to reprint the article in our magazine.

1 | 2 | 3 | 4 | 5 | 6 | 7 | 8 | 9 | 10 | 11 | 12 | 13 | 14

Part 2 ▪ Timed Writings

Test Speed/Accuracy

1 Take 3-minute, 5-minute or 10-minute timing(s). If you have your choice, choose an easy writing for speed, an average writing for speed/accuracy, and a challenging writing for accuracy.

2 Calculate net words per minute:

NWPM = (total words ÷ number of minutes) – 2 for each error

3 It's a good idea to keep a record of your timings so that you can keep track of your progress. A Keyboard Speed Record sheet for this purpose is provided at the end of this book. You may make a photocopy of the record sheet.

Build or Stabilize Speed

1 From the first fifteen easy, average or challenging timed writings, select the paced material that is closest to the gross words per minute **speed** you wish to achieve. GWPM is your speed *before* subtracting for errors.

2 Take 3-minute or 5-minute timing(s) during which a tape, or someone, signals each minute. If, when the signal is given, you are typing more than three characters behind or ahead of the superscript minute marker in the text, adjust your speed (faster or slower) so as to be as close as possible to the next marker when the next signal is given.

Brain Games

28 GWPM

This timed writing is a collection of brain games designed to test not only your typing speed, but your mental agility too. When you are done, check your answers with the timed writing on the next page. — 12 12 / 26 26 / 39 39 / 41 41

In this first group of games, explain why the odd fact in each story is true. My friend held an egg over a concrete floor, then dropped the egg one metre without breaking it. Two mothers and two daughters were shopping. Although each of them bought a new coat, only three coats were purchased. A thief and a doctor sat talking. The thief was the doctor's son, but the doctor was not the thief's father. Two girls played three games of tennis one morning, and they each won three games. — 55 55 / 68 68 / 81 81 / 94 94 / 107 107 / 120 120 / 133 133 / 140 140

32 GWPM

Next, try your skill at these riddles. A man has a fox, a goose, and a bag of grain. He has to cross the river, but his boat is small and he can take only one thing with him at a time. Figure out how he can transport all three safely. On a high shelf are three boxes which you can reach but cannot see into. The boxes are labelled red balls, blue balls, and red and blue balls. Somehow the labels were mixed up and each box has the wrong label on it. By reaching up and removing just one ball, how can you determine which box contains what? In a drawer are twenty socks, ten blue and ten brown. The light in the room is burned out, and you must find a pair of socks in the dark. What would be the minimum number of socks you must remove from the drawer to be sure that you have a matched pair? — 13 153 / 27 167 / 40 180 / 53 193 / 67 207 / 81 221 / 94 234 / 108 248 / 121 261 / 134 274 / 147 287 / 160 300

36 GWPM

A boy scout is lost in a forest. At last he finds a path but doesn't know which way to go. In the forest live two brothers, one of whom always tells the truth and the other always tells a lie. Along comes one of the brothers, but the scout can't tell whether he is the truthful one or the liar. What one question can the scout ask to learn the direction out of the woods? — 12 312 / 25 325 / 38 338 / 52 352 / 66 366 / 74 374

Now see how well you can respond to this quiz. Take your time and try not to jump to conclusions. Some months of the year have thirty days and some have thirty-one. How many months have twenty-eight days? Two days ago, my son was two years old. Next year he will be five years old. How can that possibly be? Your friend has just one match. She enters a cabin that has a wood stove, a candle, and an oil lamp. Tell which she should light first. If you take three grapes from ten grapes, how many grapes do you have? — 87 387 / 100 400 / 114 414 / 127 427 / 140 440 / 154 454 / 168 468 / 180 480

1 | 2 | 3 | 4 | 5 | 6 | 7 | 8 | 9 | 10 | 11 | 12 | 13 | 14

Brain Game Answers

40 GWPM

This timed writing gives you the answers to the brain games. `12  12`
Are you ready? Here we go. Because my friend dropped the egg from `26  26`
a height of two metres, the egg fell one metre without breaking; of `39  39`
course¹ it broke when it finally hit the concrete floor. The two `52  52`
mothers and two daughters who went shopping were a daughter, a `65  65`
mother, and a grandmother. The doctor was not the thief's father `78  78`
because² she was his mother. The two girls who played tennis didn't `92  92`
play together. `95  95`

The man who had to cross the river faced a serious dilemma. `108  108`
He could not leave the fox and goose alone together lest the³ fox eat `122  122`
the goose. Neither could he leave the goose and the grain alone, for `136  136`
the goose would eat the grain. To solve his problem, he took the `149  149`
goose across and left it on the other side. He came back⁴ and took `162  162`
the grain across, left it there, and brought the goose back. Leaving `176  176`
the goose on the first side, he took the fox over. Then he left the `189  189`
fox with the grain while he came back for the goose⁵. `200  200`

44 GWPM

The only box of balls that will solve your problem is the one `13  213`
marked red and blue balls. Since all the boxes are wrongly labelled, `27  227`
the ball you pick from this box has to be the colour of all the balls `41  241`
in the box. Once¹ you have this information, you can figure out the `54  254`
contents of the other two boxes. `61  261`

To be sure of getting a matched pair of socks, you need pick `75  275`
just three socks from the drawer. Should the first two be one of² `88  288`
each colour, the third sock has to match one of them. `98  298`

To learn the direction out of the woods, the scout's question `111  311`
should be worded something like this: If I were to ask your brother `125  325`
if this is the way out of the woods³, what would he say? No matter `138  338`
which brother it is, if he answers no, the direction indicated is the `152  352`
way out. If he answers yes, the scout must go in the other direction. `166  366`

All twelve months of the year have twenty⁴-eight days. My son's `180  380`
birthday is on the thirty-first day of December and the statement `193  393`
in question was made on the first day of January. Your friend would `207  407`
be wise to light the match first. You should have three grapes⁵. `220  420`

1 | 2 | 3 | 4 | 5 | 6 | 7 | 8 | 9 | 10 | 11 | 12 | 13 | 14

In the Words of Sir Winston

48
GWPM

We tried again and again to prevent this war, but now we are | 13 13
at war. One bond unites us all: to wage war until victory is won and | 27 27
never to surrender ourselves to servitude and shame, whatever the | 41 41
cost and the agony may be. The long night of barbarism will descend | 55 55
unless we conquer – as conquer we must; as conquer we shall. | 68 68

Come then. Let us to the task, to the battle and the toil – each | 82 82
to our part, each to our station. Fill the armies, rule the air, pour | 96 96
out the munitions, strangle the U-boats, sweep the mines, plough the | 110 110
land, build the ships, guard the streets, succour the wounded, uplift | 124 124
the downcast, and honour the brave. Let us go forward together. | 137 137
There is not a week, nor a day, nor an hour to lose. We shall defend | 151 151
our island home – if necessary, for years; if necessary, alone. We | 165 165
shall not flag or fail. We shall go on to the end. We shall fight in | 179 179
France; we shall fight on the seas and oceans; we shall fight in the | 193 193
air. We shall defend our island whatever the cost may be. We shall | 207 207
fight on the beaches; we shall fight on the landing grounds; we shall | 221 221
fight in the fields and in the streets; we shall fight in the hills. We | 235 235
shall never surrender. | 240 240

52
GWPM

Now, the old lion with her cubs at her side stands alone against | 13 253
hunters who are armed with deadly weapons. It has come to us to | 26 266
stand alone in the breach and face the worst that the tyrant may do. | 40 280
Should the invader come, there will be no placid lying down of the | 53 293
people in submission before him as we have seen in other countries. | 67 307
We shall defend every village, every town, and every city. If the villains | 81 321
drop down upon us from the skies, we will make it clear to them that | 95 335
they have not alighted in the poultry run, or in the rabbit farm, or | 109 349
in the sheepfold; but that they have come down into the lion's den. | 122 362
Let us therefore brace ourselves to our duties, and so bear ourselves | 136 376
that, if the British Empire and its Commonwealth last for a thousand | 150 390
years, men will still say that this was their finest hour. | 162 402

Put your confidence in us. Give us your faith and your blessing; | 176 416
and under providence, all will be well. We shall not fail or falter; we | 190 430
shall not weaken or tire. Neither a sudden shock of battle nor the | 204 444
long-drawn trials of vigilance and exertion shall wear us down. Give | 218 458
us the tools and we will finish the job. | 226 466

We have not flinched or wavered; we have not failed. Alone, but | 240 480
upborne by every generous heartbeat of mankind, we have defied the | 253 493
tyrant in the height of his power. | 260 500

1 | 2 | 3 | 4 | 5 | 6 | 7 | 8 | 9 | 10 | 11 | 12 | 13 | 14

Trivia

56 GWPM

From this fantastic world we live in, we now bring you a collection 13 13
of facts, plus a few figures, to amaze and amuse you. 24 24

Did you know that a homing pigeon saved a group of soldiers? 38 38
The soldiers had sent ahead for air assistance, but before it arrived 52 52
they won a surprise victory. They now had to deliver a fast cancel- 65 65
lation to their air base or be bombed by their own planes. Their 78 78
only hope lay with the speed and safety of a pigeon. The bird got 92 92
the message through just in time. 99 99

Some birds lay their eggs in the nests of other birds. The 112 112
unwitting foster parents hatch the eggs and feed the chicks. As most 126 126
foster chicks are larger birds, often they knock the natural chicks 139 139
right out of the nest so they can take over the roost. Although the 153 153
kiwi bird is about the size of a domestic hen, it lays an egg that is 167 167
eight times larger than a hen's. Vultures crack hard eggs by dropping 181 181
them on stones. If an egg is too large to pick up, the birds drop 194 194
stones on the egg. 198 198

Crocodiles may not have tooth brushes, but some do have tooth- 212 212
picks – not our common wooden kind, but real live ones. A bird 225 225
called the plover picks out and eats the bits of food lodged between 238 238
the crocodile's teeth. Not all fish out of water are out of their 251 251
element. As well as gills, some fish, like the walking catfish, have 264 264
lungs with which they can breathe air. They are also able to walk 277 277
on their fins. 280 280

At one time, golf balls were made from pieces of leather stuffed 294
with feathers. Raincoats made out of crude rubber were worn 307
hundreds of years ago by South American natives. Long ago, the 320
Chinese used to waterproof cloth by coating it with tallow. A whip 333
cracks in mid-air, not because it has struck something, but because 346
its tip is moving faster than sound. Early clocks were built with 360
only one hand, an hour hand. 366

Some American Indians made their tomahawks so that they 379
served a dual purpose. With a hollow handle and a pipe bowl as 392
well as a blade, the tomahawk was a weapon in times of war and 405
a pipe in times of peace. One Chinese ruler was prepared to do 418
battle even in death. When he died, he was buried with an army of 431
six thousand clay soldiers and horses, all built to life size. 444

1 | 2 | 3 | 4 | 5 | 6 | 7 | 8 | 9 | 10 | 11 | 12 | 13 | 14

60
GWPM

There really is a vampire bat. At night, the vampire leaves its   13   13
roost to seek out sleeping prey. With its sharp teeth, it bites its   27   27
victim gently so as not to waken it. The bat does not suck the blood,   41   41
but laps it up from the wound. The ermine and the weasel are one   54   54
and the same animal. When the brown weasel dons its white fur   67   67
coat for winter, it is transformed into a lovely ermine.   78   78

Before theatres were designed so that the actors and the viewers   92   92
were separated, viewers sat on the stage. An actor who gave a poor   106   106
performance had to be careful, for the viewers would try to bump   119   119
him or her off the stage. The rarest stamp in the world has a face   133   133
value of one cent but is worth many thousands of dollars. If a French   147   147
horn were straightened out, it would measure seven metres.   159   159

The eyes of the squid are almost human. Its eye has an iris   172   172
and pupil, and a lens that can focus for any distance. Some squids   186   186
even have eyelids. The bee hummingbird, weighing in at a mere two   199   199
grams and measuring just five centimetres from stem to stern, is   212   212
the smallest bird in the world. One type of male moth can locate   225   225
from eight kilometres away a female of its species from her scent   238   238
in the air. The bat is the only mammal that can fly. The dragonfly   251   251
can reach a flying speed of more than sixty kilometres per hour on   264   264
wings that are thinner than paper. A flea can jump one hundred   277   277
times its own height. This is like your or my jumping to the top of   291   291
a building that stands sixty storeys high.   300   300

You can use a magnet to check out brass items. If it attracts,   314
it's not brass. Before printing came into being and set up some   327
rules, words were written all strung together with no spaces or   340
punctuation. In the old days, tablecloths were used not so much to   354
cover the table as to serve as a towel for wiping one's mouth and   367
hands after a meal. The same two letters are found in many of the   381
words that are used in connection with fowl: duck, chicken, cock,   394
pluck, cackle, cluck, and peck. A different set of two letters occurs   408
in many words that have to do with the nose: sneeze, snout, snort,   421
snooty, snarl, snoop, and sniff.   428

1 | 2 | 3 | 4 | 5 | 6 | 7 | 8 | 9 | 10 | 11 | 12 | 13 | 14

Even More Trivia

64
GWPM

The platypus has survived for thousands of years in spite of its   13   13
weird make-up. It is covered with fur. It has a tail like a beaver,   27   27
a bill like a duck, and webbed feet with cat-like claws at the ends.   41   41
On each hind leg is a spur which carries poison. This fine swimmer   55   55
lays eggs like a reptile and nurses its young like a mammal.   67   67

The Arctic is an ocean with land around it, while the Antarctic   81   81
is a land mass with ocean around it. In reading a barometer, it does   95   95
not matter what weather sign the needle is pointing at. What one   108   108
must know is in which direction the needle has moved. If the needle   121   121
moved up, the weather will improve; if it moved down, the weather   134   134
will worsen. Our hair will still be around when we are long gone.   148   148
Keep human hair away from fire and it will take a long time to   161   161
decay. It is not affected by cold, heat, water, or many chemicals.   175   175
That is why hair clogs sinks and drains.   184   184

All live coral has some colour; only dead coral is white like   197   197
chalk. There is one type of catfish that floats upside down near the   211   211
water's surface to make it easier to feed from the surface film. When   225   225
a pride of lions has a successful hunt and feast and then lies down   239   239
to sleep, it could be as many as four days before the pride wakens.   253   253
When it starts to get cold in the late summer and early fall, some   266   266
bugs seek overnight lodgings in flowers that close their petals at   279   279
night. When the blossoms open in the morning, the bugs continue   292   292
on their way. Many folks think that cooties is just a name that chil-   306   306
dren have made up for bugs, but cooties really are a type of body lice.   320   320

An odometer was in use in the horse-drawn wagons of China   333
in the early part of the first century. In the wagon were two wooden   347
figures, each of which held a drum stick. Each time the cart travelled   361
half a kilometre, one of the figures struck a drum. It's much easier   375
to smile than it is to frown; in fact, it takes fewer than half as   388
many muscles to smile as it does to frown. The shortest verse in   401
the Bible has just two words, Jesus wept.   410

A snake's eggs, with their soft cover, grow up to one-third larger   424
after they are laid. A snake may not have a meal for over a year,   438
but when it does eat, it can swallow an animal much larger than   451
its mouth. The snake has no need to chew its meal, for its juices   464
dissolve bone, teeth, feathers, and all. A tomato may be a vegetable   478
in your book and mine, but strictly speaking, it is a berry and   491
therefore a fruit.   495

1 | 2 | 3 | 4 | 5 | 6 | 7 | 8 | 9 | 10 | 11 | 12 | 13 | 14

Beauty Salon

We are the beauty salon you have been waiting for. Our staff 12   12
are a friendly bunch and we are located right in your neighbourhood. 26   26
What's more, we offer you a new kind of styling. It's called no-risk 40   40
hairstyling. We call it no-risk styling because if you don't like it, 54   54
you don't pay for it. In other words, you risk nothing by trying us.[1] 68   68
We can make this offer because we are confident in ourselves. We 81   81
are certain that we can please you better than any other salon, and 95   95
for very good reasons. 100   100

The first reason is that we match the stylist to your needs. 113   113
When you call us for your first appointment, we will ask you some 126   126
brief questions. As a result of the information[2] you give us, we will 140   140
book you with the stylist who, we feel, would best meet your hair's 154   154
needs. Just as with all other professions, hair stylists have their 168   168
specialties and we want to make sure that you get the one who is 181   181
special for you. 184   184

The second reason for our confidence is that we listen to you. 197   197
At your first visit, you and[3] your stylist will discuss your hair. You 211   211
will talk about style preference, hair problems, the amount of time 225   225
you like to devote to your hair, etc. In other words, we study your 239   239
hair and your likes and dislikes before we undertake the work. 252   252

The third reason is that in our shop you are the judge of any 265   265
haircut or style we give you.[4] We do our utmost to combine your 278   278
tastes with our design expertise to create a look that is best suited 292   292
to your hair, your features, and your personal style. We try to come 306   306
up with a style that not only looks nice when you leave our store, 319   319
but that you can maintain until your next appointment. We even 332   332
give you tips on how to look after it.[5] 340   340

Lastly, we give you our no-risk guarantee. Our aim is to make 354
you beautiful and happy. If you decide that you are not satisfied 367
with our services, you don't pay for them. It's as simple as that – 381
no fuss, no hassle. So why not do yourself and your hair a favour? 395
Give us a call today. You just can't lose, and you have much to gain. 409
By the way, if you book your appointment for a Monday, Tuesday, 422
or Wednesday, we will give you a ten per cent discount on all of our 436
services. 438

1 | 2 | 3 | 4 | 5 | 6 | 7 | 8 | 9 | 10 | 11 | 12 | 13 | 14

Childhood

72
GWPM

My childhood days in the north of Scotland were happy times. 12 12
Life was simpler then. They were the days of candles to light one to 26 26
bed and cooking on an open grate over a wood fire. Travel was by 39 39
foot, or by horse and buggy, or by bicycle. In winter, there was lots 53 53
of snow. There was an old saying that a black Christmas meant a full 67 67
kirkyard. We believed[1] it, and so it was counted a bad omen if there 81 81
was no snow by the end of the year. 88 88

Most New Year's, or hogmanay as we termed it, my parents threw 102 102
a party. Father used to draw up a program and act as the master of 115 115
ceremonies. There were games like postman's knock, pass the scissors, 129 129
and yes please and thank you. The last was a card game, and as you 143 143
have[2] probably guessed, quite a polite one. There were musical solos 157 157
and singsongs, and after it all a grand tea was laid on. 168 168

In the summer, we ran barefoot. Children played in the streets. 182 182
The boys had marbles and balls and bikes. Girls played with dolls, 195 195
knitted, and played games like catty. The catty was a thick piece of 209 209
wood that was tapered on both ends.[3] It was laid on the ground and 222 222
one end was hit with a stick which made the catty catapult up and 235 235
over. Sometimes we girls would decide to have a picnic up the hill 249 249
below which the town nestled. We would gather gooseberries from the 263 263
garden, and buy half a penny's worth of sweeties and a big bag of 276 276
broken biscuits for a penny. That, plus a few wild raspberries[4] and 290 290
brambles that we picked on the hill, was our picnic feast. 302 302

Because so many people in the region had the same names, it 315 315
was a common custom to tack identifiers onto names. For instance, 328 328
there was Bill the wright, Dinny the grocer, and Jock the goose. My 342 342
father was renowned for his fine tenor voice, and he was widely known 356 356
as Murd the bird.[5] 360 360

There were vagrants who wandered into town from time to time. 373
Some were tinkers, or tinks as we called them, who came to peddle 386
their wares. Some were gypsies who camped in an old quarry on the 399
outskirts of town and made a few shillings at telling fortunes. Some 413
were unusual characters like Peter the Great, a hermit who lived in 427
a small hut way up on the hill, or Eppy Cacky who would arrive round 441
the top of our street dressed in petticoats to her ankles, a wide cape, 455
and a broad-brimmed hat. She danced and sang and played the 468
harmonica and we were all enchanted. 475

1 | 2 | 3 | 4 | 5 | 6 | 7 | 8 | 9 | 10 | 11 | 12 | 13 | 14

Other Side of the Window

76
GWPM

Finally, one day I decided it was time. For years, I had worked 13 13
the nine to five shift cooped up in a plush office or running from 26 26
one meeting to the next, trying to keep things running smoothly 39 39
and, at the same time, to fan the flames of new ideas. For the most 53 53
part, I enjoyed what I was doing and the nice people with whom I 66 66
worked. Why then did I suddenly up and leave it all? I left for a 79 79
number of reasons. Perhaps the most important was that I was 92 92
drawn more and more to the wonderful world on the other side of 105 105
the window in the large office in which I worked. 115 115

For the greater part of the threescore years and ten, I had 128 128
longed to have the freedom to watch spring emerge, not only in the 141 141
gardens, but in the meadows, along the hedgerows, in the woods 154 154
and beside the creeks and marshes. I wanted to respond to the call 168 168
of the frogs, the song of the robins, and the buzz of the bees. Every 182 182
day that passes brings me closer to that great spectrum of life repre- 195 195
sented by the flora and fauna of our native landscape. They are my 208 208
friends and I must know them better. 216 216

But the time is short, and their numbers are so great. I will 230 230
never recognize them all by name, but I will begin to know what to 243 243
expect according to their ecology. I will know that where there is 257 257
goldenrod, I am apt to find the spindle gall. I'll learn that it is 271 271
the home of a moth caterpillar, but I will likely not remember its 284 284
name, for it's so long and difficult. I will remember that wherever 298 298
I see monarch butterflies, I will expect to find milkweed; that in the 312 312
wetlands, the three-sided stems of grass-like growth are not a grass 326 326
at all but rather one of a number of sedges; and that where I hear 339 339
the frog in early spring, it will not be long before marsh marigolds 353 353
will beam from the still pond water. I simply must drink my fill of 366 366
all of these wonders and learn what I can while there is still time. 380 380

Now and then, I will take some people with me to introduce to 394
my new friends. Some of my friends can't move, but those that can 407
will wave at me in the breeze. None of my friends can talk. Never- 421
theless, they will delight my people companions with their beauty, 434
their strange but wonderful ways, and their unique roles in this vast 448
stage called life. 452

1 | 2 | 3 | 4 | 5 | 6 | 7 | 8 | 9 | 10 | 11 | 12 | 13 | 14

Salt

Salt is much more than just a food seasoner. In fact, salt has   13 13

some fourteen hundred known uses. Many of these can be applied   26 26

in the home. For instance, salt is a great cleaning aid. A paste of   40 40

salt and vinegar smeared on brass, copper, or stainless steel for an   54 54

hour or more will remove tarnish. The paste should be rubbed off   67 67

with a soft cloth; and then the item can be washed and polished   80 80

with a clean, dry cloth.   85 85

Wicker furniture can be cleaned with a solution of warm water   99 99

and salt. As well as cleaning, the salt solution will stiffen the wicker   113 113

and promote longer life. A deep vase may be cleaned by letting a   126 126

solution of salt and vinegar stand in it for a time. Then shake well   140 140

and rinse with clean water. A fair amount of salt added to quite hot   154 154

water will set the colour in fabrics and help to prevent the colour   168 168

running. Just plunge the garment into the solution and let it stand   182 182

until the water is cold.   187 187

Here's a tip for people who use a clothesline. Wet a cloth in   201 201

water to which a good portion of salt has been added. Wring out   215 215

the cloth and wipe it along the clothesline. This will leave a salty   229 229

film that will prevent clothes from sticking to the line in cold weath-   243 243

er. Salt sprinkled on sidewalks and in damp corners will help deter   256 256

snails and earthworms.   261 261

Some vegetables can be placed in cold, salted water for a few   274 274

minutes to allow any worms they may harbour to float to the top   287 287

of the water. Vegetables, like sprouts and spinach, may be cleaned   301 301

by adding a handful of salt to the water in which they are to be   314 314

rinsed. Any sand in the greens will sink to the bottom.   326 326

Salt can also be a beauty aid. A mixture of two parts salt to   339 339

one part olive oil makes a cheap, but good, facial lotion, one that   353 353

can help teenage skin problems too. Massage the lotion into the face   367 367

and throat with gentle, upward strokes. Leave it on for five minutes   381 381

or so; then remove gently with soap and water. Follow with a warm   394 394

rinse and then a cold one.   <u>400</u> 400

After handling onions, rub your hands with salt and then rinse   414

to remove any onion odour. Tired feet can be soothed by soaking   427

them in a foot bath to which a handful of salt has been added. Salt,   441

by itself or mixed with baking soda, is a great teeth whitener. Also,   455

it slows the build-up of tartar, hardens the gums, and sweetens the   468

breath.   <u>470</u>

1   2   3   4   5   6   7   8   9   10   11   12   13   14

Letter Writing

84
GWPM

Before you can begin to write a thing, you must have a clear   12   12
understanding of why you are writing; so collect all of the data you   26   26
will need for your letter. Then you must decide what you want to   39   39
say and how you are going to say it. Make a plan or outline of your   52   52
letter in point form. A plan can be a big help because it lets you   66   66
change your mind and add or delete items before you start to write   80   80
or dictate. Too,[1] if you were interrupted while you were writing and   94   94
had to come back to it at a later time, your thoughts would still be   108 108
there in point form and you could pick up right from where you left   121 121
off.   122 122

Next, sort the points into a logical sequence. Then check the   135 135
points to be sure that you have not missed any. When you are writing   149 149
the letter from your plan, you will use paragraphs to group points   162 162
which relate to one main[2] idea. From your plan, you will soon see   175 175
which points belong together in one paragraph. Paragraphs make a   188 188
letter look nice, and they help to get the message across quickly.   201 201

As a rule, a business letter will have three or more paragraphs: 215 215
an opening one, one or more which contain the data, and a closing   228 228
one. Short paragraphs are easy to read and are more pleasing to   241 241
the eye than long ones. For this reason, it is good[3] practice to use   255 255
fairly short paragraphs in letter writing. Do not use a succession of   269 269
two- or three-line paragraphs, though; these do not look pleasing on   283 283
the page and force the reader to jump too quickly from one idea to   297 297
the next.   299 299

The opening paragraph should be short. It should tell the reader   313 313
the subject of the letter and the reason for writing. It should catch   327 327
the reader's attention and put him or her[4] in the right frame of mind   341 341
for grasping the message. The closing paragraph is just as important,   355 355
if not more so. Its purpose is to convince the reader to take the   368 368
action you desire, or to inform him or her of what action is being   382 382
taken and what the next step will be. The middle paragraphs give   395 395
the information and the details. Each should contain just one main   409 409
idea and be no more than nine or ten lines long.[5]   420 420

When your letter is done, check it over to make sure that it is   433
clear and concise, complete and correct, and last but not least, that   447
it is courteous.   452

1 | 2 | 3 | 4 | 5 | 6 | 7 | 8 | 9 | 10 | 11 | 12 | 13 | 14

On Time

88
GWPM

Boy, do I hate to get up in the morning. The trouble is I have 13 13
to be at work by nine o'clock. Sometimes I get there by five after 26 26
nine. Sometimes it's nine-thirty. I'm hardly ever on time but nobody 40 40
says anything about it. I like my job. I am a transcription typist 54 54
in a big office. My boss dictates her letters onto a tape; then I 67 67
listen to her voice and type the letters. 75 75

Well, this morning it's eight-thirty and I am still in bed.[1] Boy, 89 89
I'm really going to be late today. I jump into my clothes and run a 103 103
comb through my hair. Thank goodness my hair is short! I get into 117 117
my car and drive – fast. I make good time, park the car in the lot, 130 130
and dash into the office building. Everyone is working hard when I 143 143
get in. A couple of the girls look up. When I say hi, I get a cool 157 157
reception. I settle down at my desk. My boss is out, thank goodness. 171 171
I turn on the transcriber[2] and hear my boss's voice on the tape. She 185 185
tells me to type a letter to Ann Jones. Hey, that's me! She gives me 199 199
the address – the whole works, just like a letter to someone I don't 213 213
know. This is nuts. I type, and here is how it reads: 224 224

"You have been working for this company for four months. During 238 238
that time I have found you to be a willing, intelligent worker and 252 252
a very fine typist. There is one serious problem, however.[3] You never 266 266
come to work on time. Some days you are five minutes late. Sometimes 280 280
you are as much as thirty minutes late. There are fifteen people 293 293
working in this office. Fourteen of them get to work on time. You 306 306
do not. I think we all feel irritated when we see you coming in late. 320 320
You do not have special privileges here. I have heard the staff talk- 334 334
ing about your lateness. One person suggested that maybe everybody 348 348
should come in[4] late. If you don't have to be on time, why should 361 361
they? I don't think you realize that your office friends resent you 375 375
for coming in late. It is very bad for office morale. Besides, the 389 389
company pays you for a full day, and you do not give it to us. In 402 402
six weeks you will be eligible for a raise. If you can correct this 416 416
bad work habit, I will recommend you for the raise. If you do not, 430 430
I will have to fire you. Sincerely, Jane Dunn."[5] 440 440

Boy, is my face red. I put the letter on my boss's desk. When 454
she returns, she sees the letter and asks whether I have any ques- 467
tions. I say no and she hands me a package. I open it. It's an 480
alarm clock. "I will try hard, Mrs. Dunn," I say. "I just never 493
realized that being on time was so important." 502

1 | 2 | 3 | 4 | 5 | 6 | 7 | 8 | 9 | 10 | 11 | 12 | 13 | 14

Vine Giant

92
GWPM

If you should ever come across a green giant of a plant with 12
pretty flowers, it is more than likely that you are viewing kudzu. 25
Kudzu is a vine that drapes its leaves over ordinary things until 38
they look like spooky creatures. It will shroud anything in its path. 52
It can cover an old junked car in a few weeks or an empty house 65
in just one summer. Kudzu grows so fast that some people call it 78
the mile-a-minute vine. Others say you can measure its growth in 91
miles or kilometres per hour, just as you would measure the speed 104
of a car. I have heard one tale which tells of a farmer who planted 118
some kudzu behind his barn. The story says the kudzu grew so fast 131
that it beat the farmer back to his house. I must admit that kudzu 145
does grow fast, but not that fast. At most, a stem can grow about 158
one foot or thirty centimetres per day. 166

Kudzu did not always grow in North America. It came from 179
Asia where it is used in many ways. The Japanese use the vines to 193
make cloth, baskets, and paper. They make hay from the leaves. The 207
Chinese grind up the vine's roots to make flour. 217

Americans first saw kudzu at an exhibit over a hundred years 230
ago. They liked the way it looked so much that they began to plant 243
the vine to shade their porches from the hot summer sun. Farmers 256
found that their animals liked to eat kudzu too; and when kudzu 269
grew, it made the soil richer around its roots. Then someone found 283
that the fast-growing plant helped keep the soil from washing away 297
along new roads and highways. Kudzu was good for so many things 310
that people began to call it the miracle vine. 320

Kudzu grew especially well in the southern United States. There 334
it grew, and grew, and grew. In fact, it grew too well. Now, most 347
southern folks think kudzu is a curse. Foresters don't like the way 361
it sneaks into forests and kills the trees by blocking out the sun- 374
light. Farmers don't like the way it invades their fields and crowds 388
their crops. Telephone companies don't like the way it sometimes 401
pulls down their poles and wires with its heavy, grasping vines. 414
Today, people no longer call kudzu a miracle vine. Instead, they call 428
it a weed. But this fast-growing vine is neither all good nor all bad. 442
Like so many other things in life, kudzu is a monster only when it 456
gets out of control. 460

1 | 2 | 3 | 4 | 5 | 6 | 7 | 8 | 9 | 10 | 11 | 12 | 13 | 14

Pygmalion

96
GWPM

The old Greek myths are full of unusual tales – of gods and men, of strange creatures, of brave heroes and high adventure – and they even talk of love.

One of these myths tells the love story of a sculptor named Pygmalion. He was a young man who was well known for his talent and his desire to produce perfect works of art. So much did he seek perfection that he began to demand it in his personal life as well.

Pygmalion's friends urged him to marry and settle down,[1] but none of the girls he knew could meet his high ideals. Not wanting to settle for less than perfection, he set about to sculpt his vision of the flawless woman. He applied himself wholly to the task, and under his gifted hands the statue took shape and each day became more beautiful. Day and night he worked until, at last, not a flaw could be found. His ivory maiden was lovely beyond compare and was so lifelike that she appeared to be alive and simply to have paused for a[2] moment.

Soon after the work was completed, it became apparent that a strange thing had happened to Pygmalion. He had fallen deeply and madly in love with his creation. For some time, he pretended his statue really was alive. He spoke to her and pretended that she was too shy to reply. He kissed her and brought her gifts of flowers and fruit, and pretended that she was pleased. At long last, he had to face the truth. He was in love with a lifeless piece of stone.[3]

On the feast day of Venus, the goddess of love, Pygmalion was one of thousands who came to the temple to seek aid in their love affairs. When it came his turn to pray, Pygmalion asked that he find a maiden like his ivory statue. As he rose to leave the temple, the flame on the altar in front of which he stood flared up three times. If only this were a sign!

Pygmalion returned home in better spirits than he had been in for a long time, but still his heart was sad.[4] Would he find a maid, and if so, could she ever take the place of his beloved stone lady? He went in to his statue and touched her arms. He imagined they felt soft and warm. He kissed her lips and could almost swear they mellowed under his. He clasped her body in his arms. Her cold stiffness vanished. She was alive! He looked into her face, and she smiled and took his hand. Pygmalion called her Galatea. They were married soon after and lived happily ever after.[5]

| 13 |
| 27 |
| 31 |
| 44 |
| 57 |
| 71 |
| 84 |
| 98 |
| 111 |
| 125 |
| 139 |
| 153 |
| 166 |
| 180 |
| 194 |
| 207 |
| 221 |
| 234 |
| 248 |
| 262 |
| 276 |
| 288 |
| 301 |
| 314 |
| 328 |
| 342 |
| 356 |
| 361 |
| 374 |
| 388 |
| 402 |
| 416 |
| 429 |
| 442 |
| 456 |
| 470 |
| 480 |

1 | 2 | 3 | 4 | 5 | 6 | 7 | 8 | 9 | 10 | 11 | 12 | 13 | 14

New World

100
GWPM

It must have been late at night when I finally awoke, for the · 12
room was as black as could be. All of my limbs ached. I felt as · 25
though I had been the victim of a hard and powerful blow. How I · 38
had gotten here and for what purpose, I did not know. I yearned · 51
for something or someone; yet I didn't know what, whom, or why. A · 64
feeling of loneliness crept over me, and then for some strange reason, · 78
I began to cry. A blinding light came on and a gigantic creature · 91
dressed in white came into view. I felt¹ helpless and scared. The · 104
creature walked over and stared down at me. Then it began making · 117
weird noises and distorting its face in the most peculiar manner. · 130
Somehow it seemed to relax me and I fell into a deep sleep. · 143

When morning came, I awoke more refreshed. Looking round · 156
me, I found that I was encaged in a glass cubicle which offered just · 170
enough room for my outstretched body. Now, I have always thought · 183
myself to be a gentle and harmless person, and so I found my imprison- · 197
ment both² puzzling and disturbing. · 204

On glancing round the room, I saw that small glass cells were · 217
to be found everywhere I looked. As my eyes focussed I could see · 230
that each one held another unfortunate inmate like myself. There · 243
must have been thirty, all told. Further probing revealed a huge · 256
glass window in the wall directly facing me. What was this window · 269
for? Was I on display in a zoo? As I pondered my plight, the door · 282
burst open and another creature, dressed in white and topped with · 295
brown fuzz, strode in³ shouting in a strange tongue. As the creature · 309
made its rounds of the prisoners, I grew angry. I was getting hungry. · 323
Was there no food in this jail? What had we done to deserve this · 336
kind of treatment? As was my wont when I was upset, I began to · 349
cry. The white creature marched over to my cell and began to make · 362
gurgling sounds to me. I could not guess what it was trying to say, · 376
but a sudden fatigue came over me and I fell asleep once more. · 389

I wakened up to find a host of faces peering down⁴ at me through · 403
the great window. Creatures tapped on the pane and made outrageous · 417
faces. I spent three weeks in that terrible place. Thinking back · 430
now, a whole year later, I would never give up my luxurious crib here · 444
at home to return to my little cell there at the hospital. I know I · 458
would not want to endure those silly "people" again, looking down at · 472
me through that big glass window, tapping and making faces and dis- · 486
turbing my sleep – even if one of them did turn out to be my mother.⁵ · 500

1 ｜ 2 ｜ 3 ｜ 4 ｜ 5 ｜ 6 ｜ 7 ｜ 8 ｜ 9 ｜ 10 ｜ 11 ｜ 12 ｜ 13 ｜ 14

Computer Novice

	WORDS
Last year, I made up my mind that it was time I learned to	12
run a computer. It seemed that everyone I knew was an old hand	25
at it. It got to the point where my lack of computer knowledge made	39
me a misfit at many social gatherings. All it took was for someone	52
to mention computers. Ears would perk up and eyes would start to	65
shine. The topic would spread like wildfire and in no time the room	79
would be buzzing with bits and bytes and scurrying mice. I was out	93
of my element, lost and alone in a world of lotus and perfect words.	107
I was so excited when I sat for the first time in front of my	120
new computer. I would soon show those computer buffs a thing or	133
two. The first instruction in the manual said to put a clean diskette	147
into the floppy drive and close the door. Well, what a fussy machine	161
this was! I took a disk out of the box, washed it thoroughly, and	174
carefully slid it into the floppy disk drive. Then I got up and closed	188
the office door.	191
A prompt on the screen told me to "press the Any key or click	205
mouse button here." Since my keyboard did not seem to have an Any	219
key, I picked up the mouse, held it to the screen, and confidently	232
clicked the button. Not a thing happened. I tried again, this time	246
making sure the mouse was pressed right up against the target spot.	260
Still no response. I decided to carry on in the hopes that the	273
computer would get its act together and start to pay attention.	286
The next few steps did not work either. The book then said to	300
put program disk number one into the drive. It was a bit of a tight	314
squeeze but I managed to get it in. I followed the next directions,	328
but to no avail. Some computer! Even with two diskettes in the	341
drive, it would not co-operate. What could be the matter?	353
Bits of computer talk flashed through my mind and then two	366
words came to the fore: bad disks. This had to be my problem. I	379
phoned a computer store and was advised to send the defective disks	393
back to the vendor with a note explaining the problem. There seemed	417
nothing else to do but comply. I wrote a note, stapled it to the disk-	421
ettes, packaged them up, and mailed them off.	431
When a computer friend came to visit me the next day, I related	445
to her my tale of computer woes. It was some time before she was	458
able to stop laughing. With her arm round my shoulders, she led	471
me to my desk and sat me down. With a flick of the switch and the	484
arrival of the C prompt, my computer lessons began.	495

1 | 2 | 3 | 4 | 5 | 6 | 7 | 8 | 9 | 10 | 11 | 12 | 13 | 14

Eppy

WORDS

Eppy was a little boy who lived with his mother in a small vil- 13
lage. Eppy loved his mother and tried very hard to please her. 26
One day Eppy was sent to visit his Grandma, who gave him a 39
piece of cake to take home. Eppy held the cake very tightly in his 53
hands so that he wouldn't drop it, but by the time he arrived home, 66
the cake was all crumbs. His mother chided him and instructed him 79
on the way to carry cake. You place the cake on your head, put on 92
your hat, and walk on home. 98
A few days later, Eppy went again to visit his grandma. When 111
he was leaving, she gave him a pat of butter to take home. Remember- 125
ing his mother's instructions, Eppy sat the butter on his head, put 138
his hat on, and trudged home. But it was a very hot day, and by the 152
time Eppy reached his house the butter had melted and was streaming 166
down his face. His mother ran to him and asked what was that all 179
over his face. When she learned it was butter, she exclaimed that 192
that was not how to carry butter. You cool it, cool it, cool it in 206
water, wrap it in leaves, put it on your hand, and come away home. 219
When next Eppy went to his grandma's, she gave him a puppy 232
dog. Eppy was thrilled. He took the puppy down to the river. He 245
cooled it, cooled it, cooled it in the water, wrapped it in leaves, 259
and held it on his hands all the way home. Eppy's mother could not 273
believe her eyes! She scolded her son and informed him that he should 287
have had a string in his pocket. He should have tied one end around 301
the puppy dog's neck, taken the other end in his hand, put the puppy 315
on the ground, and walked home. 322
A week or so later, Eppy set off again to see his grandma, and 336
this time he was careful to take along a piece of string. Grandma had 349
made fresh bread that morning, and she gave him a loaf to take home. 363
Eppy took his string, tied one end around the bread, put it on the 376
ground, took the other end in his hand, and trotted off home. 389
Eppy dragged the battered bread into the kitchen. His mother 402
turned around to see what Eppy was bringing home this time. She 415
said, "Eppy, you haven't the sense you were born with. You never will 429
have the sense you were born with. Next time, I'll go to see Grandma 443
myself! Now see those pies I've baked. They are spread out on the 457
doorstep to cool. You be very careful how you step in those pies." 471
And Eppy was very careful how he stepped in those pies. He 484
stepped right into the middle of every one of them. 495

1 | 2 | 3 | 4 | 5 | 6 | 7 | 8 | 9 | 10 | 11 | 12 | 13 | 14

Hank Got Cut

Hank and I had been eyeing each other since I moved in nearly six months previously. He had been dead for three years, or so my neighbours told me. I'd size him up from time to time, trying not to let him know what was in my mind as I gazed aloft at his bare, weighty branches. But I couldn't help feeling he knew and was getting ready for me.

Hank had to go. If I were to leave him much longer, that splendid oak would start to rot and all its firewood potential would evaporate. He measured 22 metres tall, I learned later, with a girth of two metres. He looked pretty straight from the ground up and should tumble in whichever direction suited me. I went to the store and bought a hard hat. Hank's time had come, and I meant business.

I drew a deep breath, collected my gear, and ambled across the paddock to confront Hank. I had felled a few trees in my time, but none so intimidating as Hank. He seemed to have a mind of his own.

I started up the chain saw and cut away some scrub that might have impeded my planned escape route. The power and telephone lines stretched between poles to the south of him, well within his reach; but I planned to lay him prone to the northeast, in a natural valley between his more lowly neighbours.

The saw and I took out a perfectly shaped wedge from Hank's trunk. Like a segment of cheese, it was. Then we took a breather. I looked aloft again and squinted, peering more intently up through the branches. Funny. The main concentration of Hank's branches seemed to be more to the south than I had thought, and did I now detect a breeze from the north?

I fired up the jeep and secured one end of a line to the towing hitch. I laid an aluminum ladder ever so gently against Hank's gnarled trunk and took the other end of the line above the crosstrees and secured it. Then I descended delicately, stowed the ladder, put the jeep in gear, and let out the clutch. The jeep promptly stalled. There was a creak from Hank – or was it an evil chuckle from the big oak?

I restarted the jeep and tried again. The line went taut, and one of the tires went flat. As I went for the spare and the jack, I glanced back at Hank. Perhaps it was only because of the breeze, but I could swear he was shaking with mirth.

| 13 |
| 26 |
| 39 |
| 52 |
| 66 |
| 69 |
| 82 |
| 96 |
| 110 |
| 123 |
| 137 |
| 151 |
| 165 |
| 179 |
| 193 |
| 206 |
| 219 |
| 232 |
| 246 |
| 255 |
| 268 |
| 282 |
| 295 |
| 308 |
| 321 |
| 328 |
| 342 |
| 355 |
| 369 |
| 383 |
| 397 |
| 410 |
| 412 |
| 426 |
| 440 |
| 453 |
| 463 |

1   2   3   4   5   6   7   8   9   10   11   12   13   14

Hank Got Even

The saw and I returned to the common foe and started cutting	12
the trunk in from the back towards the wedge. Soon Hank was almost	26
conquered. There was a mere sliver of wood between him and defeat.	40
Back aboard the jeep, I gave it the gas. The wheels spun. I	53
backed off a few yards. Then Hank took charge. Slowly and, I have	66
to admit, rather majestically he went down with fiendish precision,	80
right across the power and phone lines. There was a bright blue	93
flash, and all our power went out. Not only our power, as I was to	106
learn very shortly, but that of most of the residents in the area.	119
At that stage in my confrontation with Hank, I was sure that	132
the most he could now do would be to infest the house with woodworm	146
when I brought in his remains for a final drying before burning. In	160
no way could I have foreseen by what devious means he would continue	174
to wreak his revenge on me.	180
I brought some of Hank's limbs back to the yard and went to	193
work sawing them to length and splitting. I consider myself quite	206
adept at hitting the bull's eye when it comes to splitting wood; yet	220
in half an hour I had missed the mark so often that the axe head	233
was barely attached to the handle. Eighty dollars later, I resumed	246
the battle, cut a few more logs, and split them. In my new mood of	260
confidence, I was in no way prepared for Hank's continued trickery.	274
At our next session, one of Hank's logs refused to split and	287
actually swallowed the whole axe wedge. It just disappeared into the	301
core of the log. Disgusted, I threw down the maul, gave the log a	314
passing kick, and limped back to the house.	323
I am superior, I reminded myself, as I hobbled down to the	336
cellar. I picked up a log from the neat stack of Hank firewood I had	350
thus far made, and headed for the wood stove. There was a crashing	364
sound behind me, and I raced back to stick my finger in a hole that	378
had appeared at the bottom of the oil tank and through which gallons	392
of heating oil were jetting out. A Hank log had become dislodged	405
and fallen uncannily so as to sever the oil supply pipe. My shouts	419
brought help from upstairs, and in a little while the serviceman	432
came to repair the damage and present his bill.	442
In all fairness, I suppose, Hank has so far done a good job of	455
providing heat. A piece of Hank seems to burn forever. I had to pay	469
exorbitantly for this, but that was Hank's price – and I was obliged	483
to pay, rot his bark!	488

1 | 2 | 3 | 4 | 5 | 6 | 7 | 8 | 9 | 10 | 11 | 12 | 13 | 14

For me, the source of all wisdom is Farmer Wight down the   12
road from our country home. He plants hay or corn in the land we   25
don't use and where the pheasants used to run. I tell him how   38
newspapers work; he tells me about farming and who knows what   51
in the area. What I learn from him is infinitely more useful than   64
what he learns from me. More interesting too.   74

It was to Farmer Wight I turned when I found hornets were bur-   87
rowing into the lawn in front of the steps to the deck. The hornets 101
were huge and lethal looking, and for a while I tried zapping them 114
with insect spray at five paces. They seemed to relish it and come 127
back for seconds. I fled to Farmer Wight when I found that the   140
colony I was spraying at led to a huge nation of hornets behind the 154
house over the sump pump.   160

After touching on politics, taxes, and the weather, while perched 174
on the back of his pickup truck, I asked him how I should handle   187
the hornets. He thought they sounded a lot like mud hornets, and   200
if they weren't bothering me, why not just leave them be.   212

I explained to Farmer Wight that the hornets were right at the   226
doorstep. Although he still thought I should leave them alone, he   239
suggested I could try boiling water. All I had to do was heat the   252
water on the stove, then dump it on them. It kills whoever gets hit. 266
I asked whether I couldn't put a hose in the ground and flood them out 280
instead, but Farmer Wight said that wouldn't bother the hornets at 293
all. It would be like rain. My next concern was what if the hornets 307
turned on me. Nonplussed, Farmer Wight suggested I wear long pants, 321
long sleeves, and be ready to run. I thanked him for his advice.   334

I went to the gardening counter of a store in town and asked   347
whether they had any remedies. They didn't, but a fellow customer 360
did. He told me to mix a can of sardines with some corn syrup and 373
lace it with chlorine bleach. The stink of sardines attracts the   386
hornets to the bait, the sweet corn syrup tempts their taste buds, 399
and the bleach kills them dead. It works every time. I was thinking 413
how nice and easy it was when he added that it kills everything   426
else too – honey bees, insects, coons, cats, dogs, birds, kids –   439
anything that gets at it.   444

So I'm back to square one. While they're hard on the nerves,   457
our hornets have never stung anyone, so I'm now prepared to co-exist 471
with them – at least until they do.   479

1 | 2 | 3 | 4 | 5 | 6 | 7 | 8 | 9 | 10 | 11 | 12 | 13 | 14

Lump in My Throat

For quite some time, my father and mother had been discussing the idea of emigrating to Canada. At long last, they decided that Father would go and see what kind of life he could make there. If all went well, he would send for my mother and me. If things did not work out, he would return home.

At the age of eleven, I was more concerned with the mark I would get on my latest math test or on my most recent essay than I was with anything my parents were planning to do. As a result, I hadn't given the matter of emigration much thought until that April day when my father took his battered old suitcase and a well stocked tool chest and walked out of our house – and perhaps out of our lives forever, I thought. I wasn't at all prepared for the large lump that formed in my throat and the silly antics I felt compelled to act out in an attempt to avoid these new feelings I did not know and could not handle.

In a short while, my mother and I had settled down to a routine. I was kept busy with my work at school, and my mother had lots to keep her occupied as well. Now and then, we went on an outing. In the summer, we had some short, but pleasant, trips to the seaside. Regularly, we received letters and parcels from my father.

At that time, every child in England, on reaching eleven years of age, had to take a nation-wide examination. Just before my father left for Canada, I had received the results of my exam and learned that I had passed for the school of my dreams. I couldn't wait for that summer to pass. Then I was busy getting settled into a new school, one that I had longed for years to attend. On the first day at my new school, I was sure I was in heaven. I loved wearing my new uniform, and I loved the long, pink stone building with the green copper roofs where I now spent my days.

In February of the following year, my father wrote us to say that he felt he was settled enough for us to join him in Canada. While I was anxious to see him again, and to see the country he had told us so much about, I was crushed at the thought of leaving my dear school. Nonetheless, preparations went ahead, and in mid-March we were ready to go. It was time to say goodbye to my school friends, to our relatives, and to our neighbours. That lump returned to the back of my throat.

| 12 |
| 25 |
| 38 |
| 51 |
| 59 |
| 72 |
| 85 |
| 98 |
| 111 |
| 125 |
| 139 |
| 153 |
| 167 |
| 180 |
| 185 |
| 199 |
| 212 |
| 225 |
| 239 |
| 251 |
| 265 |
| 279 |
| 292 |
| 306 |
| 319 |
| 333 |
| 346 |
| 359 |
| 369 |
| 382 |
| 395 |
| 408 |
| 422 |
| 435 |
| 448 |
| 462 |
| 468 |

1 | 2 | 3 | 4 | 5 | 6 | 7 | 8 | 9 | 10 | 11 | 12 | 13 | 14

Mother's Little Helper

I know it is natural for a child of three to want to help out in | 14
the kitchen, but somehow when my daughter helps, everything takes | 27
at least twice as long as it should. One day last week, I was rushing | 41
to prepare two chickens to roast for dinner, and my little one was | 54
right under foot as I scurried around the kitchen. She was helping. | 68
To speed things along, I asked the older children to take their sister | 82
outside to play for a short while, and they did. | 92

Our home is in the country and we have a stream that runs | 105
through our property. As the children went out to play this day, I | 119
chanted my familiar refrain reminding them to stay out of the creek. | 133
With the kids all outside now, the kitchen chores would be easily | 146
and quickly done, I thought. How wrong I was. | 156

It seemed only moments after the children went out that the | 169
eldest child appeared back at the door waving and shouting that his | 182
little sister was in the creek. It's a shallow, muddy creek so I knew | 196
there was no need to panic. I left the two uncooked chickens on the | 210
counter top and went to fetch the problem child. | 220

By the time I got to her, she was about knee deep in mud and | 233
very stuck. Together, the other children and I tugged and pulled | 246
until we got her out, and then with a sharp scolding I took her back | 260
up to the house. Once inside, I popped her, clothes and all, into the | 274
laundry tub; stripped off all the muddy clothes; and sent her scurrying | 288
upstairs with instructions to jump into the bath. I remained at the | 302
laundry tub trying to flush out as much of the mud as possible | 315
before running the clothes through the washing machine. | 327

I heard the bath water running and assumed that things upstairs | 341
were proceeding as they should be. Good, I thought, I can finish | 354
stuffing those chickens now and get them into the oven. Then I will | 368
check up on the bath activities. But wait. There are no chickens. | 382
They're gone. Both of them. | 388

I asked the boys if they had moved the chickens and they | 401
pleaded innocent. Could it be? No! Upstairs to the bath I ran, to | 415
discover my daughter in the bath with the two chickens, a bottle of | 429
shampoo, and a face cloth. When I shrieked at her, she simply | 442
explained that she was bathing the babies for me. Innocently she | 455
passed me one raw chicken and said, "This one's done, Mommy. You | 468
should wrap him up." I took the raw, soapy chickens from her, | 481
returned to the kitchen, and called for a pizza. | 491

1 | 2 | 3 | 4 | 5 | 6 | 7 | 8 | 9 | 10 | 11 | 12 | 13 | 14

New Country

My mother and I came to Canada by ship, since that was the common | 14
mode of travel then. The voyage was uneventful, and the weather was | 28
calm. At least that was the word of the ship's pilot, whose report of | 42
the ship's progress we read each day. Although the ship often reared | 56
and plunged and shuddered and creaked through mountainous waves, | 69
not once did the pilot describe these seas as other than a slight swell. | 83

One day I stood at the ship's rail and watched with delight as | 97
the brilliant March sunshine revealed a coastline softened by the rich | 111
green of pine trees as far as the eye could see. So this was our new | 125
country! We landed in Halifax and in no time transferred to the boat- | 139
train for Montreal. The trip would take about twenty-four hours – a | 153
long time to a child whose longest trip had lasted all of three hours. | 167

That night as we clattered across the country, too excited to | 180
sleep I peered out of our berth window. All I could see was the | 193
unfamiliar landscape, which lit up in flashes as we passed through | 206
towns and villages, and the cold, white lights of train stations where | 220
we made a few stops. | 225

It was noon the next day when we arrived in Montreal, and soon we | 239
were enveloped in a bear hug by my normally reserved father. He bore | 253
us away in a borrowed car while we looked eagerly around us and tried | 267
to take in as much as we could. The blue skies had given way to leaden | 281
grey, and the little car we rode in slithered along through freezing | 295
rain. As we watched the icy pellets clump and then melt, we joked | 309
about the Canadian climate which, we had been told, was cold but not | 323
damp so you didn't feel the cold as much as in England. Not damp, eh? | 337

After supper on the first Friday, we went to visit some friends | 351
of my father's. A blizzard was blowing as we made our way to their | 365
home well out in the country. Not having the sense to turn around | 378
and go home, we battled gamely through, our British upper lips as | 391
stiff as they could be. We were snowed in at their home all weekend. | 405

On Monday morning, our host drove the three of us to the train | 419
station to catch a train home. There I stood on the platform wearing | 433
my light English raincoat and my sturdy English shoes – no boots, no | 446
hat and no mitts – and surrounded by mountains of snow. No wonder | 460
our fellow passengers gave me strange looks! We did make it home, but | 474
our next outing was to the winter clothing section of the nearest cloth- | 488
ing store. | 490

1 | 2 | 3 | 4 | 5 | 6 | 7 | 8 | 9 | 10 | 11 | 12 | 13 | 14

Princess Passing

I suppose most people are dazzled by the rich and famous. A   12
lot of us are excited by the prospect of being near someone who is   25
out of the ordinary. Perhaps we even hope that a little bit of the   39
glamour will somehow rub off onto us. That was how I felt when I   52
had the chance to see one of the British royals.   62

My first opportunity occurred when I was ten years old. A lesser   76
known princess was paying a brief visit to the town where I lived   89
in the north of England. Our school was assigned a viewing place   102
along the royal route, and every child was issued a Union Jack on   115
a stick. I planned how broadly I was going to smile and how smartly   129
I was going to make my flag snap as I waved it with great fervour.   143

We stood in our appointed place, now and then shielding our eyes   156
from the morning sun, and waited eagerly. And waited. And waited.   169
Then a rustle of excitement swept the crowd from the direction in   183
which the royal party was to appear. A long, sleek, black car was   196
slowly making its way towards us. My moment had come. I beamed   209
my most brilliant smile and waved as hard as I could while, along   222
with my schoolmates, I peered into the car as it glided by.   234

The person in the car was definitely not the one we were waiting   248
for. Perhaps this car had been sent on ahead to make sure the route   262
was clear. My smile and the snap of my flag had been perfect,   275
though. I congratulated myself on a fine dress rehearsal. Now I was   289
ready for the real thing.   294

We waited some more, constantly glancing along the street for   307
signs of the royal entourage. At last, we were rewarded by the sight   321
of another black car. From the way the crowd went wild, we knew   334
this one had to contain the princess. She was upon us and gone   347
before we knew it. Somehow, this time I wasn't able to get my flag   361
waving quite right, and my smile was nowhere near as eye catching.   374
In a way I was glad she was looking the other way when she passed   387
my spot.   389

My classmates and I couldn't help feeling let down that it was   403
all over so quickly; but at least, we told ourselves, even the most   416
demanding teacher could not expect us to write an account of the   429
day we so briefly saw a princess. Consoled, we raced one another   442
back to school.   445

1 | 2 | 3 | 4 | 5 | 6 | 7 | 8 | 9 | 10 | 11 | 12 | 13 | 14

Small Town Life

Two years ago I moved from the city to a house in a small town. 13
I looked forward to the slower pace of life that I had always thought 27
was the norm in small towns. Since then I've learned that slower 40
is not the right description. Decidedly different would be more 53
accurate. 55

Small town folk own their community far more than city dwellers 69
do. Since most of us know at least one member of the town council, 83
we know more about, and have more control over, how our town is 96
run. It does have a drawback though. It can make five thousand 109
people harder to govern than five hundred thousand would be. 122

In the city we mingled mostly with people who were much like 135
us. Our friends were people we worked with, or neighbours down 148
the street. Here in town, we know people from all walks of life – 161
tradespeople, professionals, farmers, and so on – and find our lives 174
much the richer for it. 179

In the city, a tradesperson would come to our house, do a job, 193
and disappear, never to be seen again. Here, the tradesperson and 207
I are on a first name basis, and we curl together in the winter. So, 221
while sweeping down the ice, I simply remark that some work needs 234
doing at my house and could he or she drop by sometime. 246

I can buy just about all I need in my town, although shopping 259
often takes longer than it did in the city because I stop and chat 272
with all those people I met at the curling rink. On a recent trip to 286
a city mall to buy the few things I can't get here, I did not notice 300
one conversation taking place. All I heard was music and sales talk. 314

I certainly don't miss rush hour in the city, cramming myself 327
into the subway train and not getting a seat until the stop before 340
I get off. Here, rush hour is called rush minute because that's as 354
long as it lasts. It's so nice to get home in three to five minutes on 368
the best transportation made – my own two feet. 378

When I lived in the city, visiting friends or going to concerts 392
was pleasant, but the drive home through the city was not. No 405
matter what the hour, traffic was heavy. Now, when we go out for 418
an evening, we drive home on almost deserted roads, under the light 131
of the moon and stars, real stars, millions of stars. 442

I must stop before I convince you of all the benefits of living 456
in a small town. Then, my small town would become a big city and 469
I'd have to move somewhere else. 476

1 | 2 | 3 | 4 | 5 | 6 | 7 | 8 | 9 | 10 | 11 | 12 | 13 | 14

Last week I received a card from Uncle Herbert. As his cards	12
and letters always do, it brought back fond memories of the fun	25
times my sister and I had with him in New Zealand when we took	38
a trip there a few years ago.	44
It was a long and tiring journey of over thirty hours. More than	58
half of that time was spent in the air, while the rest was spent	71
changing planes or waiting for the plane to fuel. Our feet were quite	85
swollen as a result of sitting for so many hours in the plane and at	99
airports. Of course we had consumed a lot of food and drink en route	113
and that had not helped at all. For the first few nights in New	126
Zealand, we slept with our pillows under our feet, instead of under	139
our heads, to aid in reducing the swelling.	148
For the next few days, Ann and I visited the sights. We wandered	161
along the city streets and looked into the shops. We stood on the	174
harbour dock and watched the sailboats float by. We strolled through	188
the gardens and sighed over plants and flowers and trees that we	201
knew would not grow in our own climate. We took a bus tour of the	214
city and the countryside, and sang along with the bus driver on the	228
return trip. Then we headed south.	235
We stopped for two or three days in the thermal region of New	248
Zealand. Here we saw sights we had only seen in movies or read	261
about before. We exclaimed over geysers and boiling mud flats,	274
steaming crevices and ponds that contained water hot enough to cook	287
your dinner. At the end of each day, we were glad to sit on the bank	301
of the river, take off our shoes, and soak our feet in its nice, warm	315
water.	317
From there we flew to the capital city. It was a small plane	330
but the flight was smooth – right up to the moment the plane began	343
its descent. Then we were bumped and joggled and jolted and shaken	357
until we were sure we would never make it. The wheels glanced off	370
the runway two or three times, then found their footing. The pilot	384
reversed the engines, and the plane ground to a halt. We had arrived	398
in New Zealand's windy city.	404
We stayed overnight with friends and, the next day, bounced	417
our way back into the clear blue sky and struck out for Christchurch	431
and Uncle Herbert.	435

1 | 2 | 3 | 4 | 5 | 6 | 7 | 8 | 9 | 10 | 11 | 12 | 13 | 14

Most days Herbert drove Ann and me on an outing. One day it | 13
was to the beach, another day to picnic in a park, and another to visit | 27
a sheep farm. And always there was the scenery to admire along the | 41
way. Of course, the best place from which to view the scenery is the | 55
front seat of the car; so, to be fair, Herbert decreed that Ann and I | 69
would take turns, day about, sitting in the front seat. | 80

On the way home from one of our excursions, the muffler on the | 93
car suddenly gave way and was dragging noisily along behind us. My | 107
uncle stopped the car and got out. After a quick look at the problem, | 121
he opened up the trunk and produced a rope. He wrapped the rope | 134
once around the muffler, and brought an end of the rope up each side | 148
of the car and in through the rear seat window. He then commanded | 161
my sister, who was occupying the back seat that day, to hold on tightly | 175
to the ends of the rope. Not once as we drove home did my sister let | 189
the muffler drag. Herbert was so pleased that she got roped in again | 203
the next morning when Herbert summoned her, even though it was my | 216
turn for the back seat, to hold the rope while he drove to the garage. | 230

Herbert decided to take photos of Ann and me in his garden. His | 244
grape vines, of which he was very proud, were in full fruit. He posi- | 258
tioned us in front of the vines and began to snap pictures. A number | 272
of times, Ann and I moved off to other parts of the garden, thinking | 286
to provide a different setting. However each time, Herbert coaxed us | 300
back in front of the vines and shifted us this way or that in order to | 314
expose yet another bunch of grapes. | 321

Herbert liked to spoil Ann and me with breakfast in bed. He | 334
served up two trays full of food and I ate all mine except for a | 347
biscuit-like cereal. Not having the heart to tell my uncle I didn't | 361
like them, each day I put the biscuits into the drawer of my night | 375
table with the intention of removing them before we would leave. | 388

When our visit was up, Ann and I sadly hugged and kissed our | 401
uncle, thanked him for the marvelous time, and boarded the plane. We | 415
stowed our hand luggage and settled back in our seats. All of a sud- | 429
den I remembered that I had left the cereal in the night table. | 442

Three weeks after we got home, I received a letter from my | 455
mother who had gone to stay with Herbert just after we left. She | 468
mentioned that she had found a stack of cereal biscuits in the night | 482
table. She had thrown them out without telling Herbert but thought | 496
a night table a weird place for him to store cereal. | 507

1 | 2 | 3 | 4 | 5 | 6 | 7 | 8 | 9 | 10 | 11 | 12 | 13 | 14

Those walnut trees down the side drive have got to go. The four	14
in the backyard are messy too, but we've learned to live with them.	27
There used to be a fifth, but we cut it down a few years ago. It	40
cast too much shade on the vegetable garden, and we had heard it	53
was toxic to the tomato plants.	59
The four walnut trees down the edge of the driveway are another	73
matter. They are messy, destructive, and they have no respect for	86
their owners. Not only that, but they harbour birds and animals	99
with the same nasty traits. As mature trees of fifty years or so,	112
they really should know better. Let me tell you a few things about	126
our unfriendly giants.	131
Spring has to be nature's most joyous time of the year. The	144
weather begins to warm, the days get longer, and showers sprinkle	157
the earth. Plants and trees react by budding forth and greening the	171
country once more. Our walnut trees join the parade with bright	184
green leaves and long catkins so dainty you don't know they're there	198
– until they begin to float down to cover the driveway and our	211
vehicles. When at last the trees get tired of celebrating spring, we	225
are glad to put the broom away and look forward to summer.	237
Walnut trees love summer almost as much as they do spring.	250
It makes them so happy, they shed tears, real walnut tears. Their	264
tears of sticky sap drip all over my sporty red Mustang and my	277
husband's brand new car. Great stuff for the paint! Out come the	290
hose, the chamois, and the buckets, and I'm sure you can guess what	304
we have to do at least once a week. It doesn't take long for word	317
to get around. Only first-time visitors park in our driveway. Every-	331
one else parks in the schoolyard across the street.	341
Fall is such a pretty season of the year, when greens turn to	354
autumn hues and harvest time arrives. Our walnut trees produce	367
an abundant harvest. They are loaded down with walnuts. In case	380
you've never seen a whole walnut, it is somewhat like a peach, about	394
the same size and containing a large rough stone, or nutshell in this	408
case, in the centre. However, don't try biting into a walnut; you'll	422
break your teeth. The hard husk is a deep green similar to a lime	435
or an unripened lemon. As a matter of fact, last fall a lady stopped	449
at our house to ask my husband where all the lemons in our driveway	463
were coming from and would he mind if she took a few. Without	476
batting an eye, Cam pointed to the trees and told her to help herself.	490

1 | 2 | 3 | 4 | 5 | 6 | 7 | 8 | 9 | 10 | 11 | 12 | 13 | 14

Walnut Woes – Part 2

Now as you know, squirrels love nuts. Squirrels especially love walnuts. The squirrels around our house love to picnic on the walnuts in our trees. To get at the nuts in the walnuts, they have to remove the husks. Walnut husks are not very good to eat, so the squirrels simply drop them – on our cars. The husks ooze walnut oil which leaves dark brown stain marks. These are very hard to scrub off.

Squirrels also like to drop whole walnuts onto our cars. What walnuts the squirrels miss, the wind blows down onto our cars. Did you know that whole walnuts are as hard as rocks? Our cars have many dents to prove it. Some of the walnuts fall on my neighbour's roof. She calls to complain that the racket is keeping her awake at night.

Fall, of course, is the time when trees and shrubs shed their leaves and prepare to bed down for the coming winter. Our walnut trees do likewise; but in addition to dropping leaves and walnuts, they release thousands of long, slim sticks that litter the lawns, the gardens, the walks, and the driveway. They gather in corners, clog the eavestroughs, and get stuck in my car's air vents. Yes, fall is definitely clean-up time.

At last our walnut trees finish unloading their excess baggage and settle down to sleep for the winter. One would think that our problems would be laid to rest for a while too, but not so. The walnut trees are now bare and leave us open to a whole new form of attack.

During the spring, summer, and autumn when the birds perch in the walnut trees, the leaves tend to shield our cars from most of their droppings, although there are a few weeks in the month of July when this is not the case. That's when the mulberry tree is full of fruit and attracts a lot more birds than we normally have around. The birds eat their fill of mulberries and then rest in the walnut trees which are close by. Before long, splat come down gooey red gobs on our cars. It is a nuisance but it's only for two or three weeks and we have to wash the cars anyhow. In winter, on the other hand, with the trees bare there is no protection for our cars and the birds splatter them to their hearts' content all winter long.

As soon as the snow is gone this year and before the sap starts to run, those four walnut trees will be history. So come on back, everybody. You can park in our driveway!

| 13 |
| 27 |
| 41 |
| 55 |
| 68 |
| 81 |
| 94 |
| 108 |
| 122 |
| 136 |
| 150 |
| 163 |
| 176 |
| 189 |
| 203 |
| 216 |
| 230 |
| 235 |
| 249 |
| 262 |
| 275 |
| 288 |
| 290 |
| 303 |
| 317 |
| 330 |
| 343 |
| 356 |
| 370 |
| 384 |
| 398 |
| 411 |
| 424 |
| 437 |
| 451 |
| 464 |
| 473 |

1 | 2 | 3 | 4 | 5 | 6 | 7 | 8 | 9 | 10 | 11 | 12 | 13 | 14

Windmill

One of the highlights of our trip to Portugal last year was a 12
visit to a real, working windmill. We had seen a few windmills 25
before, but only from a distance and most were in ruins. This was 38
our first venture inside one that was still in use. It was like step- 52
ping back in time. 56

The windmill was a round white tower structure three storeys 69
high and topped with a dark, domed roof that looked like a cap. A 82
weather cock was perched on the highest point of the cap. Through 95
the roof protruded the windshaft to which were attached the arms 108
of the sails. The arms were painted white with bright blue and red 121
bands, and the canvas sails were a cheerful yellow. What a pretty 135
sight it was. 138

The man who owned the windmill was in his fifties and his 151
skin was well darkened from the sun and wind. He was short and 164
stocky, with bare feet and pants rolled up to the middle of his calves. 178
It was easy to see that the windmill was his pride and joy. As a 192
matter of fact, it was also his home. 200

Through an interpreter, we learned that the blowing wind turns 213
the sails and the windshaft to which they are connected. Inside the 226
mill, the revolving windshaft drives big wooden gears which, in turn, 240
rotate the main central shaft which extends through the floor to the 254
first level. The main shaft drives more wooden gears on each floor 267
level causing the large millstones to revolve. The stones grind corn, 281
wheat, or other grain that is fed in through funnels or hoppers on 294
the upper floors. With a good, strong wind, up to four grinding stones 308
could be put to work all at the same time. 317

When we were shown the top floor, we were surprised to find 330
that the entire roof rests on wooden wheels. This enables the whole 344
cap to revolve when the wind changes direction, so that the sails 357
are always facing the best direction to catch the wind. If the winds 371
become too strong and erratic, though, the miller will furl the sails 385
and secure the roof inside the mill with iron hooks and stout ropes. 399

As we left the windmill, we stopped to listen to the whistling 413
of the wind as it blew through the sails strung with pretty objects. 427
When the miller pointed out that the objects were plastic jugs, we 440
were quickly brought back to the twentieth century. With a last 453
wistful look, then a smile and a wave, we climbed into our car and 466
drove on to our next destination. 473

1 | 2 | 3 | 4 | 5 | 6 | 7 | 8 | 9 | 10 | 11 | 12 | 13 | 14

Renovation

28 GWPM

The room was small and certainly not designed with two boys in mind – especially two who fought constantly. The three-quarter bed they shared was a front line battle zone. Twin beds did little to improve matters; the bickering and fighting continued. The only solution seemed to be to give each boy his own room. There was just one problem: there was only one other bedroom, and it was ours. There were three ways to acquire a third bedroom: give up my hobby room, buy a larger house, or enlarge our present home. The more we thought about it, the more we liked the idea of expanding. Not only would we acquire another bedroom, but we would gain a larger master bedroom, more closet space, etc.

13 13
26 26
39 39
53 53
67 67
81 81
94 94
108 108
122 122
135 135
140 140

32 GWPM

We drew up a plan to expand the upstairs from half a storey to a full storey. We called in several contractors to price the job and learned we could hire a contractor to do the structural work and finish the outside; then we could finish the inside ourselves. Being reasonably handy people, we decided this option was tailor-made for us and we signed a contract. We managed to cram all of the bedroom furniture into the living and dining rooms, leaving a narrow passage that wound its way through the maze to the front entrance. Because of a chest of drawers in front of it, the door couldn't be opened, but we were able to shout through the door to direct callers to the rear entrance. In the midst of the furniture were two makeshift beds for the children, while we occupied the basement.

13 153
27 167
41 181
54 194
68 208
82 222
96 236
110 250
124 264
137 277
151 291
160 300

36 GWPM

After the workers removed the roof, we stood in our former bedroom looking up at the stars and praying that these people knew what they were doing. They did. The new roof was constructed and the outside was completed. Then it was our turn. We installed insulation between the wall studs; then we covered the walls and ceilings with a plastic vapour barrier. A drywall expert put up the walls and ceilings, and a plasterer taped, filled, and sanded the joints. All the while, we cleaned – before, during, and after each job. Painting was our next task, followed by installing wood trim. Then the broadloom was laid and the furniture was put in place.

13 313
27 327
41 341
54 354
68 368
82 382
96 396
110 410
124 424
133 433

Finally, it was finished and ready for habitation. What a pleasure it was to have bedrooms again. That evening, each boy settled happily and quietly in his own room. It had taken three months of chaos, but we had found peace at last.

146 446
159 459
172 472
180 480

1 | 2 | 3 | 4 | 5 | 6 | 7 | 8 | 9 | 10 | 11 | 12 | 13 | 14

Baby Bonus

40 GWPM

When we arrived, Mrs. Nagle was sitting in a wheel chair under a   13   13
big maple tree. Her hair was white now and cut quite short, but her   27   27
face, although looking smaller and more delicate, had not changed at   41   41
all; and you could tell by her twinkling eyes that her fine spirit and   55   55
sense of humour were still intact. While my mother and Mrs. Nagle   68   68
reminisced, I recalled my own memories.   76   76

When I was young, the Nagles came regularly to visit my parents.   90   90
John Nagle was a quiet, pleasant man with a dry wit. He was tall, and   104   104
I remember thinking that I had never seen anyone so thin. Kay Nagle   118   118
was short and pretty with dark hair and eyes. I knew they had been   132   132
friends of my parents since they were next-door neighbours before I   145   145
was born. I also knew they had many, many children.   155   155

Kay was brought up on a farm north of Toronto. While in her   169   169
early twenties, she moved to the city where she worked as a bookkeep-   183   183
er. She met and married John Nagle, a carpenter, and soon they were   197   197
raising a family.   200   200

44 GWPM

With the onset of the Depression, John fell out of work and they   13   213
joined the many other families on public relief. Their family con-   26   226
tinued to grow. By 1935 the Nagles realized they had a chance to   40   240
figure in a rather large legacy left by a bachelor lawyer who had died   53   253
nine years before. He had bequeathed the bulk of his estate to the   66   266
mother in Toronto who bore the greatest number of children in the ten-   80   280
year period following his death. Kay entered her name as a candidate   94   294
and quickly found herself engulfed in a whirl of publicity that was to   108   308
continue for years. Newspapers vied for sole rights to her story,   121   321
companies wanted her to endorse their products, and the city promised   135   335
to bill for welfare monies paid out to winners. The family became the   149   349
butt of praise, support, jokes, and threats.   158   358

When the ten years were up, Kay Nagle had borne ten children dur-   172   372
ing the period, nine of whom were eligible according to the terms of   186   386
the will. A year and a half later when the courts concluded the liti-   200   400
gation, she was declared one of the four mothers who were entitled to   214   414
share equally in the estate.   220   420

The sudden transition from welfare to wealth wrought many changes   434
in the lives of the Nagles, but one thing it did not alter was their   448
love of children. Mrs. Nagle went on to have three more for a total   462
of fifteen. Most of them were present that day at the family reunion,   476
paying tribute to this bubbly lady who had made it all possible.   489

1 | 2 | 3 | 4 | 5 | 6 | 7 | 8 | 9 | 10 | 11 | 12 | 13 | 14

Garbage In, Garbage Out

48 GWPM

The saying "garbage in, garbage out" is used most often today in reference to computers. It quite simply describes the fact that if improper data is fed into a computer, then improper information will come out. Another place where[1] this saying can be applied is in the matter of eating habits.

Good eating habits are becoming more and more difficult to acquire. Increasing dependence on fast foods has become a way of life. To a great extent, this is to be expected[2]. Our society moves at a hectic pace. In most homes, both partners work. There is neither the time nor the energy for spending hours in the kitchen. What is too bad is that in taking the fast way out, we too often sacrifice quality[3]. Instead of reaching for an apple or a glass of milk, we snatch a pop, a chocolate bar, white bread, or a hot dog – the heavily refined foods that are loaded with salt and sugar. Not only do they contain little of the food values our[4] bodies require, but they are loaded with chemical additives and preservatives with which our bodies must contend. Some food producers even go so far as to wax fresh foods, like apples and oranges, to give them a brighter, more appealing look[5].

52 GWPM

Our bodies need an adequate supply of nutrients in order to nourish, maintain, build, heal, fight infections, and remove wastes. The body is a wonderful machine and is likely to withstand abuse much longer than will a computer; but if the proper nutrients[1] are not forthcoming, sooner or later the body will react. Often it is some time before the effects are actually felt, for the body has a way of compensating for what it lacks.

Fortunately, there is hope on the horizon. More and more people are learning[2] about the importance of wholesome food. They are cutting down on refined foods and are turning to natural foods instead – to fresh fruits and vegetables, to nuts and whole grain products. They are learning about the chemicals that are put in our food[3], and they are checking food labels to find out what the ingredients are. Many health food stores have sprung up and, as a result, a number of supermarkets are starting to stock some shelves with natural and more nutritious products. But the biggest factor in keeping our[4] bodies healthy is us. What we buy at the store is what the grocers will keep on their shelves. If we want to look and perform our best, then we should do ourselves a favour and avoid the "garbage in" syndrome. Otherwise, we become the "garbage out."[5]

14	14
28	28
42	42
56	56
61	61
75	75
89	89
103	103
117	117
131	131
145	145
159	159
173	173
187	187
201	201
214	214
228	228
240	240
14	254
28	268
41	281
54	294
68	308
82	322
88	328
102	342
116	356
130	370
144	384
157	397
171	411
185	425
198	438
211	451
225	465
238	478
251	491
260	500

1 | 2 | 3 | 4 | 5 | 6 | 7 | 8 | 9 | 10 | 11 | 12 | 13 | 14

56
GWPM

Proficiency at the keyboard may be defined as speed, plus accur- 13 13
acy, plus thinking responses. The quickest route to proficiency is 26 26
through a daily session of concentrated drilling in which the drills 40 40
are ones that meet your personal drill needs. 49 49

Do not be surprised if you encounter[1] times in your drill program 63 63
when progress seems to have come to a standstill or even to have taken 77 77
a step backwards. Your speed may reach a plateau, or maintaining 90 90
accuracy may become a problem. These periods are only temporary, so 104 104
do not get discouraged. Keep a positive[2] frame of mind at all times. 118 118

When you are checking your drill work, be sure to proofread very 132 132
carefully. Good proofreading is important in any aspect of keyboard- 146 146
ing, and drill is no exception. Without good proofreading, you will 160 160
not have a true picture of your accuracy[3] and will proceed to work on 174 174
drills that are not appropriate for you. Here are a few things you 187 187
should not do when proofreading. First, do not assume that you have 201 201
no errors because you did not feel a misstroke while you were key- 214 214
boarding. Do not just scan your typing looking for[4] non-words. A word 228 228
may contain an error but still be a word. For example, you might type 242 242
"were" instead of the word "where." Also do not simply look at words 256 256
with no regard for their logic within the context of the sentence or 270 270
paragraph. There could be a word or a line missing.[5] 280 280

Now let's look at some of the things you should do. Do read your 294
typing for logical meaning. Do read what has actually been typed, not 308
what you know it should say. Do check for obvious spacing or align- 322
ment errors and do circle errors to make them easier to see and count. 336
With good proofreading, you will know where your accuracy stands. 349

If maintaining reasonable accuracy becomes a problem, use an 362
error analysis chart to help you analyze your errors and to find out 376
what corrective steps to take or drills to do. Typing by letter re- 390
sponse – that is, where you say each and every character and space as 404
you keyboard – can also help you to acquire accuracy. This forces you 418
to pay attention to your stroking and the letters you are typing. If 432
accuracy is good but speed is a problem, you should forego accuracy 446
for a short period of time so that all effort can be put into increasing 460
speed. 461

1 | 2 | 3 | 4 | 5 | 6 | 7 | 8 | 9 | 10 | 11 | 12 | 13 | 14

Buying a Used Car

60
GWPM

The difference between the price of a new car and a used one, 12   12
plus the difference in the rate of depreciation, can make the purchase 26   26
of a good used car instead of a new one quite appealing. Choosing a 40   40
used car, however, can be somewhat risky. Unless you are an automo- 54   54
bile expert, you could wind up[1] just inheriting someone else's prob- 68   68
lems. But do not feel discouraged; there are a number of checks you 82   82
can make when looking into a prospective purchase that will help to 95   95
keep risks to a minimum. 100   100

When phoning about a used car for sale, as well as asking the 113   113
usual questions about make, model,[2] price, condition, and special fea- 127   127
tures which you may be seeking, enquire about the paint. Is it still 141   141
the original? If not and it was recently painted, there is a strong 155   155
possibility that the new paint job was done to conceal rust or body 169   169
work. When you are satisfied that the car sounds promising,[3] you will, 183   183
of course, go to see it. When you do, be sure to check under floor 197   197
mats (both inside the car and in the trunk or hatch) for moisture or 211   211
holes indicating advanced rusting in the underbody. Look inside front 225   225
and rear windows for water stains caused by leaky windows. Try out 239   239
the horn,[4] radio, windshield washers and wipers, and all lights. Open 253   253
and close all doors (including the one on the glove compartment) and 267   267
windows to ensure that they function properly. The cleanliness and 280   280
condition of the interior and trunk are often indicators of how well 294   294
the car has been maintained.[5] 300   300

Now for the test drive! Notice the efficiency, or lack of it, of 314
the start-up. As you are driving, listen for unfamiliar noises and 328
check for the car's ease of handling. Travelling at about 50 km/h on 343
a straight stretch of road, loosen your grip on the steering wheel and 357
notice whether the car continues in a straight line or veers off to 370
the right or left. If the car veers, it may have had front-end damage 384
which causes it to lose its alignment. Ask about it. If possible, 398
take to the highway for part of the test. Accelerate to the highway 412
speed limit and watch out for vibrations caused by improper wheel 425
balance. Finally, if you feel satisfied that this is the car for you, 439
make your offer right then and there, for a good used car sells quick- 453
ly. If you have any doubts, bow out. 460

1 | 2 | 3 | 4 | 5 | 6 | 7 | 8 | 9 | 10 | 11 | 12 | 13 | 14

Roles

64
GWPM

It used to be that the roles of husband and wife were quite | 12 | 12
clearly defined. The husband had the overall responsibility for the | 26 | 26
family's well-being. He was the breadwinner, the person who went out | 40 | 40
to work every day. The wife usually did not go to work. She stayed | 54 | 54
at home and was responsible for things inside the[1] home – cooking, | 67 | 67
cleaning, bearing children and attending to them. All this began to | 81 | 81
change a few decades ago. | 86 | 86

As the cost of living increased, a number of wives found it | 99 | 99
necessary to go to work in order to make ends meet. More and more | 112 | 112
women chose or were forced to continue to work after they married and | 126 | 126
while the[2] children were growing up. Before long, it became clear that | 140 | 140
wives could not handle the double workload and that husbands would | 153 | 153
have to pitch in and help. As a result, many home duties became | 166 | 166
shared tasks. In time, better jobs began to open up for women, and | 180 | 180
many females moved into positions that gave them more money[3] and pres- | 194 | 194
tige. At home, the male/female roles continued to evolve so that, | 208 | 208
today, equal-sharing roles are common. | 216 | 216

A few families have gone a step further and opted for a reversal | 230 | 230
of traditional roles. In this situation, the wife is the financial | 244 | 244
provider while the husband stays home and takes on the functions[4] and | 258 | 258
duties that used to belong to the wife. There is, however, one func- | 272 | 272
tion that he cannot take over, that of child bearing. In the human, | 286 | 286
this is the sole domain of the female. There is at least one animal | 300 | 300
species, however, in which the male does bear the young. The one that | 314 | 314
comes to mind is the sea horse.[5] | 320 | 320

Swimming along in an upright position and looking for all the | 333
world like a carved chess piece, the sea horse is the steed of many a | 347
child's dream. Not only is the appearance and swimming style of this | 361
fish unusual, but so is its method of bearing its young. Contrary to | 375
accepted practice, it is the male, not the female, that gives birth to | 389
the little sea colts. The female places her eggs in a pouch on the | 403
belly of the male. The eggs are fertilized in the pouch and are nour- | 417
ished there. When the colts are ready to be born, father attaches | 430
himself by his tail to a sea plant. He experiences the pangs of | 443
childbirth and soon the baby colts, looking just like dad, are ejected | 457
from the pouch. The newborn do not stay around long, but soon strike | 471
out to make their own way in the big wide sea. | 480

1 | 2 | 3 | 4 | 5 | 6 | 7 | 8 | 9 | 10 | 11 | 12 | 13 | 14

Lady Godiva

**68
GWPM**

It is interesting to note how a name from the pages of history | 14 | 14
can evoke an instant picture in people's minds. Too often, though, | 28 | 28
the picture has lost the historic significance of the person or the | 42 | 42
event and, instead, has latched onto the specific feature which origi- | 56 | 56
nally fired the imagination and made the name memorable. For example, | 70 | 70
at mention of the name Lady Godiva, most people will automatically | 84 | 84
conjure up the portrait of a naked lady riding a horse through the | 97 | 97
streets. What many people either don't know or tend to forget is the | 111 | 111
reason for that famous journey. Let me make it clear here and now | 124 | 124
that it was not, as is often inferred, the act of a naughty² lady. | 137 | 137
Rather, it was the fulfillment of a deal that would bring much relief | 151 | 151
to the poor in the region in which she lived. | 160 | 160

Lady Godiva, the wife of an earl, was a beautiful and devout | 173 | 173
woman. She gave her support to many churches and she helped to estab- | 187 | 187
lish a monastery. Her heart went out to the people of Coventry who | 201 | 201
toiled long and³ hard, only to have their rewards eaten up by heavy | 214 | 214
taxes. She appealed constantly to her husband, the earl, to relieve | 228 | 228
the people of their tax burden. Finally, tired of listening to her | 242 | 242
constant pleas, he retorted that he would comply with her request if | 256 | 256
she would condescend to ride nude through the town. It is quite like- | 270 | 270
ly that the⁴ earl believed his gentle, pious wife would not deign to | 284 | 284
expose herself in such a fashion, and would thus be forced to retreat | 298 | 298
and refrain from nagging him further. If that was his intent, his | 311 | 311
ploy was doomed to failure, for he was dealing with a woman of great | 325 | 325
courage, strong will, and bold determination. Godiva accepted his | 338 | 338
challenge⁵. | <u>340</u> | 340

On the day appointed, with only her long hair to cover her body, | 354
Godiva mounted her horse and rode through the streets. Some accounts | 368
say that all of the townsfolk were instructed to stay indoors and to | 382
keep their windows shut during the time of the ride. It is also said | 396
that a man by the name of Tom was caught looking out through the shut- | 410
ters. This "peeping tom" was, it is told, immediately struck with | 424
blindness. | 426

The earl kept his side of the bargain and eliminated most of the | 440
taxes in the area, and, as a result, the populace enjoyed a long | 453
period of comfort and prosperity. Now and then, a festival is still | 467
held to honour Lady Godiva and her noble deed. | <u>476</u>

1 | 2 | 3 | 4 | 5 | 6 | 7 | 8 | 9 | 10 | 11 | 12 | 13 | 14

Billy Bishop

WORDS

72
GWPM

Billy Bishop was a rotten student. His report cards were terrible. His principal didn't think he would amount to much. The one thing he was good at was shooting. He was a crack shot with a rifle. 12 26 40

At the start of World War I, Billy joined up. He hated the mud of the military camp. Standing on the parade ground one day, he gazed up into the sky and¹ saw a cleansing sight: a trim little fighter plane zooming out of the clouds. Then and there, Billy made up his mind to fight the war in the air. 54 68 81 94 101

Flying was not the breeze Billy had imagined. On his solo, he pancaked his training plane. As a pilot he could barely manage a decent take-off or landing. In the air, he handled his plane like a spirited steed.² But he had an advantage: he couldn't miss with a machine gun. He was so accurate he could shoot down enemy planes before they knew he was behind them. He developed the quick, darting attack as his personal style. 114 127 140 154 167 181 187

One day, after destroying one enemy plane and forcing down two more, Billy ran headlong into the Red Baron. With the odds five to two in³ his favour, the Baron was out for blood. As the seven planes swirled and crisscrossed in the air, the Baron poured a stream of bullets at Billy. One entered the fold of Billy's flying coat; another pierced his instrument panel. Billy lost his temper and charged. Black smoke poured from the Baron's plane. For a moment, Billy thought he had him, but the Baron⁴ had merely used an old escape trick. He dove over twelve hundred metres, flattened out, waggled his wings and was gone. They never met again. 200 214 228 241 254 267 280 294 308 317

Billy was sure that if he could reach the enemy airfields, unseen, at first morning light, he could launch himself into reckless attack before the enemy could recover from the shock. He started flying alone.⁵ 330 344 357 360

By the end of the war, Billy Bishop had won every cross, medal, and honour available to him. He had shot down seventy-two enemy planes confirmed. Counting the many hits made alone, far behind enemy lines where no allied witness could spot and confirm the wreckage, the real total, however, was certainly more than a hundred. Billy Bishop, the Lone Hawk, had become the world's greatest living air ace. 374 387 400 413 427 441 443

1 | 2 | 3 | 4 | 5 | 6 | 7 | 8 | 9 | 10 | 11 | 12 | 13 | 14

Nullarbor Plain

76
GWPM

The Nullarbor Plain is noted for containing the longest straight 13 13
stretch of railway line in the world – over three hundred kilometres 27 27
without a curve. I had often thought I would like to take the journey 41 41
by train across the plain to Perth, a distance of more than five thou- 55 55
sand kilometres. The opportunity finally came when I learned that 68 68
Trevor, an old friend who was born in Perth[1], wanted to visit his home 82 82
town. Trevor had lung cancer and was keen to see his birthplace 96 96
once again before he died. He did not want to travel alone, so I 110 110
offered to make the trip with him. 115 115

The morning we departed Melbourne, we were given a rousing send- 129 129
off by family and friends. Our first stop was at Adelaide, and after 143 143
a hearty lunch in the station restaurant, we[2] began the long journey 157 157
across the Nullarbor Plain. Nullarbor, which is Latin for "no trees," 171 171
proved to be an apt name, for the only vegetation we could see was 184 184
just low scrub. We did, however, manage to catch sight of several 197 197
bright, colourful, and noisy parrots, as well as a few kangaroos and 211 211
other animals, which broke the monotony of the landscape. The four- 225 225
day trip was a[3] mini-holiday in itself. Excellent food was served, 238 238
live entertainment was provided in the lounge car, and there were 251 251
stops in several towns along the way. We particularly enjoyed the 264 264
singsongs we had around the piano, and we joined in with great gusto 278 278
and enthusiasm. 281 281

At last we arrived in Perth, a city of great beauty and one in 295 295
which many architectural styles exist side by[4] side. It also contains 309 309
many lovely parks; in fact, even its freeways are landscaped. Perth 323 323
is probably the most isolated city of its size in the world. Located 337 337
on the banks of the Swan River and blessed with mild winters, warm dry 351 351
summers, and many sunny days, Perth is a city where beaches and boats 365 365
play an important part in its way of life. Sailing is a regular 378 378
pastime[5]. 380 380

Our ten-day visit was over before we knew it, and our parting 393
from Trevor's family and the friends we had made was touching. We 406
began the long trek back to Melbourne, a tired but satisfied pair. 420
We had each fulfilled a wish. 425

1 | 2 | 3 | 4 | 5 | 6 | 7 | 8 | 9 | 10 | 11 | 12 | 13 | 14

Potatoes

80
GWPM

Not only are potatoes cheap, but they are good for us. They are   13   13
a low-calorie food that fills us up, not out – unless, of course, we   27   27
dress them up with butter and sour cream. Spuds are a good source of   41   41
vitamin C and thiamin, as well as iron and potassium. How much of   54   54
these nutrients is available to the eater depends on how the potato is   68   68
cooked.[1] Because most of the nutrients are close to the skin, it is   81   81
best to cook and serve potatoes in their skins. Potatoes being boiled   95   95
should be cooked in as little water as possible. Potatoes are ex-   108   108
tremely versatile. They may be cooked and served in a variety of   121   121
ways. They may be baked, boiled, roasted, or fried. They may be   134   134
served stuffed, mashed, scalloped, in stews, in soups, in pies, etc.   148   148

Canadians are one of the potato's biggest fans, consuming[2] about   162   162
seventy-five kilograms per person per year. Canada grows over fifty   176   176
varieties of spuds.   180   180

Potatoes will grow almost anywhere if they are planted in a rich,   194   194
acid soil with good drainage, in a place where they will receive lots   208   208
of sunshine. Pieces of potato, each containing at least one eye (a   221   221
small depression from which sprouts will grow), are used as seed.   234   234
When they are planted, the sprouts[3] from each eye produce a bright   247   247
green, leafy plant above the earth and clusters of potato tubers   260   260
below. Farmers mound up earth, straw, or leaves around the plants to   274   274
protect the tubers developing close to the surface.   284   284

In many areas, two crops can be planted: one in early spring as   298   298
soon as the frost is out of the ground, and another in summer after   312   312
the early crop has been harvested.[4] Harvesting of the tubers can be   326   326
started when the potato flowers are in bloom, about eight weeks after   340   340
planting. These first young spuds are the "new" potatoes that we so   354   354
highly prize. Potatoes left in the ground will have grown to full   367   367
size by the time the plant withers and dies down. The late spud crop,   381   381
harvested in the fall, may be washed and stored in a cool, dark place   395   395
for use over the winter.[5]   400   400

Although potatoes are native to South America where they grow   413
high up in the Andes Mountains, they are grown in many other parts   427
of the world as well and have become a staple food in a number of   440
countries.   442

1 | 2 | 3 | 4 | 5 | 6 | 7 | 8 | 9 | 10 | 11 | 12 | 13 | 14

Timed Writings – Average

Olympic Games

84
GWPM

The first Olympic games were held in Olympia, Greece, hundreds of | 13 13
years before Christ. The most important contest at those games was | 27 27
the stadion. This was a short foot race in which contestants ran from | 41 41
one end of the stadium to the other. In the beginning, the games | 54 54
lasted one day, but as more events were added, the festival was ex- | 68 68
tended to five days, with the main contests taking place on the third | 82 82
day. Sports like running, long jump, leaping, wrestling, boxing, | 95 95
javelin throwing, and chariot racing were popular. The rules and | 108 108
regulations for the various contests appear to have been somewhat | 121 121
different from the ones we follow. The naked wrestlers were doused | 135 135
with oil to make holds more difficult, and it was common for boxers to | 149 149
have ears torn off during the games. In another event, everything but | 163 163
biting was permitted. | 167 167

The fifth day of the games was a day of parades and banquets, a | 181 181
day when the victors were crowned with garlands of olive branches | 194 194
picked from a sacred tree. The name of each winner, his father, and | 208 208
his country was loudly proclaimed. Winners were highly honoured. | 221 221
They received many presents, songs were written and sung about them, | 235 235
and statues were erected to them. | 242 242

At first, only free-born Greeks were allowed to compete in the | 256 256
games, but as Roman influence increased, other athletes were allowed | 270 270
to take part. Even slaves, trained by their wealthy owners, competed. | 284 284
Gradually, the character of the games changed – for the worse. To | 298 298
claim the honour of nurturing winners, cities bought top athletes. | 311 311
Slaves who had been promised their freedom if they won were caught | 324 324
cheating. Gladiators fought to the death, and wild animals were | 337 337
introduced into the fighting arena. When the emperor Nero decided he | 351 351
would compete in a chariot race, all the other racers, afraid of what | 365 365
he might do to them if they beat him, withdrew from the race. Al- | 378 378
though Nero's performance didn't quite set the world on fire, needless | 392 392
to say he won the race. At last in the year 393, a Christian emperor | 407 407
banned the games, putting an end to the slaughter and bloodshed. | 420 420

The Olympic games were reborn through the efforts of a French | 433
baron, and the first games as we know them took place in Athens | 446
in 1896 with thirteen countries taking part. Today, athletes from | 460
almost all of the civilized world compete, and the Olympics have | 473
become a symbol of international goodwill. | 480

1 | 2 | 3 | 4 | 5 | 6 | 7 | 8 | 9 | 10 | 11 | 12 | 13 | 14

Disaster

88
GWPM

This story describes but one of many natural disasters which have   13 13
struck an area of the globe that seems prone to such catastrophes.   27 27
The place is a valley high up in the Andes Mountains where the highest   41 41
peak rises to a height of over seven thousand metres above sea level.   55 55
Towards six o'clock in the evening, the clouds that had enshrouded the   69 69
summit dispersed. The view of the peak, which is never more beautiful   83 83
than at this time of the day when its vast snowclad slopes are en-   96 96
livened by the warm tints of the setting sun, was magnificent.   109 109

Suddenly, the scene changed. Thousands of tonnes of solid ice   123 123
broke off from the northern peak and came hurtling down the mountain-   137 137
side. Clouds of snow and ice blotted out the enchanting scene of a   151 151
few moments ago. An ever louder roar accompanied the cloud in its mad   165 165
downward career. Gathering volume and ferocity as it descended, it   179 179
carried everything before it. Two and a half million tonnes of rock   193 193
and ice had split off from the summit to leave a scar and a trail more   207 207
than nine kilometres long.   213 213

In the first village in its path, it was just at the time of the   227 227
evening meal and all of the inhabitants were either in their homes or   241 241
hastening to be there before dusk. Only two minutes elapsed between   255 255
the first warning of trouble and the arrival of the avalanche. Per-   269 269
haps it was fortunate that the victims were unaware of their impending   283 283
doom till the moment it struck them, for there was no possible way of   297 297
escape. Two hundred homes and nine hundred people were wiped out   311 311
in an instant. There were only eight survivors.   320 320

Sweeping along at three hundred kilometres per hour to the next   334 334
village, the avalanche swallowed up another four hundred people. It   348 348
left no survivors in its wake nor any trace of the village. With a   362 362
sickening roar, the avalanche raced on to engulf the third and largest   376 376
village. Half of the town was wiped out and a thousand souls were   389 389
lost. Within a matter of minutes, all the villages in the path of the   403 403
avalanche between the summit and the river had been erased from the   417 417
face of the earth, leaving nothing more than a scar of torn earth that   431 431
was four kilometres deep to tell the tale.   440 440

When the avalanche reached the river, the sudden rise in the   453
water level sent a wall of water ten metres high racing down the val-   467
ley to the sea. Bridges, farms and villages along the way disappeared   481
in a trice. The flood reached the ocean and was borne out to sea.   494

1 | 2 | 3 | 4 | 5 | 6 | 7 | 8 | 9 | 10 | 11 | 12 | 13 | 14

Writing Is Easy

Writing a collection of stories is really very easy. You have   13
just to sit at the typewriter and type all those wonderful notions and   27
ideas that are swirling around in your head. Normally, this works   40
well, but I must admit there are times when you just stare at the   53
machine for hours, your mind a complete void, until tiny drops of   66
perspiration start running down your face and your fingers become   79
stiff from being poised so long in position ready to strike.   91

At[1] this point, you realize that you need a little diversion and   105
then the thoughts will flow. So you make yourself a cup of tea; you   119
leaf through a few magazines; you tidy up the kitchen. That should do   133
it, and you plunk yourself down again in front of the typewriter. Not   147
a word nor even a letter appears on the paper. You cannot think of a   161
solitary thing to say. Usually your fingers stumble all over each   174
other in their rush to record your thoughts and words,[2] but not today.   188
All you can do is stare. Today you are Ms. Blank from Empty City, and   203
your brain has turned to mush. Your confidence has exited through the   217
back door and panic has entered through the front.   227

You try a few more change-of-pace tactics. You put some clothes   241
into the washing machine, listen to some music, and have another cup   255
of tea. It doesn't work. Nothing you do is setting the wheels in   268
motion. Gradually it occurs to you that[3] your talent has up and de-   282
serted you, leaving you dumb and stupid. The gift is gone and you   295
will probably never write again. All you feel now is terror. You   308
check out the folders of interesting clippings you have been saving   322
over the years, your books of famous quotations, also the Bible.   335
Nothing twigs even a glimmer of a story in your mental mush. The end   349
has come. Your career is over. You've failed. Everyone and every-   363
thing is against you. Even[4] your typewriter, for so long your obedient   377
helpmate, is laughing at you; and you deserve it, you dull, stupid,   391
untalented author. You may as well be dead. At least that would give   405
someone else something to write about.   413

So you go to bed hoping you may never wake up. You toss and turn   427
and finally slumber begins to settle. Then it hits you – the next   440
story. You scramble out of bed and rush downstairs to your beloved   454
typewriter and start to write.[5]   460

1 | 2 | 3 | 4 | 5 | 6 | 7 | 8 | 9 | 10 | 11 | 12 | 13 | 14

Uncanny Tale

It was a moment of joy and triumph for Morgan Robertson when he 13
learned that his latest novel, Futility, had been accepted by a pub- 27
lishing house. After a long and difficult struggle, his determination 41
and hard work had paid off. It was a thrilling story he had written, 55
a wild tale he had concocted about a passenger liner that was larger 68
and more luxurious than any that had, as yet, been built. She was a 82
huge, triple-screw vessel that could travel at twenty-four knots. The¹ 96
finest design and workmanship had gone into her making. Her interior 110
was a showcase of glamour and opulence. She could accommodate 123
three thousand people, although the lifeboats strapped to her side 136
had room for only a small fraction of that number. This was not 149
viewed as cause for concern because the liner was unsinkable. 162

When Robertson's ship set sail on her maiden voyage, she was 175
filled with rich and prominent people. Nothing was too good for these 188
passengers, and the² staff catered to their every whim. They were 201
treated to the best of food and liquor, both of which they consumed 214
in huge amounts. Gambling, games, sports, and music were provided 227
for their entertainment. Nothing had been overlooked in the way of 240
comfort and amusements. 246

The liner had been at sea a few days when the first ice floes 259
appeared. The floes were widely scattered, but they added an inter- 273
esting new element to the seascape and, for a brief while, were a 286
topic of³ conversation. According to Robertson's yarn, it was a chilly 300
night that April when his ship hit a great iceberg. The lifeboats 313
were launched but there were not nearly enough to go around. The 326
unskinkable ship went down with most of its passengers and crew on 339
board. 340

Little did Morgan Robertson know that this novel, published in 353
1898, was almost prophetic, and that fourteen years later his story 366
would be enacted live and for real. The similarities between his tale 380
and the later event⁴ are uncanny. The two ships were of similar size, 394
mass, and speed. They each had about the same passenger capacity. 407
Both were luxury liners on their maiden journeys and had many well- 421
to-do passengers on board. Neither ship had nearly enough lifeboats 435
for the number of people on board, but then both ships were labelled 449
unsinkable. Both vessels struck an iceberg and sank on a cold April 463
night. Robertson had named his fictional liner the Titan; the real 476
ship was the Titanic.⁵ 480

1 | 2 | 3 | 4 | 5 | 6 | 7 | 8 | 9 | 10 | 11 | 12 | 13 | 14

Wood

Of the many materials with which nature has provided us, wood   12
must be the most wonderful and the most useful. Our pioneer fore-   25
fathers would never have survived without it. With it, they acquired   39
such necessities as shelter, warmth, tools, and fire over which to   52
cook their food.   55

To some extent, wood has since been replaced by other materials.   69
For the most part, gas, oil, and electricity have replaced it as fuel.   83
Aluminum has replaced it as home siding. Plastic and chrome steel   96
have replaced it in¹ some types of furniture. In spite of all this, we   110
still put wood to abundant use. Everywhere we look, we see wood in   124
some form or another. It may be the framework of a doorway, the fence   138
around a garden, crutches that are helping someone to walk, the bowl   152
in which a salad is served, the letter opener on a desk, or the cross   166
on the wall of a church. Wood has made fortunes for many and is a   179
sought-after commodity in the world trading market. Countries with   193
large preserves of trees are deemed² wealthy indeed.   203

Each wood has its own unique character – its own grain, its own   217
colour, its own smell. Its value is measured by its strength, the   230
texture of its grain, and its versatility. Some woods are better for   244
certain uses than others. Most softwoods come from evergreen trees   258
(also called conifers because of the cones in which their seeds are   273
formed). They include fir, pine, cypress, hemlock, and spruce. Soft-   287
woods are commonly used for building materials and for the production³   301
of pulp and paper. Hardwoods are usually derived from deciduous trees   315
– that is, trees that shed their leaves each autumn. Hardwoods, like   329
cherry, birch, walnut, oak, and mahogany, are popular in furniture mak-   343
ing. Solid hardwoods have become so expensive that now most pieces of   357
furniture are made from pressed board, rather than solid wood, which   371
is covered with a wood veneer to provide the wood grain. Pressed   385
board is composed of sawdust and wood chips pressed together into   398
sheets or⁴ boards. Wood veneer is a very thin sheet of natural wood.   412

Almost everyone has an affiliation with wood. Some love to whit-   426
tle it, some build with it, some admire its handsome grains, sculptors   440
carve it, many folks rock in chairs made from it, and sometimes chil-   454
dren even get paddled with a stick of it. For many people, one of the   468
most pleasant associations with wood is watching it crackle and burn   482
in a fireplace, breathing in its scent, and basking in its light,   496
warmth, and comfort.⁵   500

1 | 2 | 3 | 4 | 5 | 6 | 7 | 8 | 9 | 10 | 11 | 12 | 13 | 14

Bionics

Although the word bionics was coined in this century, the idea	13
goes back a few thousand years. The word was formed from the Greek	27
words bios, which means life, and ics, which means to have the nature	41
of. Bionics covers a wide range of equipment that functions in place	55
of living parts. These range from prosthetic parts, such as dentures	69
and limbs which are worn outside the body, to internal replacement	83
parts like synthetic arteries, to machines like the kidney machine	96
that takes on the function of an organ.	104
One of the earliest bionic devices was false teeth, an item with	118
which we are all familiar. In ancient Egypt, missing teeth were re-	132
placed by carved bone or ivory attached with fine wire. False teeth	146
have continued to be made and worn down through the ages, but it was	160
not until the development of the technique of using moulds from which	174
the plates could be designed that dentures became comfortable to wear.	188
Peg legs and hooks are bionic parts which were used for hundreds	202
of years and even into recent times to replace lost legs and arms.	215
These are probably best known through the literary characters of the	229
pirate Long John Silver, who lost his leg in a duel and replaced it	243
with a peg leg, and Captain Hook, whose hand was bitten off by a croc-	257
odile and replaced by a hook. It's certain that neither of these	270
bionic parts was of much use for fine manipulations, but at least they	284
could carry out some functions.	290
In the last few decades, bionics has taken giant steps forward.	304
With the knowledge from research in almost every field – from animal	318
studies to miracle fibres to electronics – all kinds of bionic parts	332
have been devised. Many people are walking around today with a bionic	346
device – perhaps a lens implanted in the eye, a heart valve in the	359
heart, a pacemaker, a synthetic hip joint, an artificial vein, or a	373
bionic ankle. Peg legs and hooks have been replaced by limbs that	386
look real and are electrically connected to the wearer's muscles so	400
that they can be made to respond almost like the real things. Some	413
even provide more strength than a normal limb. Work is currently well	427
under way to produce bionic blood, eyes, livers, ears, hearts, etc.	441
The world has come a long way since Long John Silver and Captain	455
Hook. Now it's only a matter of time till the six-million-dollar man	469
becomes a fact, instead of just a fantasy.	478

1 | 2 | 3 | 4 | 5 | 6 | 7 | 8 | 9 | 10 | 11 | 12 | 13 | 14

Bluenose

Right up to the last lap of the race, the pair of graceful fish-	13
ing schooners, their white sails billowing in the wind, had been rid-	27
ing the waves almost bow to bow. Now, on the last stretch they turned	41
to windward and a surprising thing happened. While the American	54
defender Elsie struggled against the strong blow, Canada's Bluenose	68
charged ahead with her prow held high and proud. As she glided to the	82
finish line, the triumphant winner of the Fishermen's Cup, a great	95
roar went up from the jubilant crowd on shore. After the disgrace of	109
the previous year's defeat, the town of Lunenburg's faith and pride	123
had been restored. The news was flashed across the country and around	137
the world, and the Bluenose was on her way to becoming the best-known	151
sailing vessel of this century.	157
While the Bluenose was under construction, Captain Angus Walters	171
hovered about the shipyard like an expectant father. On checking the	185
framed hull and finding it allowed only 150 cm of headroom, he growled	199
that his crew were not a bunch of midgets. The bow was raised 45 cm,	213
giving it an elegant and distinctive look.	222
To both seagoers and landspeople, the sight of the Bluenose was	236
enough to take one's breath away. Riding at anchor with her tall	249
masts bare, her long plunging lines and the defiant lift of her bow	263
gave her the air of speed. Under full canvas with the breeze whistl-	277
ing merrily through her rigging, one would swear she surged with sheer	291
joy. Even in high winds and rough seas, she bore on as though there	305
was nothing that could stop or hurt her – and nothing did. It did not	319
seem to matter whether the Bluenose was fishing or racing, every fibre	333
of her make-up seemed to come alive. When Walters was at the wheel,	347
he always talked to his ship, and the crew were certain that she	360
heard and responded to his commands.	368
Right through those final years of sail, the famous windjammer	381
was acknowledged as Queen of the North Atlantic fishing fleets. She	395
held the record for the largest single catch of fish, and her racing	409
feats were the inspiration for songs, pictures, books, and poems. Her	423
home country honoured her with a stamp, and her portrait can still be	437
seen on Canadian dimes. The lofty clipper provided a fitting and	450
exciting end to the romantic era of wooden ships, billowing sails, and	464
lusty fishermen.	467

1 | 2 | 3 | 4 | 5 | 6 | 7 | 8 | 9 | 10 | 11 | 12 | 13 | 14

Bluenose to the End

With the Fishermen's Cup in the permanent possession of the	12
Bluenose and the era of windships drawing to a close, Walters was	25
asked to race once more. After much thought, he agreed.	36

In spite of a fresh overhaul, new paint, and sparkling white 49
sails, it was obvious the champion was old and tired after seventeen 63
years of weathering the rigours of working the fishing grounds – and 77
the first of the five meets proved it. The younger American schooner 91
established a lead in the first round and held onto it to the finish. 105
In the second race, Bluenose found her speed and won. Under light 119
winds in the third of the series, she won again. In the fourth meet, 133
her backstay parted and the challenger darted ahead to take the race. 147
With the competition in a two-two tie, the fifth and final race would 161
decide the victor. 165

Sailing well in a light breeze, the Bluenose took an early lead 179
and held onto it. With the finish line almost in sight, suddenly her 193
topsail halyard block gave way. With no time for repairs and her 206
opponent bearing down on her, Walters pleaded with his beloved vessel, 220
"Just one more time." Like an old war horse with a new surge of ener- 235
gy, Bluenose gathered every breath of wind into her sails and crossed 249
the finish line with less than three minutes to spare. For a moment, 263
the crowd of Americans on shore stood in awed silence; then a loud 276
roar of applause and cheering filled the air. There was no doubt that 290
this was a true champion. 295

After Walters retired from the sea, the Bluenose lay idle for 308
several years, losing money. No longer able to afford her, he finally 322
sold her to a freighting firm. After four years of lugging molasses, 336
bananas, sugar, and tobacco, the Bluenose struck a coral reef off the 350
coast of Haiti and sank. 355

Some years later, a brewery company built a full-scale replica, 369
Bluenose II, and invited the seamen from the original ship as guests 383
on her first sailing trial. Soon after the cruise got under way, 396
Walters was asked to try her out. Holding the wheel in his gnarled 409
old hands, he cocked his head to one side and seemed to be listening 423
for a long-lost voice. After the trip, the old hands agreed she was a 437
fine vessel, but there was only one Bluenose and there'll never be 450
another like her. 454

1 | 2 | 3 | 4 | 5 | 6 | 7 | 8 | 9 | 10 | 11 | 12 | 13 | 14

Break-in

We were probably rather smug about the fact that in the twenty	13
years we had lived in our home, we had never had a break-in. A break-	27
in was one of those things that happened to other people, but not to	41
us – at least not until about eleven o'clock one morning last year	54
when a young man came knocking at our front door.	64

Down in the recreation room, my teenage son Greg was annoyed that
his guitar practice was being disturbed, but he went upstairs and
looked out the window to see who was there. A chap was standing at
the door, while another appeared to be waiting at the sidewalk. When
the latter fellow shouted to his friend to knock louder, Greg became
suspicious and decided not to answer the door.

In a few minutes, there was a noise, at the rear entrance this
time; and Greg rushed to the kitchen window to investigate. Just as
he got there, he heard the sound of breaking glass, then the back door
opening. Grabbing the nearest weapon at hand, a frying pan, Greg ran
shouting and threatening to the back door. Well, the would-be burglars were so startled, they took off at a gallop – out the door and
down the driveway with Greg in pursuit, shouting and brandishing his
frying pan.

As the burglars fled down the street, Greg hurried back to the
house and telephoned the police. In a matter of minutes, four cruis-
ers had arrived and sealed off the immediate area. After a quick
briefing, Greg and two policemen set off for a cruise of the neighbourhood. They drove up one street and down the other, but the burglars were nowhere in sight. Finally giving up, the cruiser headed
home. They were almost there when Greg spotted a couple of figures
that looked awfully familiar. The cruiser halted immediately and the
police were out of the car in a flash. A short chase and a tussle
later, they had their men. A search at the police station produced
gold chains and other small wares from the pockets of the two sus-
pects. It was obvious their burgling had been more successful earlier
in the morning.

Greg arrived home from the police station a hero that day. Not
only had his surprise tactics scared the burglars off, but he had been
involved in their apprehension. It was certainly a day of excitement,
drama, luck, and pride.

| 78 |
| 91 |
| 105 |
| 119 |
| 133 |
| 152 |
| 166 |
| 180 |
| 194 |
| 208 |
| 222 |
| 236 |
| 250 |
| 252 |
| 266 |
| 280 |
| 293 |
| 307 |
| 321 |
| 335 |
| 349 |
| 363 |
| 376 |
| 390 |
| 403 |
| 417 |
| 420 |
| 434 |
| 448 |
| 462 |
| 467 |

1 | 2 | 3 | 4 | 5 | 6 | 7 | 8 | 9 | 10 | 11 | 12 | 13 | 14

Brownbagging

It may be that an American president was the first executive to give brownbagging a touch of class. True, a chef cooked, assembled, and packed the gourmet delights in the wicker basket and the president's wife carried it to her husband's private office and laid out its yummy contents, complete with silver service and linen napkin; but despite the grand style, it was still brownbagging. The habit has since caught on with a number of Canadian executives in the top and middle management groups who were quick to see its merits.

Brownbagging is a good way to avoid lining up every day for the business lunch at which you often eat too much and feel obliged to run or jog it off at night, and drink too much causing you to be in a dull stupor at the afternoon meeting with your superior and the person who has an eye on your job. Brownbagging is also a time saver and a money saver.

It is important, however, to brownbag it in the right way. Some executives restrict themselves to a piece of fruit and a slice of cheese; then they take a brisk walk and return to the office looking slim, but bored. Others throw together a peanut butter or ham sandwich which they sneak into the office concealed in their briefcases and gulp down when no one is around. This kind of brownbagging is bad, bad; it can cause indigestion, gas, heartburn, and perhaps even ulcers.

Good brownbagging involves a bit of planning, shopping, and a lot of self-indulgence. If you're a sandwich toter, liven it up with fillings like asparagus or lobster with mayonnaise, pate with slivers of cucumber, or cream cheese topped with slices of smoked salmon. At least one side dish to go along with the sandwich is a must to dispel thoughts of the packed lunches we used to take to school and to add a touch of sparkle and glamour. If you live in the city, there's no need to go to a lot of fuss making up your own. Chances are you will find there are many specialty take-out places that offer all kinds of delectable things, like quiche, croissants, exotic salads, stuffed tomatoes, fresh fruit tarts or pecan pie.

With lunches like these, you won't have to sneak your noon-day meal any more; you'll be the envy of the whole office staff. Not only that, but you'll feel relaxed and satisfied and ready to tackle the rest of the day. So if you're going to brownbag it, do it in style. Give it a real touch of class.

| 13 |
| 27 |
| 41 |
| 55 |
| 69 |
| 82 |
| 96 |
| 108 |
| 122 |
| 136 |
| 150 |
| 164 |
| 178 |
| 179 |
| 193 |
| 206 |
| 220 |
| 234 |
| 248 |
| 261 |
| 275 |
| 277 |
| 291 |
| 304 |
| 318 |
| 332 |
| 346 |
| 360 |
| 373 |
| 387 |
| 401 |
| 414 |
| 422 |
| 436 |
| 450 |
| 464 |
| 478 |
| 484 |

1 | 2 | 3 | 4 | 5 | 6 | 7 | 8 | 9 | 10 | 11 | 12 | 13 | 14

Burglars

WORDS

By the time you have finished typing this page, one or more homes 13
or apartments in this country will have been struck by burglars. In 27
most of these cases, the break-ins will have occurred when the homes 41
were unoccupied. One of the ways, then, in which you can deter bur- 55
glars is to ensure that your residence always has a lived-in look. 68
You can do this by eliminating the clues that tell a burglar the home 82
is empty. 84

If you are going to be away for a few days or a few weeks, stop 98
all deliveries, such as the newspaper. Arrange for someone to pick up 112
your mail, handbills, etc.; mow the lawn; shovel the snow; and check 126
your home regularly. Home timers attached to lights in various loca- 140
tions throughout the house will help to make the place look occupied. 154
Even better are programmable timers which will turn lights on and off 168
more than once during the evening. Outside lights at entrances will 182
also help to discourage would-be burglars, who prefer to work in the 196
dark. Be sure to use a timer, however; outside lights left on all day 210
are a good indicator that the folks are away. 219

Home timers can also be used to turn radios and televisions on 233
and off. The sound will help to reinforce the illusion that someone 247
is home. Pull some, but not all, window shades and leave blinds 260
slightly open. Be sure to lock all doors and windows, including those 274
in the basement, the second floor, and the garage. If possible, leave 288
a car parked in the driveway. 294

If, when you return, you notice any evidence of a break-in, do 307
not enter. The burglar, who could be armed, may still be inside. Get 321
to a telephone and call the police at once. If, in spite of all your 335
efforts, your home is robbed, you will be required to itemize the 348
things that are missing, not only for the police but for your insur- 362
ance company as well. It is important, then, that you have available 376
a list of all your expensive items, along with models, serial numbers, 390
dates of purchase, costs, and, if possible, pictures. Keep this data 404
tucked away in a safe place, such as in a safety deposit box. 416

Last, but not least, to help you and the police to identify your 430
property should it be recovered after a theft, have all of your valu- 444
ables marked with your personal identification. This can be engraved 458
onto metal objects or marked with an indelible marker on other materi- 472
als. In many places, the marking tools may be borrowed free of charge 486
from the local police department. 493

1 | 2 | 3 | 4 | 5 | 6 | 7 | 8 | 9 | 10 | 11 | 12 | 13 | 14

Business Conferences

Some people love them; some people hate them. Whether you agree	13
with the first group or with the second, the fact remains that the	26
business conference is a necessary part of our professional lives.	39
On the plus side, a conference gives you a chance to get away	52
from your daily routine, to visit another city, stay in a hotel, renew	66
some old friendships, and make some new friends. If you are manning a	80
display booth, as I often do, it is quite interesting to find out	93
which of your products is receiving the most attention from potential	107
buyers, and to see whether the competition's booth is attracting more	121
or fewer people than yours is.	127
On the down side, it's sometimes hard to arrange to be away from	141
home for the required number of days. As well, many people don't	154
sleep well away from home and end up fighting exhaustion instead of	168
enjoying the conference. If they have come from a different time	181
zone, the problem may be compounded by jet lag. Being away from home	195
often involves eating different foods at odd hours. To add to the	208
stress, meeting a lot of new people can be demanding, especially when	222
you want to make a good first impression.	231
Still, conferences can have their funny moments. On one occa-	244
sion, a colleague and I got caught in a heavy downpour while out at	258
lunchtime doing some shopping. We were soaked to the skin, and our	271
hairdos were ruined. For the rest of the day, we stood at our display	285
booth looking like two drowned rats, fearing that we were being com-	299
pared with the representative in the competing booth next to ours who	313
was always perfectly and elegantly groomed.	322
At one conference, we were squeezed into a section of a high	335
school cafeteria for lunch. Suddenly, we heard the command, "All	348
rise." With great difficulty, we hoisted ourselves up from the packed	362
benches to say grace, or so we thought. After a few minutes of con-	376
fused silence, we all sheepishly sat down again. What we had really	390
heard was not a request to rise, but the school's short-order cook	403
shouting, "Small fries!"	408

1 | 2 | 3 | 4 | 5 | 6 | 7 | 8 | 9 | 10 | 11 | 12 | 13 | 14

Caves Below

The world holds many natural wonders both on the ground and in | 13
the sea, but some of the most beautiful of all are found in caves | 26
beneath the earth. The natural splendour of caves has oft been | 39
described as fairylands and wonderlands, but sometimes even these | 52
words do not do them justice. These underground worlds of endless | 65
passages, vast halls, gleaming walls, swift rivers, cascading water- | 79
falls, crystal lakes, and unbelievable formations seldom fail to cast | 93
their magic spell on anyone who sees them for the first time. | 105

A cave can best be defined as a natural underground cavity that | 119
is large enough for a human to enter. It may be a single cavity or a | 133
group of cavities called a cave system. Some caves have been formed | 147
by the flow of volcanic lava, some by ocean waves hurling rocks and | 161
gravel against cliffs, some by the frequent bombardment of rock by | 174
high-speed winds carrying grit and sand, and some by ice; but most | 187
caves have been formed by the continuous action of acid water on lime- | 201
stone rock. | 203

Like the cave of Tom Sawyer, a limestone cave is made up of a | 216
maze of shafts, passages, and chambers. The outer area of a cave, | 229
where light still penetrates, is known as the twilight zone. Inside | 243
the cave proper, there is no light, no reflections, no distant glows, | 257
just total darkness. In some caves, the only noise is the constant | 271
dripping of water, the roar of a raging river, or the thunder of a | 284
teeming waterfall. In others, there is no sound at all. The presence | 298
of so much moisture in a cave creates a constant high humidity. | 311
Often, too, there is almost a complete lack of air currents so that | 325
the cave temperature remains constant and moderate in spite of exter- | 339
nal weather changes. | 343

Probably the most spectactular feature of many caves is the vari- | 357
ety of glistening white formations that have developed in them. Some | 371
hang from the ceilings like great icicles or rise up from the floor | 385
like dunce caps. Some hang in sheets like curtains or are shaped like | 399
flowers or sparkling jewels. | 405

Caves in all their glorious beauty can be viewed in many places | 419
throughout the world where they have been lit up and transformed into | 433
dazzling tourist showcases. | 438

1 | 2 | 3 | 4 | 5 | 6 | 7 | 8 | 9 | 10 | 11 | 12 | 13 | 14

Caves from Limestone

It may sound too simple to be true, but the fact of the matter is | 13
that most of the caves that exist in the world today were hollowed out | 27
over eons of time by the actions of three elements: carbon dioxide, | 41
water, and limestone. Even as you are reading, these elements are at | 55
work enlarging existing caves and forming new ones, perhaps below your | 69
very feet. The process is lengthy but simple. | 78

Large amounts of carbon dioxide are present in the soil as a re- | 92
sult of the decay of plants and other organic matter. As water seeps | 106
through the soil, it picks up the carbon dioxide and they combine to | 120
form carbonic acid. This acid water carries on down and slowly makes | 133
its way through the joints and cracks in the limestone rock below. | 146

Now limestone is mainly a mineral called calcite which breaks | 160
down in the presence of carbonic acid. As a result, as the water | 173
passes, it dissolves some of the limestone and carries it along in | 186
solution. This slow but constant action enlarges the cracks in the | 200
rock. Some grow bigger than others and are able to take in more water | 214
and grow still faster. The water in these large channels becomes tur- | 228
bulent and robs the water from the small ones. The motion and the | 241
increase in water speeds up the dissolving action in the large chan- | 255
nels, rivers may enter and help with their enlargement, and the chan- | 269
nels grow into cave passages. | 275

What is perhaps most appealing about caves is their strange land- | 289
scape formations. The interesting thing is that these formations are | 303
the result of the reversal of the cave-forming process. As the caves | 317
grow and the water level drops, large air spaces develop into which | 331
the water solution seeping down through the rock begins to drip. The | 345
air contains much less carbon dioxide than the water, which causes the | 359
carbon dioxide to leave the water in favour of the air. This loss | 372
permits calcite to come out of its water solution and be deposited. | 386
Ever so slowly, the deposits grow and take on a variety of shapes. | 399
The best known are the stalactites that hang from the ceilings of | 412
caves and the stalagmites that have built up from the ground. It's | 426
easy to remember which of these are which if you notice the "c" for | 440
ceiling in stalactite and the "g" for ground in stalagmite. | 452

The amazing sizes and shapes of caverns and their formations have | 466
inspired such names as Giant Dome, Hall of the Thirteen, the Big Room, | 480
Bamboo Grove, Frozen Fountain, Leaning Tower of Pisa, Bridal Veil, | 494
Jewel Cave, and Paradise. | 499

1 | 2 | 3 | 4 | 5 | 6 | 7 | 8 | 9 | 10 | 11 | 12 | 13 | 14

Caves Have Life

WORDS

Caves offer a constant, moderate climate, but it is in a world 13
of total blackness. In view of the conditions of cave living which 27
this imposes, the variety of life found in caves is quite surprising. 40

Many animals, like bears, moths, owls, frogs, snakes, and even 53
humans, may shelter in a cave entrance or in the twilight zone where 67
there is light, but seldom will they venture into the black depths 80
beyond. Some animals, however, can and do find their way in the dark. 94
The best known are bats, which use sonar sounding to navigate in 108
darkness. Some bats use caves just for winter hibernation. For 122
others, caves are daytime resting places. At dusk, they leave their 136
caves en masse, sometimes looking from a distance like a dense cloud 150
of smoke. They forage for food, usually insects or fruit, and return 163
to their caves at dawn. 166

Two birds which nest in caves also appear to have sonar vision, 180
although not as highly developed as the bat's. These are the oil bird 194
and the salangane, a type of swallow. The nest of the latter is built 208
with spittle secreted from under the bird's tongue, and is the main 222
ingredient in the well-known Chinese dish, bird's nest soup. Another 236
animal which manages to travel in the dark is the pack rat, but this 250
creature relies on memory and its own scent markers for navigation. 264
None of these animals, however, can be considered true cave creatures, 278
for they live outside as well as inside caves. 287

True troglobites spend their entire lives in caves. Their total 301
population is normally quite small, mainly due to the keen competition 315
for a meagre food supply. Without light, the only plant life in caves 329
is fungi and bacteria which provide some food, and, of course, some 343
cave animals feed on their neighbours. Most of the food, however, is 357
brought in from the outside, either via flowing water which contains 371
plant debris or other food, or by animals, like bats, which occupy the 385
caves and leave organic matter behind. 393

Among the many troglobites are cave forms of fish, flatworms, 406
spiders, crayfish, shrimps, and salamanders. They tend to be small, 420
white, and blind. Some have only vestiges of eyes, and others have no 434
eyes at all. Their sense organs, however, are extremely well devel- 448
oped and they survive by hearing, smell, and touch. 459

1 | 2 | 3 | 4 | 5 | 6 | 7 | 8 | 9 | 10 | 11 | 12 | 13 | 14

Caving Spelunkers

Have you ever secretly thought that some day you would like to — 13
engage in a really daring sport, something that would test your stam- — 27
ina and courage, that would offer excitement and adventure, perhaps — 41
even give you the thrill of discovery? For myself, I could not imag- — 55
ine doing such a thing, but I know there are a lot of people who not — 69
only dream of adventure, they get right out there and do something — 82
about it. Why, the news is full of the daring exploits of people like — 96
mountain climbers, deep sea divers, and spelunkers. Actually, I — 109
haven't seen too many stories about spelunkers, but I just thought I — 123
would throw that in. Oh, you've never heard of a spelunker? Well, a — 137
spelunker is another name for a caver, one who explores caves for the — 151
sport of it. — 153

I have explored a few caves and I love it. Of course, my idea of — 167
caving may be a little different from that of true spelunkers. I — 180
rather like the smooth paths, stairways, bridges, elevators, and — 193
superb lighting found in commercial caves. True cavers, however, go — 207
in more for dangling in mid-air on ropes over plunging rock caverns, — 221
crawling on their bellies through mud in low tunnels, squeezing — 234
through tiny openings not designed for their girth, swimming and wad- — 248
ing in cold water, or climbing strong waterfalls. This kind of caving — 262
is a real challenge but it takes a lot of skill and experience. If — 276
you think you'd like to try it, let me give you some advice. — 288

Start with a nice, easy cave where you can build up some experi- — 301
ence. Having the right equipment is a must, and the most important is — 315
light – not just one light source, but several in case of failures. — 329
Most cavers use a headlamp attached to a hard hat as their main light — 343
source. A map if there is one available, a compass, drinking water, — 357
some energy food, a watch, and a long rope would also be useful. — 370
Caves are cool, damp, and dirty so warm clothing, stout boots, and — 383
tough gloves would be in order. — 390

Caves do contain hazards, so never go caving alone. Also, let — 404
someone on the outside know where you are going and when you expect — 417
to return. Always stay within the bounds of your proven strength and — 431
endurance. Lastly, observe the rules of conservation. A cave is a — 444
closed and fragile environment that took perhaps millions of years to — 458
develop. Leave it just as it was when you arrived; the next spelunker — 472
wants to enjoy it too. — 477

1 | 2 | 3 | 4 | 5 | 6 | 7 | 8 | 9 | 10 | 11 | 12 | 13 | 14

Country Mouse

The little country mouse prepared her nest in a field of wheat | 13
and, in due course, six tiny pink babies were born. As the wheat | 26
matured, the baby mice also grew. Mother mouse told her youngsters | 40
that the wheat was almost ready for cutting, and before that happened | 54
they would have to vacate the field or be cut to pieces by the | 67
combine. | 69

One day while mother mouse was foraging for food, the young mice | 83
overheard the farmer and his son as they walked in the field discuss- | 97
ing the harvest. The farmer was telling his son that he expected the | 111
neighbours to come the following day to assist in harvesting the | 124
wheat. The mice were very excited and impatient as they awaited | 137
their mother's return. At last she arrived and they stumbled over | 151
each other in their haste to recount what they had heard. When they | 165
had finished, mother mouse did not appear at all concerned and in- | 179
formed her children that there was no need to relocate yet. The | 192
following day, the young mice were alert for signs of harvesting, but | 206
the day passed and the wheat continued to stand uncut – much to the | 220
relief of the young mice. | 225

The farmer and his son strolled through the field again. The | 238
young mice strained to listen and overheard the farmer comment that he | 252
had invited his relatives to assist with the harvesting the next day. | 266
The youngsters were very worried and anxious, and when their mother | 280
got home they related the latest revelation. Again, mother mouse took | 294
the news calmly and assured her offspring that they were in no danger. | 308
Mother mouse was right, for the relatives did not arrive and the wheat | 322
did not get cut. | 325

Once more, the farmer and his son appeared in the field. As they | 339
passed by, the little mice overheard the farmer inform his son that | 353
because his neighbours and relatives had failed him, it looked as | 366
though they would have to harvest the wheat themselves the following | 380
day. The young mice were in a panic and relayed the conversation to | 394
their mother. This time, mother mouse replied, "Now, my children, we | 408
will prepare to move to safer quarters before morning, for when the | 422
farmer decides to do the work himself, it will get done." The family | 436
moved immediately, and the following day the wheat was harvested. | 450

1 | 2 | 3 | 4 | 5 | 6 | 7 | 8 | 9 | 10 | 11 | 12 | 13 | 14

Cruising used to be only for those who knew they had good sea | 12
legs and for those who were willing to find out. Although many people | 26
thought of a cruise as the ultimate vacation, when the choice came, | 40
often the cruise was bypassed in favour of dry land. After all, who | 54
wanted to work hard all year to earn a few weeks' holiday and then | 67
take a chance on having to spend it seasick on a boat? Now, all that | 81
has changed. Seasick pills have almost eliminated that bane of sail- | 95
ing, and cruises have reached a new peak in popularity. | 106

Cruise ships are virtual pleasure resorts afloat, and all kinds | 120
of fun and games await their passengers. It seems that food is a star | 134
attraction on these floating spas. It is available in great abundance | 148
and variety. With breakfast, lunch, dinner, morning and afternoon | 161
snacks, and sumptuous midnight buffets being offered, almost any time | 175
is mealtime and anything from fresh fruit to lobster may be served. | 189

All the tasty temptations can play havoc with one's diet, but | 202
exercise classes and lots of activities are provided to help compen- | 216
sate. Tennis courts, shuffleboard, a swimming pool, and other facili- | 230
ties are available to the sports enthusiast. Even the golfer can keep | 244
his hand in at the driving range, although it is suggested that golf- | 258
ers do not attempt to retrieve their balls; it's a long way down to | 272
the ocean floor. | 275

The sundeck is a popular spot for sunbathing and reading. In the | 288
evenings, entertainment and dancing are the order of the night. Talent | 302
shows, costume parties, and other special attractions are common too. | 316
For those who like to try their luck at the tables or slot machines, a | 330
casino is usually available. Cruise ships stop at several ports at which | 344
passengers may go ashore for sightseeing and shopping. These stops | 358
are an important feature of a cruise and add a nice change of scene | 372
and pace. | 374

Movies have so often depicted a cruise ship as the place where | 388
boy meets girl that many folks have developed the notion that it is a | 402
great man-woman meeting place. Sad to say, the records show that | 416
women guests far outnumber the men. This may be quite satisfactory | 430
from the man's point of view, but it clearly indicates that the woman | 444
seeking romance on a ship is more than likely to be disappointed. | 457

1 | 2 | 3 | 4 | 5 | 6 | 7 | 8 | 9 | 10 | 11 | 12 | 13 | 14

Different Days

Whenever my children and I get into a discussion and I endeavour	13
to compare their circumstances to mine when I was their age, they	26
always remind me that those days were different. When I stop to think	40
about it, many things then were different.	48

Throughout the Depression, during which our family grew to eight people, we lived in a rented, three-room cottage. The woodstove was in the basement and that was where Mother did her cooking and then carried the food upstairs to the kitchen table.

Like so many other men, my father was on public relief. Until the food voucher system came in, the men on welfare went to a downtown warehouse to pick up their relief food. There was a variety of goods available, but each family was allowed only a limited quantity of each item. It wasn't long before the men started trading items among themselves – perhaps a can of beans for a jar of peanut butter – so that each took home a better supply of the things his family used.

Each morning, Dad walked downtown to the employment office. Sometimes he would be sent out on a job shovelling snow, delivering coal, painting, or doing odd jobs, and, if he were lucky, would earn a few dollars. Once he came home with three chairs instead of money because the employer claimed to have no money with which to pay him.

Our landlady was an elderly widow who lived with her son in the country. They raised hens and when she came to collect the rent, she sometimes brought us a freshly-killed chicken. We children had lots of fun plucking it.

During the war, everyone had to observe the blackouts. All streetlights were out and there could be no light showing from homes or buildings. Wardens patrolled the streets to ensure that darkness prevailed, and as soon as ours had passed, we would peep out beneath the blinds and watch him disappear out of sight. Then, with a little coaxing, my older sister would entrance us with one of her wonderful tales.

Of course there were no televisions in those days. The old floor radio was our indoor family entertainment and we children sat around it on the floor and listened to mystery shows like The Shadow. On Saturday afternoons, we were allowed to go to the cinema, a small local one that we dubbed Dutchy's Palace. Admission was all of five cents. En route we passed under a railway bridge where we picked up bits of tar to chew along the way.

The word counts in the right margin: 62, 76, 89, 98, 112, 126, 140, 154, 168, 182, 194, 207, 221, 235, 248, 262, 276, 290, 304, 308, 321, 335, 349, 363, 377, 391, 392, 406, 420, 434, 447, 461, 475, 482

1 | 2 | 3 | 4 | 5 | 6 | 7 | 8 | 9 | 10 | 11 | 12 | 13 | 14

During the war, Remembrance Day held special meaning, for every-   13
one had a son, father, husband, brother, or friend fighting overseas.   27
I can remember quite clearly the siren sounding all over the city at   41
eleven o'clock in the morning on Remembrance Day, and every vehicle on   55
the road and every person on the street coming to a standstill for the   69
two minutes of silent remembrance.   76

The war was well along before my father finally found permanent,   90
full-time work. Just before I turned seven, we moved into our own   103
house and, shortly after, our first telephone was installed. It   116
became my job to go to the store every day after school. Because we   130
had no ice box, it was necessary to shop for perishables on a daily   144
basis. Milk and bread were delivered to the door, but meat and fresh   158
produce were purchased from the corner store. In the summertime, our   172
milk was kept cold by standing the bottle in the kitchen sink under a   186
constant drizzle from the cold water tap.   194

Old clothes and other items for which we no longer had any use   208
were kept in a rag basket in the basement. When the ragman came driv-   222
ing his horse and wagon up the lane behind our house and ringing his   236
bell, my mother would take out the rag basket and sell him the con-   250
tents for a quarter, or sometimes even a dollar or two.   261

Often on the way to or from school, we would hitch a ride with   274
the local breadman or milkman in his horse and wagon. It was always   288
a thrill when he allowed us a turn at the reins.   298

Although we sometimes managed to excel in a few subjects, for   311
the most part we children tolerated school as a necessary nuisance.   325
Most of our efforts were expended at recess time on games like volley-   339
ball, rounders, and ledgers, and I especially liked to play alleys in   353
the snow in winter.   357

Rounders is similar to baseball except that the ball is larger   370
and softer, and there is no pitcher. Instead, the person who is up   384
throws the ball into the air, hits it with the hand, and runs the   397
bases. Ledgers involves throwing and catching a tennis ball. The   410
ball was thrown overhand to strike the sloped concrete ledge of the   424
school's foundation wall in such a way that it bounced into the air   437
like a fly ball.   440

1 | 2 | 3 | 4 | 5 | 6 | 7 | 8 | 9 | 10 | 11 | 12 | 13 | 14

Different Ways

Every summer, we spent a week or so visiting our former landlady.	13
We loved the change from the city – picking apples and cherries, feed-	27
ing the hens and trying to gather the eggs without getting pecked,	40
investigating the woods across the road and bringing back toads. We	54
were longing for a pet, and I adopted one of the hens as my favourite.	68
There was a big old cat called Jack on the premises, but he permitted	82
no one near him except his owners. When the cat's food was ready,	95
Mrs. Marks would stand at the open door and sharpen her long carving	109
knife. The sound would bring the cat running for his dinner.	121
Each bedroom in the old farmhouse was equipped with a wash basin	135
and pitcher for bathing, and we slept in the biggest, softest feather	149
bed you could ever imagine. We never had to be asked twice to pump	163
water at the old hand pump outside the kitchen door, and of course we	177
pumped far more than was needed. Somehow we didn't have the same	190
enthusiasm for the outhouse facilities, but we became adept at holding	204
our breath and at closing the door quickly in an attempt to keep the	218
flies out.	220
Our modes of transportation at that time were our legs, public	234
transit, and bicycle. Even Dad had his bicycle which he rode to and	248
from work every spring, summer, and autumn workday for over fifteen	262
years. Eventually my brothers taught him to drive, and in 1960 he	276
bought his first car. It was his pride and joy, and every night he	290
dusted and polished it until it gleamed. That car represented the	304
culmination of a lifetime of hard work and the beginning of a more	318
leisurely future.	321
Yes, many things were different then. We certainly did not have	335
the affluence that we enjoy now. We were perhaps more independent at	349
an earlier age. We did not have the gadgetry and conveniences that	363
are now widely prevalent, nor did we have the influence of television	377
on our lives. But were people and values really so different? We	390
were brought up to believe in kindness, honesty, hard work, fair play,	404
respect for other people and their property, and respect for our-	417
selves. Aren't those values still applicable today? I think so, and	431
I believe our children will too when their sons and daughters inform	445
them that things were different way back then.	454

1 | 2 | 3 | 4 | 5 | 6 | 7 | 8 | 9 | 10 | 11 | 12 | 13 | 14

English – From Olden Times

Language is the vital tool by which we are able to think, read 13
write, speak, understand, and learn. For most of us, that language is 27
English. 29

In the past fifteen hundred years, English has made tremendous 43
strides. From a few thousand words spoken by a few hundred thousand 57
people on a small island, it has grown to a million or so words spoken 71
by over 250 million people in every corner of the globe. This is more 85
than double the number who communicate in the next most widely spoken 99
tongue, French. 102

One of the intriguing sides of English is where it came from and 116
how it developed. Its evolution is commonly broken into three peri- 130
ods. The first of these is known as Old English. It dates back to 144
the rough and tumble Anglo-Saxons who invaded and settled in England 158
after driving the native peoples into the north and west of the 171
island. Their language, Englisc, was complex. Its pronunciation was 185
quite different from ours; and its nouns, adjectives, and verbs had an 199
array of endings, called inflections, which showed the function of the 213
words in a sentence. 217

The language reigned supreme for some six hundred years until the 231
country was conquered by the French Normans, one of the most cultured 245
people of the time, who set up their royal court in England. For 258
quite a number of years, the new reign saw two distinct languages 271
being spoken: French by the ruling class and English by the working 285
mass. 286

In time, the rulers began to learn English to enable them to 299
improve their dealings with the bulk of the people. This set the 312
stage for the Middle English period, during which the language under- 326
went a great many changes. A lot of the older words fell out of use. 340
Because the complicated word endings were difficult to learn, many of 354
them were dropped and more importance was placed on the order of words 368
in the sentence. A large number of French words were absorbed into 382
the language, not so much to replace English words, as to add to them. 396
This brought new colour and dimension to the language and greatly 409
enriched it. As the years went by and more and more Normans took up 423
English, their mother tongue was abandoned and English became the one 437
official tongue. 440

1 | 2 | 3 | 4 | 5 | 6 | 7 | 8 | 9 | 10 | 11 | 12 | 13 | 14

English – To Modern Times

The Middle English period saw a great evolution in the English language. From the Old English were retained the short, homey words which form the basis of the tongue today. Man, foot, wife, sun, night, heart, mother, and good are but a few. Of the vast number of words injected from the French, many had to do with the arts, fine living, government, law, property, and war. These included words such as dance, council, judge, rent, parliament, and armour. Often words from both sources, even though they held the same meaning, persisted – the Old English as the common form and the French as the more literary form. Examples of these are begin and commence, work and labour, meet and assemble, hit and assault, need and require, and clothes and garments.

The next important event which was to greatly affect the language came about shortly before the start of the sixteenth century. The event was the start-up of the first printing press in England. At that time, the language was in rough shape with many dialects and no standards for grammar or spelling. Words were spelled the way they sounded to the writer. As a result, the same words were found spelled perhaps half a dozen ways. The printers set about to rectify the situation by setting up some standards. This marks the beginning of the period we term Modern English.

For the most part, the setting of standards was a good thing, but it did have its adverse effects. One of these had to do with spelling. While spelling was becoming constant, pronunciations continued to change. This produced words like knight, knit, gnaw, wrong, wrench, and write, which contain silent letters that used to be sounded but the sounds were eventually dropped.

Throughout the Modern English period, which extends to this day, the English language has continued to expand. Shakespeare was, perhaps, the biggest single contributor. He was a great language innovator who did not hesitate to switch words from one part of speech to another, to accept and use new words from any source, and to coin his own new words and phrases as he required them.

Trade, travel, and classical learning have added a host of new words, many taken from other languages all over the world. From politics, war, industry, and science have come many more. A vast number of words have evolved in this century alone, and more are yet to come.

| 13 |
| 27 |
| 40 |
| 54 |
| 67 |
| 81 |
| 95 |
| 109 |
| 123 |
| 137 |
| 150 |
| 152 |
| 166 |
| 179 |
| 206 |
| 220 |
| 234 |
| 247 |
| 261 |
| 268 |
| 282 |
| 296 |
| 310 |
| 323 |
| 336 |
| 345 |
| 359 |
| 373 |
| 387 |
| 401 |
| 415 |
| 424 |
| 438 |
| 452 |
| 466 |
| 480 |

1 | 2 | 3 | 4 | 5 | 6 | 7 | 8 | 9 | 10 | 11 | 12 | 13 | 14

Exercise Needed

WORDS

"Exercise should be a must for all office workers." This strong | 14
statement was made by a well-known doctor at a meeting held in | 27
Calgary. His comment was met with quick support from all of his | 40
colleagues, one of whom went so far as to say that it is the place of | 54
all employers to make sure that employees do, in fact, exercise. At | 68
first, you may think that this suggestion is extreme, but when you | 81
hear some of the facts about worker absence, you may change your mind. | 95

Studies have shown that the worker who exercises on a regular | 108
basis or is active in sports is seldom absent from work. The studies | 122
show further that the fit employee is a much more productive staff | 135
member. With these facts before you, you may want to consider start- | 149
ing an exercise program for the staff in your office. We offer just | 163
such a program. It has been adopted by more than five hundred firms | 177
across the country, and in all cases, attendance at work has shown a | 191
major improvement. The details of the program are fully explained in | 205
the attached brochure, but let me summarize them for you. | 216

First of all, a trained fitness expert will come to your office | 230
to discuss how an exercise program would best fit into your office | 244
routine. It would require setting aside ten minutes a day for exer- | 258
cises right at the work station. A pamphlet describing the exercises | 272
would be handed out to each employee for previewing. A few days | 285
later, the expert would return to your office to conduct the first | 299
ten-minute exercises to taped music and instructions. A volunteer | 312
from among your workers would then be called for. This person would | 326
take on the task of setting up and starting the tape each day at the | 340
appointed time. If you wish, this role may be rotated each week or | 354
each month among the people involved. | 361

Also, a one-hour class would be arranged for one day a week at a | 375
suitable location, either on your premises or in our gym, for all | 388
those interested. A more rigorous program can be set up for anyone | 402
wishing it, but for this, a medical check-up would be required. We | 415
know you will be amazed at the pep, drive, and increased feeling of | 429
well-being that our program will induce in your workers. Stress is | 442
reduced and attendance improves. | 448

Our fitness expert will call you next week to arrange an appoint- | 462
ment that will start your workers on the right road to fitness. | 475

1 | 2 | 3 | 4 | 5 | 6 | 7 | 8 | 9 | 10 | 11 | 12 | 13 | 14

Family Roots

Tracing one's family roots has become a favourite pastime. More | 13
and more people are seeing the value of tying their family's past with | 27
the present to form a picture for the future. Tracing one's lineage | 41
is a lengthy project, but also a highly rewarding one. It promotes a | 55
better understanding of oneself. It fosters a sense of pride and | 68
belonging. It strengthens family ties. | 76

If you have ever wondered just who you are, from whence you came, | 90
and what kind of genes have been at work to help make you what you | 103
are, then you have already begun the search for your roots. Perhaps | 117
soon you will be ready to take the next step, an active pursuit of | 130
your forebears. When you are, the place to start is right in your own | 144
home. | 145

First gather information about yourself and your siblings. Then | 159
you can work backwards to parents, grandparents, and so on. You will | 173
want names, places, dates, and relationships. Search your own memory, | 187
family papers, scrapbooks, clippings, letters, the family bible, etc. | 201
Even check out the backs of pictures for names and dates. Write down | 215
all of the data in a systematic way, such as in chart form. | 227

When your home sources are exhausted, tap into other sources. | 240
Phone, write, or visit relatives who may have information. Show them | 254
what you are doing and offer to share the fruits of your labour with | 268
them. Kindle their interest and they will bend over backwards to | 281
help. When you are reading or listening, be alert for clues that may | 295
not fit into the picture now but may prove to be a missing link later. | 309
As well as gleaning the vital details, find out whether someone else | 323
has started a family tree; ask about pictures, stories, what people | 337
worked at, and traditions of the family. Mark everything down and be | 351
sure to record the source of your information in case you should have | 365
to retrace your steps. | 369

As a result of some clues, you may find yourself poring over | 382
public records or wandering through graveyards trying to decipher the | 396
writing on the stones. Wherever your search leads you, you will find | 410
the path interesting and challenging. There is a mystery to solve and | 424
you are the detective. Whether your ancestors turn out to be famous | 438
or infamous, they are part of your history; and when you are ready to | 452
set out on your ancestral journey, they will be waiting to meet you. | 466

1 | 2 | 3 | 4 | 5 | 6 | 7 | 8 | 9 | 10 | 11 | 12 | 13 | 14

Fashion Craze

WORDS

Down through the ages, the world of fashion has supported a num- 13
ber of unusual and sometimes amusing styles – at least from our modern 27
point of view. One of these fashions can be seen in paintings showing 41
the long fingernails of both men and women of old, upper-class China. 55
Long nails were a mark of great beauty and a clear sign of status, 68
indicating that the owners did not have to work with their hands. 81
Nails sometimes grew to over five centimetres long, and special gold 95
or silver covers were worn to protect them. 104

Recent generations have not been the only people to put their 117
money where their mouths are. Instead of using gold, however, the 130
Mayan Indians filled the cavities in their teeth with pieces of jade. 144

For a while in Europe, hair was literally the height of ladies' 158
fashion. With the addition of wigs, coiffures rose to over a metre 172
high. These were elaborately styled and were decorated with flowers, 186
ribbons, plumes, and/or veils. Designers got so carried away that 199
some creations included little figures of people and one was topped 213
off with a model sailing ship. The hairdos were powdered and coated 227
with lard to hold them together; however this attracted bugs and mice 241
so great care had to be taken to avoid these pests. Because the cre- 255
ations required so much work to construct, they had to last a while 269
and were often maintained for a few months. The wearers slept on 282
special pillows and wore huge bonnets to keep their hair in place. 296

Another curious fashion which women adopted and which got out of 310
hand was the hooped skirt. As the fad spread, so did the hoops, and 324
skirts became wider and wider. When a few ladies in their hooped 337
skirts became wedged together in the entrance to a royal ball and pre- 351
vented the rest of the guests from getting in, King James I decided 365
the craze had gone too far. He let it be known that that style of 378
dress was no longer welcome at court. 385

At various times throughout history, men have rivalled women in 399
ornateness of dress. In their zeal, they have donned powdered and 412
curled wigs and fancy jewellery. They have worn brightly coloured 425
fabrics, including velvets and brocades with lavish designs. Clothes 439
have been trimmed with lace, fur, ruffles, and frills, and decorated 453
with jewels, braid, embroidery, buckles, plumes, buttons, and bows. 467

1 | 2 | 3 | 4 | 5 | 6 | 7 | 8 | 9 | 10 | 11 | 12 | 13 | 14

Fashions Revived

Fashions might be defined as the personal grooming, mode of dress	13
(or undress), and the ornaments and accessories used to adorn oneself	28
which are in vogue and enhance one's appearance and status in the eyes	42
of one's contemporaries.	47

      From early times, men and women have been concerned with fashion. 61
Body paint; simple garments such as loincloths; strings of shells or 75
beads around the neck, wrists, and/or ankles; and flowers or feathers 89
in the hair were common fashions among primitive peoples. As civili- 103
zation advanced, however, so did fashions. 111

      It is interesting to look back in time and find that many fash- 125
ions that we consider current or recent are, in fact, revivals of 138
styles that were popular hundreds of years ago. The bikini, for ex- 151
ample, was worn by Roman women when they were engaged in exercise or 165
sports. The wearing of the kilt dates back to ancient Egypt when men 179
wore skirts that sometimes extended to below their knees. Headbands 193
were often worn by Egyptian women. Gloves with separate fingers were 207
worn in the days of the Persian empire, and dress slits were common in 221
China in days of old. Hair nets, many of which were made with gold 235
mesh, were the "in" thing nearly a thousand years ago. At that time, 250
too, linings were attached to gowns and cloaks. Usually in a con- 263
trasting colour, they added that certain touch of dash. Even leg 276
warmers were fashionable way back then, although they usually came up 290
just to the knee and were found on men, rather than on women. 302

      Neither are platform shoes new to this era. Platforms were worn 316
by the ladies of Venice in the sixteenth century. As the style caught 330
on, the platforms became higher and higher until they reached an amaz- 344
ing half a metre. As one can well imagine, walking on these stilts 358
was rather difficult; however, as a rule, the gentlemen were more than 372
glad to lend their assistance. 378

      In that same century, men were wearing close-fitting tights that 392
would have made them feel right at home in today's gymnasiums. It's 406
hard to say when men began to wear ties that were completely separate 420
from their shirts, but they must have been the height of fashion in 434
the early 1800s when, the records tell us, an enterprising fellow 447
started up a school at which he taught the fine art of knotting ties. 461

1 | 2 | 3 | 4 | 5 | 6 | 7 | 8 | 9 | 10 | 11 | 12 | 13 | 14

Gardening Indoors

One of the joys of growing plants indoors is that their beauty	13
can be enjoyed year-round. It's like having a little bit of summer in	27
your home all year, even in the middle of winter.	37

House plants have so many uses – from brightening up a window sill; to adding a fresh, natural touch to the decor; to making a welcome gift for friends and relatives; and even to tempting the tastebuds. Too, they come in all manner of shapes, sizes, and habits. They can be small trees, like palms and figs, and require a fair piece of floor space. They may be medium-sized, like ferns and caladiums, that rest nicely on a table. Like African violets and geraniums, they may deliver gorgeous displays of flowers. They may even be vines or trailers, such as ivy or spider plants, that will cascade over a large planter or hanging basket, or may be trained on a trellis. Some gardeners see indoor gardening in a more culinary light. They grow herbs and tiny tomatoes which will provide fresh garnishes and seasonings for their gourmet dishes.

The selection and placement of indoor plants will depend on the quantity and quality of light that is available. A number of green plants will prosper in low and medium light; but a far greater number have high light needs, and most flowering plants require a good share of sunshine. However, light can be supplemented by artificial lights, and special grow bulbs are available for that purpose.

Plants also require a moderate temperature and moisture. Just as people tend to dry up in heated buildings in winter, so do plants. Most plants love humidity; that is why they perform so well in bathrooms and near the kitchen sink. All plants need food and water – how much depends on the plant. The tendency is to water plants too much, which keeps the tiny air spaces in the soil filled with water instead of air, and in time the roots literally drown and rot.

One of the nice things about most plants is that you can propagate them. Depending on the type of plant, this may be done by taking leaf or stem cuttings and rooting them, or simply by splitting the plant, roots and all, in two. The new plant can decorate another spot in the home, replace a plant whose days are numbered, or be given away as a gift to give pleasure to someone else.

| 50 | 64 | 78 | 91 | 105 | 119 | 133 | 147 | 161 | 175 | 189 | 203 | 208 |

| 222 | 236 | 250 | 264 | 278 | 289 |

| 303 | 316 | 330 | 344 | 358 | 372 | 383 |

| 397 | 411 | 424 | 438 | 452 | 461 |

1 | 2 | 3 | 4 | 5 | 6 | 7 | 8 | 9 | 10 | 11 | 12 | 13 | 14

Hogs

The hog dates back to prehistoric times and is believed to be the oldest domestic animal still in existence. The hog was introduced to America by an explorer in the mid-sixteenth century. Indians adopted the delicious pork meat as part of their diet and raided settlements to obtain hogs for breeding. Pioneer settlers took hogs with them when they moved west. They began to develop the pork industry, and trail drives of as many as three thousand hogs were made to assembly points.

The hog of today has been bred to provide more meat and less fat than its ancestors. Ham is the meat from the hind leg of a hog. Most hams are cured or cured and smoked, and may or may not require further cooking. If there is no label to say, it is advisable to cook the ham. Canned ham is always cured and is fully cooked in the processing. Fresh ham is fresh pork; it has not been cured in any way and should be cooked like any other pork roast. Although it is called ham because it is from the hind leg, it tastes like pork, not cured ham.

Ham and other pork cuts can be frozen for later use, but should be used within six months. Because freezing may alter the flavour and texture of cured meat, it is not usually recommended that cured hams be frozen. If one does decide to freeze a cured ham, it should not be kept for more than two months. A whole ham is often cut into several pieces. The upper half, which is rounder and meatier, is usually called the butt, but is also known as the rump. The lower half is not as rounded and is called the shank. Often, centre slices are removed between the butt and the shank for sale as ham steaks. When meat is removed in this manner, the remaining cuts are called butt portions or shank portions.

The danger of contracting trichinosis, a disease caused by eating meat containing parasitic worms, from eating undercooked pork is well known. Because of this fear, however, many persons tend to overcook pork. Recent research has shown that it is not necessary to roast pork at such high temperatures or for as long as is recommended in many old cookbooks. For a well-done, tender roast, pork should be cooked in a moderate oven until the internal temperature reads eighty degrees Celsius. It is better to rely on an easily-read thermometer than to determine the cooking time by mass, as roasts of the same mass vary in length and thickness.

1 | 2 | 3 | 4 | 5 | 6 | 7 | 8 | 9 | 10 | 11 | 12 | 13 | 14

Homemaker

Much has been said which maligns the role of homemaker. No wonder it used to be so hard for me to feel like a person, let alone feel important or interesting or worthy. Then someone suggested that perhaps there was another way of looking at things. A new picture began to emerge of a person who, by choice, is at the centre of things that are important to her, a person who can give love and support and joy to a spouse and child, a person who sees and cherishes the value of peace and quiet contentment and fun, the need to lie in the sun and watch the clouds pass by, the fun of romping in the living room having a pillow fight. Seldom are the virtues of these things extolled, but then their value is beyond reckoning.

The fact is that homemaking poses more challenges than any other lifestyle. Like the job of a senior executive, the role becomes what the person makes of it. There are homemakers who handle a broader spectrum of responsibilities and decisions, and purchase a wider range of goods and services than any other workers, except perhaps the self-employed or the high executive. They may buy everything from skating lessons to a new roof for the house. They may take the car in for repair and supervise tradespeople in the home, in many cases deciding on their own the standards of workmanship which will be acceptable. When guests come for dinner, it is often the homemaker who sets the tone. When the family goes for a weekend outing, the homemaker organizes clothing, food, and so on, to make it a success.

What's more, homemakers work on their own – alone and independent. Day after day, they must provide not only the answers, but the questions as well. There is no boss to watch, direct, instruct, or report on their performance. When the homemaker solves a tricky problem, there is no one there to know it. There is no praise from a manager, no pats on the back from colleagues. Homemakers must realize that they deserve these things but must supply the recognition and support from within themselves.

If homemakers should ever disappear from society, and I hope they never will, they will leave behind them a gaping emptiness and an irreplaceable loss.

13
27
41
55
69
83
97
111
125
139
146
160
174
187
201
215
229
242
256
270
284
298
309
323
337
351
365
378
392
405
411
425
438
442

1 | 2 | 3 | 4 | 5 | 6 | 7 | 8 | 9 | 10 | 11 | 12 | 13 | 14

Household Science

Last week, I attended open house at my daughter's school. During | 13
my visit, I was greatly impressed with all of the modern tools and | 26
equipment which today's students have at their disposal. I couldn't | 40
help but reminisce about facilities in my old school some fifty years | 54
ago when one of my favourite subjects was Household Science. | 66

There was a house located on our school premises which had been | 80
remodelled to serve the Household Science classes. On the main floor | 94
of the house, the living room and kitchen had been combined to make | 108
one large area for cooking. In this area was the teacher's demonstra- | 122
tion table, around which the work areas for the students were arranged | 136
in a circle. Each girl had her own supply cupboard and her own Bunsen | 150
burner for cooking, and she learned to produce individual portions of | 164
basic recipes. In a corner of the room were an ice box, a large stove | 178
for baking, and a double sink where two or three girls would be de- | 192
tailed for clean-up after each class. | 199

Also on the main floor was a dining room containing a mahogany | 213
dining suite which we dusted with tender loving care. Here, we | 226
learned how to set a table, how to serve a meal, and how to eat and | 240
behave with good manners at the table. | 248

Upstairs was a furnished bedroom in which we learned the art of | 262
making a bed. The wall between the other two bedrooms had been re- | 276
moved to make a large, bright sewing room. This housed several large | 290
work tables and a number of treadle sewing machines. It was in this | 304
room that we learned the intricacies of making a nainsook slip and | 317
other garments. | 320

In the basement were cement washtubs and scrub boards on which we | 334
washed our dirty tea towels, then hung them on a clotheshorse to dry. | 348
In an effort to teach us thrift, even paper towels were washed, hung | 362
to dry, and reused. | 366

Through the years, Household Science went through a few name | 379
changes, which included Home Economics and Family Studies. Its male | 393
counterpart, Manual Training, also took on new names like Shop and | 406
Industrial Arts. It never occurred to anyone when I was young that a | 420
boy might benefit from taking Household Science; and for a girl to | 433
take Manual Training was unheard of. Today, boys are busy learning | 447
how to prepare meals, and girls are working lathes and sanding table | 461
tops. My, how times have changed. | 468

1 | 2 | 3 | 4 | 5 | 6 | 7 | 8 | 9 | 10 | 11 | 12 | 13 | 14

Humour

Once I might have taken my pen in hand to write about humour | 13
with the confident air of a known professional. But that time is past | 26
Such claim as I had has been taken from me. In fact, I stand un- | 39
masked. A reviewer writing in a literary journal, the very name of | 53
which is enough to put contradiction to sleep, has said of my writing | 67
that there is little in my humour but a rather ingenious mixture of | 81
hyperbole and myosis. | 85

The man was right. How he stumbled upon this trade secret, I do | 99
not know; but I am willing to admit, since the truth is out, that it | 113
has long been my custom in preparing an article of a humorous nature | 127
to go down to the cellar and mix up two litres of myosis with half a | 141
litre of hyperbole. If I want to give the article a more literary | 154
flavour, I find it well to add in a cup of paresis. The whole thing | 168
is amazingly simple. | 172

I only mention the foregoing by way of introduction and to dispel | 186
any idea that I am conceited enough to write about humour with any | 199
professional authority. All that I dare claim is that I have as much | 213
sense of humour as other people. Oddly enough, I notice that everyone | 227
else makes this same claim. People will admit, if need be, that | 240
their sight is poor, that they cannot swim, or that they shoot badly | 254
with a rifle; but to question their sense of humour is to give them a | 268
mortal affront. | 271

The other day, a friend of mine admitted that he never goes to | 285
the opera; then he added with an air of pride that he has absolutely | 299
no ear for music. He went on to say that he can't tell one tune from | 313
another and can't tell whether someone is tuning a violin or playing a | 327
sonata. He seemed to get prouder and prouder over each item of his | 341
own deficiency. He ended by saying that he had a dog at his house | 354
that had a far better ear for music than he had. | 364

When he had finished, I made what I thought a harmless comment to | 378
the effect that I supposed his sense of humour was deficient in the | 392
same way since the two often go hand in hand. In a moment, my friend | 406
was livid with rage. He lashed out with a defense of his sense of | 419
humour, and from that turned to bitter personal attack on mine. He | 433
said that my sense of humour seemed to have withered altogether. With | 447
that, still quivering with indignation, he left me. | 457

1 | 2 | 3 | 4 | 5 | 6 | 7 | 8 | 9 | 10 | 11 | 12 | 13 | 14

Inuit Art

Canadian Inuit art as a part of the world art scene is still | 12
fairly new. It began some thirty years ago when the federal govern- | 26
ment took steps to establish a cottage craft industry that would help | 40
to relieve a highly welfare way of life. A southern artist was hired | 54
to get the program under way. | 60

Two modes of expression soon came to the fore: lithograph and | 74
sculpture. Prints, at first, were made from stencils cut from dried | 88
sealskins, but the true lithograph, or stone-cut print, was soon | 101
favoured. Attempts at etching did not meet with wide-spread success, | 115
although the technique was mastered by a few artists who made changes | 129
such as hacking copper plates with an axe, rather than using the more | 143
common tools, which produced some highly effective results. | 155

Sculpture is practised by most of the artists. Whalebone, tusk, | 169
caribou antler, and types of soft stone are the chief materials used. | 183
The tools used are simple and few. Gross carving is begun with hack | 197
saws or hatchets, followed by a progression of files or rasps and then | 211
sandpaper of ever finer grades to achieve a fine polish. An amazingly | 225
wide range of work is produced – from the most simple or primitive to | 239
the most fragile and fine – which rivals the sculpture produced by | 252
more advanced and more complex means. | 259

Some remarkable traits could soon be seen in Inuit art. Not only | 272
was the work of specific artists easy to recognize, but communities | 286
were often just as individual. With prints, the locale of the artist | 300
could be determined by the theme, as well as by the style used. With | 314
sculpture, until recent years the place where a piece was made was | 328
known by the kind of material used – such as bone versus stone, or by | 342
the kind of stone – as well as by the theme of the work. | 354

The results of the program went far beyond all hopes and expecta- | 368
tions. Inuit art in general, and a number of artists in particular, | 382
are now recognized and acclaimed by the worldwide art community. | 395

The end or decline of Inuit art had been prophesied almost from | 409
the start, but still it persists. What is astounding is the variation | 423
still produced on what could be termed the old themes. What's more, | 437
an evolution can be seen in both the prints and in the sculptures as | 451
more exposure to southern culture and technology occurs. Perhaps the | 465
purely Canadian art that has been so long sought after may be found in | 479
the work of these, one of Canada's first native peoples. | 490

1 | 2 | 3 | 4 | 5 | 6 | 7 | 8 | 9 | 10 | 11 | 12 | 13 | 14

Joseph

Joseph was the second youngest of twelve sons. His father's favourite child, he always wore the beautiful coat of many colours his father had made for him. His ten older brothers were jealous and hated him.

Joseph was a dreamer and he was in the habit of telling his brothers his dreams. One night he dreamt he had grain growing tall and straight in a field. His brothers had grain growing there, too, but their grain was bowed down before his grain. On another occasion he dreamt that the sun and moon and eleven stars paid homage to him. When he told these dreams to his brothers, they became angry and swore the day would never come that they would bow themselves before Joseph.

When Joseph was seventeen, his older brothers were far off in the country feeding their father's flock. They were gone for some time and their father began to worry. He sent Joseph to find them, learn what progress they were making, and report back to him. Joseph set off, and after making inquiries along the way, headed for his brothers' camp. The brothers saw Joseph in the distance and recognized him by his colourful coat. They decided this was an opportune time to rid themselves of this boy whom they hated, so when he entered their camp they seized him, tore off his coat, and threw him into a pit.

While deliberating how to kill him, the brothers saw a company of merchants approaching, and they saw a means of disposing of the boy without having his blood on their consciences. They sold Joseph to the merchants for twenty pieces of silver and congratulated themselves on having found such a simple solution to their problem. Then they dipped Joseph's coat in goat's blood and took it home to their father. Jacob, thinking that his beloved son was dead, was beside himself with grief and mourned for days, and none of his family could comfort him.

The merchants journeyed into Egypt where they sold Joseph to a high-ranking official. Joseph was put to work and was so successful at everything he undertook that eventually he was made overseer of all his master owned. The master's wife had eyes for Joseph and she tried to attract his interest, but he would have none of it. It chanced one day that they were alone in the house and the mistress caught the edge of his garment to flirt with him, but he ran away leaving his cloth behind. She was so enraged by his rejection that she falsely accused him of misbehaviour and her husband clapped him in prison.

| 1 | 2 | 3 | 4 | 5 | 6 | 7 | 8 | 9 | 10 | 11 | 12 | 13 | 14 |

Joseph in Egypt

It happened that the king's chief butler and baker were in the | 13
same prison as Joseph. There, they each had a dream and described | 26
it to Joseph. He interpreted their dreams saying that in three days | 40
the butler would be restored to his former position, but the baker | 53
would be executed. In three days' time, the events occurred just as | 67
foretold. | 69

Two years later, the king had a dream but no one could explain | 83
its meaning. The butler remembered Joseph, who was called before | 97
the king. Joseph listened to the king's dream and then unfolded its | 110
meaning. For seven years, Egypt would have bountiful crops and great | 124
prosperity. This would be followed by seven years of drought and | 137
famine. The king was impressed and he appointed Joseph to rule over | 151
his dominion and prepare it to withstand the famine. | 161

Joseph governed wisely, and during the seven prosperous years | 174
laid up great stores in preparation for the lean years. Then the hard | 188
times began. As the famine worsened, people arrived from near and far | 202
to purchase food from Joseph. One day, ten men knelt in front of him, | 216
and when they lifted their faces he knew they were his brothers. They | 229
did not recognize him. Joseph dealt roughly with them, bound one up | 243
and sent the rest back to their homeland with supplies and instruc- | 257
tions not to return unless they brought their youngest brother. The | 271
brothers returned to their father's house and related everything that | 285
had happened, and when they opened their sacks of provisions they | 298
found their money resting on the top, and they were afraid. | 310

When their corn was almost gone, their father sent them again to | 324
Egypt to buy stores, and after much persuasion he allowed the youngest | 338
to go too. They came again to Joseph and he was overjoyed to see his | 352
young brother. He returned the captive brother to them, feasted them, | 366
and sent them off with their goods. Again, their money was returned, | 380
but this time he also planted his silver cup in his young brother's | 394
sack. After they were gone, he sent servants to overtake them and | 407
find the cup, and they all returned to Joseph's house. | 418

Joseph declared he would retain the young lad as his servant | 431
because he had stolen the cup, but an older brother offered to serve | 445
in his place, lest their father die of sorrow at the loss of the boy. | 459
Joseph could contain himself no longer and he revealed himself to them | 473
and there was much crying and kissing. He sent for his father and all | 487
of his family, and they came and dwelled in the land of Egypt. | 499

1 | 2 | 3 | 4 | 5 | 6 | 7 | 8 | 9 | 10 | 11 | 12 | 13 | 14

Klondike Gold Rush

It all started nearly a hundred years ago when a trio of men 13
filled a pan with gravel from a creek, washed it out, and stared down 27
at gold. Unknown to them at the time, they had just discovered one of 41
the world's largest deposits of free gold. Excitedly, they checked 55
out more of the creek to confirm their find. Before long, their 68
claims were staked and they were hurrying off to the registry office 82
to file them. 85

The word spread like wildfire, and prospectors from across the 99
valleys and up and down the rivers converged on Bonanza Creek. In a 113
short time, almost all of the creek area had been staked and the 126
claims recorded. At the junction of the Yukon and Klondike Rivers 139
just a few miles north of the strike, a supply store was built and the 153
area was named Dawson City. 159

It was nearly a year before news of the strike hit the outside 173
world, but when it did it came at a time of economic depression and 187
unemployment. Fortune seekers of all kinds from all over the world 200
began to pour in — prospectors, doctors, lawyers, bankers, gamblers, 214
thieves, people of good and ill repute. Most came by steamer to 227
Alaska, then travelled on foot over a high and treacherous pass into 241
Canada. Here, those that survived the storms and blizzards stopped to 255
fell trees and construct scows which they used to traverse the lakes 269
and streams to the Yukon River, then down the river nearly nine hun- 283
dred kilometres to the gold fields. The whole journey was long and 297
full of hardships and hazards, and many gold rushers died along the 311
way from accidents, sickness, and exposure. Only one in four made it. 325

In Dawson City, tents, log cabins, shacks, stores, hotels, dance 339
halls, and saloons sprang up along the muddy roads. This was a wild 353
and wide-open town, ripe for the picking by the many toughs, con men, 367
professional gamblers, and easy women who moved in. Most of the 380
action centred in the saloons where all of the vices were at work to 394
relieve the miners of their newly-acquired wealth, and many a hard- 408
earned fortune was lost on the turn of a roulette wheel or the deal of 422
a card. Money went out also on food, lodgings, and supplies. Fresh 436
food was scarce and prices were exorbitant. Within just a few years, 450
Dawson grew from one shack to over twenty thousand people. By that 464
time, most of the placer gold which could be mined by crude methods 477
had been extracted. Soon, the hordes of people moved on, many to 490
Alaska, and Dawson was reduced to a skeleton of two thousand people. 504

1 | 2 | 3 | 4 | 5 | 6 | 7 | 8 | 9 | 10 | 11 | 12 | 13 | 14

Lightning and Thunder

Lightning is a flash of light in the sky caused by an electrical
current. The flash is really a huge spark, something like that produced by the spark plugs of a car. When a thundercloud becomes
charged, it has great electrical potential which is in proportion to
the number of water droplets it contains. A huge spark may result
when two clouds of opposite charges come near each other. When the
electrical potential of a cloud is great enough, it can overcome the
resistance of the air which is between it and the earth and normally
insulates the earth, and a lightning flash occurs.

As a lightning flash streaks through the sky, it heats the air,
causing molecules of air to expand and fly about in all directions.
As these molecules seek more room, they collide violently with cooler
air. This sets up a great air wave which gives off the sound we call
thunder. Primitive people had their own ideas about what caused thunder. Some thought it was the gods roaring in anger.

Because light travels faster than sound, we see the lightning
before we hear the thunder. Since we know that sound travels about
one kilometre in three seconds, by counting the seconds between the
lightning flash and the sound of the thunderclap we can tell how far
away from us the lightning struck. If the thunder followed in thirty
seconds, we would know the lightning hit about ten kilometres away.

Although the loud noise made by thunder frightens many people, it
can do us no harm. The lightning which accompanies it, however, may
cause property damage and loss of life. Lightning chooses the easiest
path between the clouds and the ground, even though this may not be
the shortest path. Steel buildings, tall trees, power lines, and
telephone poles are all good conductors of lightning. If a building
is properly grounded, the electricity flows through it into the ground
without causing any damage.

It is wise to take certain safety precautions during a thunder
storm. Since lightning often strikes chimneys, stay away from open
fireplaces. Do not decide to take a bath or stand near a metal
object. If it is necessary to be out of doors, stay away from lone
trees, wire fences, and open fields where you are the tallest object
around — for you could become a lightning rod. Take shelter, if possible, in dense woods, a cave, or at the foot of a cliff. If you are
caught in the open, the safest thing to do is lie down.

13
27
40
54
68
82
96
110
120
134
148
162
176
190
200
213
227
241
255
269
283
297
311
325
339
352
366
380
385
399
413
426
440
454
468
482
493

1 | 2 | 3 | 4 | 5 | 6 | 7 | 8 | 9 | 10 | 11 | 12 | 13 | 14

Martha Seeks Employment

Martha had been looking for a job since graduating from college | 13
three months before. Not one of her many interviews had resulted in | 27
even a nibble of a job offer. She was not worried; sooner or later, | 41
an employer would realize her worth. All she had to do was find the | 55
right employer. | 58

Martha glanced through the want ads to see whether there were any | 72
new jobs since yesterday. There it was – the perfect opportunity for | 86
her: "Wanted immediately. Secretary for junior executive. Recent | 100
graduate preferred. Good shorthand, typing, and machine transcription | 114
skills. Some knowledge of word processing would be an asset." With- | 128
out a doubt, this was the job for Martha. Martha called the number | 142
shown in the ad and arranged an interview for eleven the next morning. | 156
That task out of the way, she made arrangements for the rest of the | 170
day. She planned on cycling, dinner, roller skating, and a party | 183
afterwards. | 185

It was three in the morning when Martha finally climbed into bed. | 199
At ten, she awoke with a start. Why, she had to be at that interview | 213
at eleven. She dressed quickly and raced out of the house towards the | 227
bus stop. She was almost there when the bus trundled past. Oh no, | 241
that meant a twenty minute wait for the next bus. While Martha wait- | 255
ed, a sudden downpour drenched her to the skin. She had not brought | 269
her raincoat, and had lost her mother's only umbrella two weeks ago. | 283
She was so upset, she did not notice the delivery van driving close to | 297
the curb until it had spattered mud all over her legs and skirt. | 310
Martha wiped off the mud as best she could until, at last, the bus | 323
arrived and she hopped on. | 328

It was only a ten-minute ride to Martha's destination, but to her | 342
it seemed like hours. She stepped off the bus and as she walked away, | 356
the heel of her shoe caught in a grill in the sidewalk, and the heel | 370
snapped off. Martha hobbled on to the office building and got into | 384
the elevator. The elevator had started to ascend before Martha no- | 398
ticed that it did not go all the way up to the floor she wanted. Back | 412
to the main floor she had to go to catch the right elevator. Some | 425
thirty minutes after her scheduled appointment, Martha hurried into | 439
the personnel office. The manager was interviewing another job appli- | 453
cant. Martha sat in the waiting room and fumed about her bad luck. | 467

1 | 2 | 3 | 4 | 5 | 6 | 7 | 8 | 9 | 10 | 11 | 12 | 13 | 14

Martha's Job Interview

Martha's thoughts were interrupted when the receptionist gave
her a job application form to fill out. Having left her resume in her
other purse, Martha filled out the form as best she could. She was
then asked to do a ten-minute speed test. Ten minutes? Why, at
school she had never been given more than a five-minute test. Martha
looked with horror at the old manual typewriter. After the test, she
was given some shorthand dictation. She got down as much as she
could; after all, it was very fast and contained a lot of long words
which she had never heard before.

When Martha had finished typing her notes, the receptionist
offered her a cup of coffee. Martha eagerly accepted. Just as she
was settling down to drink her coffee, the personnel manager emerged
from his office and asked Martha to come in. Forgetting the broken
heel on her shoe, Martha jumped up and lost her balance. The coffee
cup in her hand fell forward, spilling coffee all over the manager.
While he was away wiping off his clothes, Martha waited in his office.
Nothing was going right for her today, but surely her test results
would be good in spite of that dreadful old typewriter.

The manager returned with Martha's graded tests and partially
completed application form. Looking at her tests upside down on the
desk, Martha could see that she had scored fifteen net words per
minute on the timing. The transcription appeared to contain a number
of spelling errors, and the marker had noted that the letter just did
not make sense.

Thinking that he might soothe this angry girl, the manager began,
"You seem to have had a few problems this morning. I'm sorry about
the typewriter; our electric one is out ...." but he got no further.
Martha could not contain her feelings any longer, and she gave a full
account of all her troubles and their causes down to the very last
detail. She was especially eloquent about that ancient typewriter.
Then she launched her sales pitch, giving reasons why she should
become the secretary to the junior executive.

When Martha finally stopped talking, the manager looked into her
make-up streaked face. "You're not going to believe this, Martha," he
began, "but ...." What do YOU think he said?

| 13 |
| 26 |
| 40 |
| 53 |
| 67 |
| 81 |
| 94 |
| 108 |
| 115 |
| 128 |
| 142 |
| 156 |
| 170 |
| 184 |
| 198 |
| 212 |
| 225 |
| 236 |
| 249 |
| 263 |
| 276 |
| 290 |
| 304 |
| 307 |
| 321 |
| 335 |
| 349 |
| 363 |
| 376 |
| 390 |
| 403 |
| 413 |
| 427 |
| 442 |
| 452 |

1 | 2 | 3 | 4 | 5 | 6 | 7 | 8 | 9 | 10 | 11 | 12 | 13 | 14

Mother's Day

As a special surprise for Mother's Day, we hired an automobile to | 13
take Mother for a beautiful drive in the country. Mother hardly ever | 27
has a treat like that because she is busy in the house nearly all the | 41
time. It occurred to Father that a better idea would be to take | 54
Mother fishing. Father said if you are going fishing, there is a | 67
definite purpose to the trip which heightens the enjoyment. Father | 81
had just purchased a new rod the previous day and said Mother could | 95
use it if she wanted to. | 100

We got everything arranged, and Mother prepared a picnic lunch | 114
although we were expecting a big dinner on our return. When the motor | 128
car arrived, there hardly seemed as much room as we had supposed, | 141
probably because we hadn't reckoned on Father's fishing gear; and it | 155
was obvious we couldn't all get in. Father said he could just as | 168
easily stay home. He said we should forget that he hadn't had a holi- | 182
day for three years; he wanted us to go ahead and have a wonderful | 195
day. Of course, we all felt we couldn't let Father stay home, espe- | 209
cially as we knew he would make trouble if he did. The two girls | 222
would gladly have remained behind and prepared the dinner, only it | 235
seemed a pity on such a lovely day; but they both agreed that if | 248
Mother said the word, they'd gladly stay. Will and I would have | 261
dropped out, but we would have been useless getting dinner. | 273

Finally, it was decided that Mother would stay home and have a | 287
lovely restful day around the house, and get the dinner. Anyway, it | 301
was slightly chilly outdoors and Father declared he would never for- | 315
give himself if he dragged Mother round the country and she caught a | 329
severe cold, when she might have been enjoying a beautiful rest. So | 343
we drove away while Mother watched us from the verandah. | 355

We had the loveliest day you could possibly imagine, and Father | 369
caught such big specimens he felt certain Mother couldn't have landed | 383
them anyhow. Will and I fished too, and the girls met two handsome | 397
young gentlemen and chatted and had a splendid time. It was late when | 411
we returned, but Mother had the dinner ready and we sat down to the | 425
grandest meal. When dinner was over, we all wanted to clear up and | 438
wash the dishes, only Mother said she would really rather do it her- | 452
self; so we could hardly argue. When we kissed Mother goodnight, she | 466
said it had been a wonderful day. | 473

1 | 2 | 3 | 4 | 5 | 6 | 7 | 8 | 9 | 10 | 11 | 12 | 13 | 14

Musical Training

	WORDS

All children at birth have the potential to produce beautiful   12
music. Using the same method by which children learn their mother   25
tongue, we can help them to develop an amazing ability in the field of   39
music. From birth to about three months of age, babies the world over   53
make the same infant sounds. At about three months, they start to   66
discard those sounds they do not hear around them, and imitate those   80
they do hear. By the time children reach six months, a trained lin-   94
guist can tell what language they are getting ready to speak. A child   108
who lives in silence has no sounds to imitate and does not learn to   122
talk. Sounds must be heard and absorbed in order to feed them back.   136

Music education also begins at birth; and some people believe   149
even a few months before birth. Too many parents wait for their chil-   163
dren to reach a level of maturity before starting them on music les-   177
sons. They do not realize that precious time is slipping away during   191
which the children are slowly losing their natural musical ability.   205
When the children do not do well at their lessons, the parents con-   219
clude they were born without musical talent.   228

An ear for music is not innate, but can be acquired by listening.   242
The earlier this listening is begun, the more effective it will be.   256
So, treat your newborn to a daily bath of music. Infants exposed to   270
good quality music will gradually learn and be able to recognize the   284
pieces, and will develop an ear for music. Just as infants absorb   298
speech patterns in preparation for the day they will start to form   312
words, so they will absorb music and be ready for lessons around the   326
age of three years.   330

It is a good idea for a parent to attend the music lessons with   344
the child and to practise with the child on a daily basis. This   357
should be a happy time for both parent and child. If the parent can-   371
not play the chosen instrument, he or she can learn the basics of it   385
and, by so doing, will understand some of the problems the child may   399
encounter. Parental support and encouragement during these sessions   413
is important. The parent needs to find things to praise and learn to   427
give correction in a positive way. The child who is shown respect and   441
approval for work well done, and who is allowed to feel the glow of   455
success after each accomplishment, will gain self-esteem and respond   469
with a keen desire to learn and to reach his or her full musical   482
potential.   484

1 | 2 | 3 | 4 | 5 | 6 | 7 | 8 | 9 | 10 | 11 | 12 | 13 | 14

Opera

An opera company on a tour was in need of chorus singers, musicians, and extras. I was young, fancy free, bone idle, and without funds. The company was offering good pay and I managed to get a part in most of the operas it was playing. All went well until Carmen, which, apart from its musical merit and popularity, contains a glorious amount of wine drinking. The stage director, who was a great admirer of the grape, did not believe his cast should be fobbed off with coloured water, so in the tavern scene, the actors were divided into four labels. The principals drank fine vintage wine in elegant glasses; the chorus, a light table wine in tumblers; the supers, the cheapest wine on the market, generously laced with the best tap water available; and the waiters, lashings of all three. I was a waiter.

From the very first performance, everyone developed a passion for the grape. There was something heady about drinking wine in front of a packed audience, especially as the issue was free. The principals had to spend a lot of their energy during that scene wrestling their vintage away from the chorus, who were trying to prevent all their table wine being swiped by the supers, who were attempting, without much success, to stop the waiters from drinking all three. By the time the dancers came on, Carmen was as merry as could be, with a vivacity that was unequalled.

Needless to say, things got out of hand, for the waiters were the only ones who had legitimate excuses to keep popping on and off stage and getting at the bottle store. This was our undoing. We never had a rehearsal; we had been marched around the stage before the curtain went up and given brief verbal instructions. They would have been difficult to follow as it was, but with three free wines around, none of the waiters had any intention of following them. We just wandered around the stage drinking, until one teenage lad fell backwards off his chair during the Toreador song. I thought this incident added to the general gaiety, but the singer was hopping mad – so mad that when he tried to down his vintage at the end, it spluttered all over his shirt. I did not let him have any more; but before the curtain came down, the wine store had run dry anyway.

The stage director had a few words to say before sacking the lot of us. He did relent, however, and I got my job back as a waiter, but there was never the same run on the raspberry syrup that replaced those dark, succulent, grape juices.

| 1 | 2 | 3 | 4 | 5 | 6 | 7 | 8 | 9 | 10 | 11 | 12 | 13 | 14 |

13
27
41
54
68
81
95
109
123
137
151
165
179
193
207
221
234
248
262
275
281
295
309
323
337
350
364
378
392
406
420
434
448
456
470
484
497
504

Timed Writings – Average

Orpheus

Orpheus was said to have been more than mortal, having been born — 13
of one of the Muses. He learned to play the lyre, and he played and — 27
sang so beautifully that he charmed everyone who heard. Such was the — 41
power of his music that no one and nothing could resist or refuse him. — 55

Orpheus fell in love with a beautiful maiden called Eurydice and — 69
in time they were married. Shortly after the wedding, the bride was — 83
walking in a meadow when she was bitten by a viper and died. Orpheus — 97
was beside himself with grief; not even his music comforted him. — 110
Unable to endure it longer, he made a bold decision. He would venture — 124
down into the underworld and use his music to charm Pluto, king of the — 138
dead, and persuade him to allow Eurydice to return to the living. — 151

He found the cave which led to the kingdom of the dead and fol- — 165
lowed its path into the depths, playing and singing as he strode. — 178
Eventually he came to a river and, with his refrain, charmed the boat- — 192
man into rowing him across. On the other side, he encountered the — 205
three-headed dog that guarded the gates of the underworld realm, but — 219
his music so entranced the animal that it permitted him to pass. — 232

Orpheus continued to play as he wandered and all of the dead that — 246
he passed stopped to listen. Finally, he found himself before the — 259
king and queen, and through words and music he pleaded his case. His — 273
sweet and mournful melody cast such a spell that he "drew iron tears — 287
down Pluto's cheek, and made hell grant what love did seek." Orpheus — 301
was given permission to take his wife back to the world of the living, — 315
but only on condition that he precede her all the way and not look — 328
back at her until they had reached the upper world. Orpheus agreed — 342
and started on the journey. — 347

As Orpheus travelled, he could detect no sound behind him and he — 361
longed to turn around and ensure that his beloved was following. At — 375
last he reached the cave entrance. He stepped into the sunshine and — 389
turned around. It was too soon, for Eurydice was still in the cave. — 403
He heard a soft farewell as she faded into the darkness. Orpheus ran — 417
into the cave to follow but she had disappeared. He continued on — 430
until he reached the river, but this time the boatman was immune to — 444
his entreaties. Orpheus returned to the earth alone. A heartbroken — 458
man, he forsook the company of humans and became a sad and lonely — 471
wanderer. — 473

1 | 2 | 3 | 4 | 5 | 6 | 7 | 8 | 9 | 10 | 11 | 12 | 13 | 14

Parachute History

There's an old saying that what goes up must come down – and one 13
way to come down is by parachute. The parachute dates back some hun- 27
dreds of years. It is believed the Chinese tried using parasols as 41
parachutes way back in the thirteenth century. However, the first 54
known parachute design was drawn by Leonardo da Vinci. His chute was 68
a large linen pyramid. It had five suspension cords, one hanging from 82
each of the four corners and one from the apex down through the middle 96
of the chute. The cords, or lines, were brought together some dis- 109
tance below the chute and were connected to a bar from which the 122
jumper hung by his or her hands. 129

It was another hundred years or more before people were reported 143
to be jumping themselves or dropping animals from high points, such as 157
the tops of towers. The sport did not arouse much interest, though, 171
until the advent of hot-air balloons made it possible for humans to 185
ascend high enough to really make use of them. The chute was fastened 199
high up on the balloon, with its lines connected to the jumper, who 213
waited in the balloon's basket until the right moment to exit. The 227
tug of the jumper's body as he or she fell wrenched the chute free of 241
the balloon. Parachuting became a sensation all over Europe and drew 255
large crowds at exhibitions and fairs. Feats like jumping from burn- 269
ing balloons, landing in the water, and performing tricks on a trapeze 283
bar while descending, made for thrills and excitement. 294

When airplanes came into being, there was great interest on the 308
part of jumpers in parachuting from moving planes. Pilots, however, 322
had misgivings; they were afraid the sudden shift as someone jumped 336
would cause the plane to go out of control. The fear proved unfounded 350
and parachuting began a new stage in its history. 360

One of the problems with jumping from a plane was that the chute 374
was attached to the aircraft and opened immediately upon the jumper's 388
exit. This meant that it could easily get caught on the plane. A 401
device called the static line was devised. This line was connected to 415
the aircraft and to the bag containing the parachute, which the jumper 429
now carried. With this set-up, the parachute was not released until 443
the jumper had fallen far enough to fully extend the static line, by 457
which time he or she was clear of the plane. Then the pull of the 470
jumper tugged the chute right out of its bag attached to the line, and 484
jumper and chute went sailing down to earth. 493

| 1 | 2 | 3 | 4 | 5 | 6 | 7 | 8 | 9 | 10 | 11 | 12 | 13 | 14 |

Parachute Jumping

It's gratifying to note the important role played by women in the   13
development of parachuting, or sky diving as it is also known. Under   27
daring conditions, the first female jumper made about forty jumps from   41
balloons. She was the first person on record to steer her descent   54
toward a specific drop zone.   60

Another female sky diver was the first person to come up with the   74
idea of packing the chute in a bag and stowing the suspension lines in   88
a way that prevented them from becoming tangled during the drop. When   102
the jump was made, the lines strung out first in an orderly way, fol-   116
lowed by the chute. This same woman was one of the first people to do   130
a double jump. Two chutes were used in this jump. The first chute   144
opened and the jumper cut it away. Then a second chute opened, which   158
the jumper used to complete the descent.   166

It was a female, too, who was the first person to do a freefall   180
jump. In this jump, the skydiver is not attached in any way to the   194
plane. After the exit, the jumper freefalls for a few seconds until   208
clear of the plane, then pulls a ripcord which releases the chute from   222
the backpack.   225

In the first part of this century, the airplane was a wondrous   239
thing, and stunt fliers were common attractions at fairs and carni-   253
vals. As interest began to wane, parachutists came on the scene and,   267
with all kinds of crazy antics, kept public interest high.   279

World War I prompted a look at the parachute as a possible tool   293
of war, but it was really in World War II that the, parachute took its   307
place in the war game. Not only did it save the lives of hundreds of   321
pilots and other war personnel, but it was used as a means of dropping   335
supplies, equipment, jeeps, and troops. After the war, parachutes   348
were put to other uses. The Russians landed a spacecraft, by para-   362
chute, on the planet Venus. The Americans used a huge chute to lower   376
the Gemini space capsule to its water landing, and three giant chutes   390
to land the Apollo spacemen on their return from the first moon trip.   404

Parachuting as a sport continued to develop and it branched into   418
new areas like parasailing. The latter sport looks like a great deal   432
of fun and more suitable to the less daring of us. The parachute is   446
tied to the back of a vehicle – a car, boat, or even a snowmobile –   460
and is towed. The wind created by the moving vehicle fills the chute   474
with air so that it rises by itself, carrying its human passenger   487
aloft.   488

1 | 2 | 3 | 4 | 5 | 6 | 7 | 8 | 9 | 10 | 11 | 12 | 13 | 14

Parachute Training

Parachute jumping is often considered to be a very risky busi- 13
ness, and the thought of it tends to invoke fear in the minds of most 27
people. Parachuting is not nearly as difficult or as dangerous as it 41
would at first appear, and the number of accidents is far less than 55
one might suppose. The major concern of non-jumpers is that the 68
parachute may not open. In fact, this rarely happens. Jumpers are 82
equipped with two chutes – the main parachute backpack and an emer- 96
gency or reserve chute in a front pack. Both chutes have been packed 110
with care by qualified riggers, and the chances that one or both of 124
them will malfunction are slim. 130

The key to successful jumping lies in having the right equipment 144
and knowing and following the safety procedures. In most cases, the 158
fee for a first-time parachute jump will cover everything a jumper 171
needs: the use of equipment, the training, the plane ride, and super- 185
vision of the jump by a qualified master. The equipment most often 199
includes a jumpsuit, helmet, goggles, gloves, boots, and of course, 213
the parachutes. The training time varies from school to school, but 227
will likely be from three to twelve hours long. 236

Classrooom instruction and films are followed by mock practice 250
jumps and landings from platforms and/or other structures. The jump 264
or exit from a plane is important and is made by springing up and out 278
from the door at the go command. Right away, the jumper must assume a 292
stable, face to earth, falling position. This involves a hard arch 306
with head up, knees slightly bent, and arms and legs spread-eagled. 319
As the parachute opens and fills with air, the jumper will slowly be 333
pulled into a more upright position in which he or she can clasp the 347
suspension lines. As with skiers, the parachutist has to learn how to 361
fall correctly so that the shock will be distributed evenly over the 375
body. The jumper must then get to his or her feet quickly, run to the 389
chute canopy and collapse it before the wind catches it and drags it 403
and the jumper along the ground. 409

The first few jumps made by a beginner will be static line jumps, 423
in which the main chute is opened automatically at a proper distance 437
from the plane by a line attached to the chute pack and to the plane. 451
A jumper may then engage in freefall jumps, in which it is the jumper 465
who opens the main chute by pulling a ripcord. To this may be added 479
manoeuvres such as turning, rolling, looping, and aiming to land at a 493
certain target, such as a small disk. 500

1 | 2 | 3 | 4 | 5 | 6 | 7 | 8 | 9 | 10 | 11 | 12 | 13 | 14

Parachuting the First Time

I cannot think of another feeling that can match the thrill and   13
excitement of diving out of an airplane at eight hundred metres. I   27
cannot begin to explain the thoughts and emotions that ran through my   41
mind when I leaped from that Cessna plane.   49

The training took about six hours to complete. The first three   63
hours consisted of classroom work during which we were given instruc-   77
tions. We watched slides and films, did exercises, and then were   90
tested. We broke for lunch, but were so excited that we could hardly   104
eat. All we could think and talk about was the jump and how nervous   118
we were. After lunch, we engaged in the practical training. Dangling   132
from a hoist, we practised our emergency procedures. From high plat-   146
forms, we made mock jumps onto foam mattresses and mock landings onto   160
gravel until we were tired and sore all over.   169

Finally, our training was over. As I was being placed in my   182
equipment, my aches and fatigue were forgotten. Instead, I was begin-   196
ning to feel edgy and scared. What if my chute didn't open? I kept   210
running the procedures over and over in my head: "Arch thousand, two   225
thousand, three thousand, four thousand, five thousand, check thou-   239
sand. On last count, check chute. If it didn't open, immediately   252
punch the emergency chute; then pull the ripcord. Remain calm. If   266
the main chute opened only partially, place left arm over the emer-   280
gency chute to prevent it from releasing right away, look at the   293
chute, and pull the ripcord. Place right hand inside the chute con-   307
tainer, catch the chute and throw it away as far as I can so that it   321
won't go straight up and get twisted in the main chute. Arch thousand   335
...."   336

We climbed into the Cessna plane and took off. The only way out   350
now was down and that was where I was headed. The four of us took our   364
jumping positions. I was the second in line. At the jump master's   378
command, the first jumper disembarked. Then it was my turn. The mas-   392
ter said "Go," and I jumped. All of my fears vanished in an instant   407
in my amazement at what I was doing. I seemed to be falling forever   421
as I watched that patched quilt below getting closer and closer.   434
Actually, forever lasted only three seconds, and suddenly I felt as   448
light as a feather and I knew my chute had opened. The thrill and   461
excitement overtook me and all sense of time and reality was lost as   475
I floated down to earth.   480

1 | 2 | 3 | 4 | 5 | 6 | 7 | 8 | 9 | 10 | 11 | 12 | 13 | 14

Pets

I never could understand why so many people kept pets around the   13
house. Somehow pets just didn't fit into my scheme of things. Now   27
don't get me wrong. I love animals – cats, dogs, you name it – as long   41
as they're someone else's. I just always figured that children to   54
cook for, to clean for, to nurture, to discipline, and to cherish were   68
quite enough me. Neither did I want a pet interfering with our free-   82
dom to pack up and get away for a weekend or a vacation when we   95
felt like it. We didn't do that very often, mind you, but I liked the   109
feeling that we were unfettered and could if we decided to.   121

My husband didn't quite agree with me, though. He believed in   135
the old theory that every boy should have a dog. I think he meant   148
that every man should have a dog. Anyhow – you guessed it – one day   162
he appeared in the kitchen with a little collie pup. The boys were   176
ecstatic, so what could I say? Actually, after that cute little mutt   190
chewed up my sweater, created odours in the basement, and did his   203
business all over my garden, I found quite a bit to say. The problem   217
was that both my husband and I worked all day, and that poor wee   230
animal was left all by himself. That was okay in the summertime when   244
he could stay outdoors, but what about the wintertime when he would   258
be cooped up alone in his kennel in the basement? It took some per-   272
suading, but my husband was finally convinced that the dog would be   286
better off with a family that could give it the attention it needed.   300
In a few weeks, it was returned to the pound.   309

Oh, I know pets can also be fun and interesting. My mother used   323
to have a pet parrot that had spent some time on a merchant ship. It   337
had quite a patter. Its favourite was, "Pretty Polly, pretty dear,   351
all the way from Kashmir. Fetch me a pint of beer quick, quick,   364
quick." Imagine all the effort, at least in those days, that went   377
into training a bird to say that. It's much easier now I discovered   391
when I was visiting relatives last week. They bought a parrot not   404
long ago and they showed me a stereo record that teaches birds how to   418
talk – in fourteen easy lessons. It contains fourteen short phrases,   432
each of which is repeated over and over and over again for three or   446
four minutes. It must be pretty boring for the bird, but I must admit   460
it's closer to my idea of pet ownership. You just turn on the record   474
and leave.   476

1 | 2 | 3 | 4 | 5 | 6 | 7 | 8 | 9 | 10 | 11 | 12 | 13 | 14

Potholes

We get them every spring. As soon as the snow melts and the | 12
earth begins to thaw, you start to hit them as you are driving inno- | 26
cently along. Plunk! There go the new shocks you had installed last | 40
year. Plunk! That's another one you must remember to drive around or | 54
over, but not into, next time. After a while, you begin to feel like | 68
an incompetent driver wheeling in and out like that, but what else can | 82
you do when you're running an obstacle course? | 91

Potholes, the scourge of northern winters, are caused by water | 105
getting under roads and causing erosion. Although most roads are | 118
covered with asphalt, water still manages to get below. Side ditches | 132
provide a ready access for water. Traffic heavier than a street was | 146
built for may cause the street to crack, providing a passage for | 159
water. Improper grading may allow water to sit in pools for extended | 173
periods, giving the water time to penetrate the road surface. If | 186
cracks and minor holes in a road are not mended, they develop into | 200
bigger cracks and holes. Add to all this the constant freezing and | 214
thawing during winter, and in spring the potholes open their gaping | 228
mouths. | 229

How subject a road is to potholes depends to a great extent on | 243
its construction. A light duty road may have a few centimetres of | 256
asphalt on a shallow sand and gravel base. Often, it will have | 269
ditches. This type of street can be fairly prone to potholes. | 282

Some medium duty roads are built with a thick layer of asphalt on | 296
a deep sand and gravel base, which gives good durability and is fairly | 310
easy to dig up, if need be, to install services. Others are con- | 323
structed with the quantities reversed – a deep layer of asphalt on top | 337
and a shallow sand and gravel base. This combination gives very good | 351
durability and saves on maintenance. | 358

The road that is the most durable, however, is the heavy duty or | 372
industrial road. This consists of a thin topping of asphalt on a | 385
thick concrete base. Now, if all our roads could have this type of | 399
construction, we should have few pothole problems. As luck would have | 413
it, however, concrete is expensive and these roads are difficult and | 427
costly to dig up to install services. We must not feel discouraged, | 441
though; new formulas and materials are being tried, and perhaps soon | 455
we will have roads that are free of potholes. In the meantime, you'd | 469
better check your shocks and alignment; spring is just around the | 482
corner. | 483

1 | 2 | 3 | 4 | 5 | 6 | 7 | 8 | 9 | 10 | 11 | 12 | 13 | 14

Property for Sale

I have been in touch with the owners of the property about which	13
you inquired. They have informed me that they have listed the prop-	27
erty with a real estate agent and it will be coming onto the market in	41
two weeks. The owners are a retired couple who have decided that the	55
upkeep and maintenance of a house is too much for them and they are	69
now seeking a suitable apartment.	76

I have been in touch with the owners of the property about which you inquired. They have informed me that they have listed the property with a real estate agent and it will be coming onto the market in two weeks. The owners are a retired couple who have decided that the upkeep and maintenance of a house is too much for them and they are now seeking a suitable apartment.

This home is clean, compact, and well maintained. It is a frame bungalow with white aluminum siding and a painted front with wooden shutters. It was recently caulked and has a new front storm door. The front verandah and stairs have wrought iron railings which have been freshly painted. A new roof was installed three years ago. The house contains a living room, a separate dining room, a kitchen, a four-piece bathroom, and two bedrooms. The floors in the living area are hardwood and the walls are plaster. The kitchen is small but modern with lots of cupboard space. The living and dining rooms are broadloomed, and the owners are willing to leave all blinds and curtains on the windows.

The full basement is poured concrete. It has a high ceiling and could be finished as a recreation room or a separate apartment. The house has a large-capacity water heater, copper piping throughout, and a new forced-air gas furnace that was installed two years ago. Taxes and the cost of heating are reasonable.

The size of the lot is ten metres by forty metres. Behind the house is a large, fenced yard that contains a hedge across the back, two mature trees, a garden, and a flagstone patio. The front of the house is nicely landscaped with flowers and shrubs, and there is a hedge down one side and across the front. The house uses city water and is fronted by a paved street with curbs, sidewalk, and sewers. Schools, shopping, bus transportation, and the highway are all close at hand.

Although this charming place does not have parking facilities on the premises, parking is available nearby. The asking price of this property is within the range you quoted me. If you are interested in viewing it, please contact me as soon as possible. I do not believe it will be on the market for long.

1 | 2 | 3 | 4 | 5 | 6 | 7 | 8 | 9 | 10 | 11 | 12 | 13 | 14

Quicksand

The perils of being ensnared in this natural deathtrap have been | 13

portrayed so frequently and with such suspense and gruesome reality in | 27

movies and novels that many of us have a tendency to tremble at the | 41

very word, quicksand. The instant vision of a person sinking help- | 55

lessly to his or her death is made even more horrible by the knowledge | 69

that the trap is so well camouflaged that the victim is taken by com- | 83

plete surprise. | 86

On top, the quicksand may look as solid and safe as concrete, but | 100

throw a rock into it and the caked surface crumbles, and the quicksand | 114

quivers and seems almost alive as it devours the object. Why is this | 128

sand so different from most sand which is quite capable of supporting | 142

things? Through a series of experiments, it was learned that the sand | 156

is plain ordinary sand, but what makes the difference is water flowing | 170

up like a spring from the bottom, forcing the grains slightly apart, | 184

and making the sand mass swell. | 190

Although quicksand pits exist in many parts of the world, they | 204

have not been the cause of nearly as many deaths as entertainers would | 218

have us believe. Depending on the speed of the upwelling water and | 232

the texture of the sand, the speed with which a human would sink | 245

varies – from immediately, to slowly enough to allow a person to turn | 259

after a few steps and get out. | 265

When it comes to quicksand, the wisest course is to avoid walking | 279

in areas that are suspected of containing quicksand pits. Should you | 293

happen to step into one, however, you have a good chance of escape if | 307

you follow these rules. The most important is don't panic. Panic and | 321

struggle are the worst reactions to the situation. They will stir up | 335

the quicksand pot and sink you all the faster. | 344

Immediately warn any companions of the danger, both to prevent | 358

their entrapment and so that they will be able to assist you. Discard | 372

any heavy items on you that might weigh you down. Slowly lie on your | 386

back with your arms spread wide. Relax your body, and your legs and | 400

feet should rise to the surface so that you are afloat. Because | 413

quicksand is heavier than water, you should be able to float on it | 426

readily. Have your companions extend a long branch or other lifeline | 440

which you can hold onto while they tow you to safety. If you can't | 454

reach the lifeline or you are alone, very gently paddle or squirm your | 468

way to firm ground. | 472

1 | 2 | 3 | 4 | 5 | 6 | 7 | 8 | 9 | 10 | 11 | 12 | 13 | 14

Quilting

Quilting of covers for beds began in North America not long after	13
the arrival of early settlers. Because of the nature of pioneer life,	27
there was little with which to decorate a home. Probably as a result	41
of this, quilts were seen as a way to brighten and decorate at least	55
one part of the home – the bedroom.	62

Quilting of covers for beds began in North America not long after the arrival of early settlers. Because of the nature of pioneer life, there was little with which to decorate a home. Probably as a result of this, quilts were seen as a way to brighten and decorate at least one part of the home – the bedroom.

Because so much work was required to make a quilt, and at night there was only the dim light of candles and coal oil lamps to work by, quilting bees soon became a way to finish a quilt quickly in the day light. Bees also served as a form of social intercourse. A quilting bee was often held at the same time as a barn raising. A bride-to-be would have prepared a few quilt tops before the bee, and, with one or two quilting frames and about ten pairs of hands around each frame, a quilt could be finished in a day.

The most common quilts were the patchwork quilt and the applique quilt. A patchwork quilt was just that: an assemblage of bits and pieces of material left over from other projects, as well as pieces cut from the usable portions of worn-out clothing. When one could afford to buy material especially for quilting, intricate patterns and colour schemes were often produced. Most patterns had names and often more than one. Many of the names, such as Jacob's ladder, had origins in the Bible. One of the most unique forms of patchwork quilting was the crazy quilt. This was an arrangement of squares of odd-shaped scraps of fabric. These were outlined with embroidery stitches, with dozens of different stitches and colours of thread being used.

Applique quilts tended to be mainly decorative, as the overall patterns depended on colour schemes that were well thought out and on patterns that were accurately cut. As a rule, this meant the material was bought especially for the project. In most cases, the result was considered to be one's best quilt.

A recent and widespread interest in quilting has occurred, with many persons and groups re-creating the patterns of traditional quilts, but also adding many bold new patterns and techniques. Some are such lovely works of art that what once was used to decorate beds and bedrooms can now be found adorning walls in any room in the house.

1 | 2 | 3 | 4 | 5 | 6 | 7 | 8 | 9 | 10 | 11 | 12 | 13 | 14

Rags

Why on earth would anyone in his or her right mind elect to write	13
about a subject like rags? What bright, witty, enlightening, or even	27
vaguely interesting things could one possibly say or tell about rags?	41
That is precisely what I asked myself right after I chose that topic.	55
However, I figured that all things have their role in history and	68
deserve to be mentioned somewhere, and surely rags should not be an	82
exception. For that reason, I now present an expose on rags.	94
Since the beginning of history, the extent to which people made	108
use of rags has tended to rise or fall according to the tides of pros-	122
perity. In our present age of affluence and consumer goods, rags have	136
a very small part to play. This was not the case in pioneer days.	149
Then, there were only limited resources with which to equip homes and	163
make them comfortable; and so it was essential that every resource	177
be used to its utmost. One of these resources was rags.	188
Every rag or scrap of useable material from torn or worn cloth	202
items was salvaged for further service. Some pieces were suitable for	216
employment as dusters or cleaning cloths. Some went into the making	230
and stuffing of rag dolls. Others were fashioned into dolls' clothes.	244
Often, strips of rags were used for tying plants to stakes in the gar-	258
den. Rags functioned as a beauty tool, too, for strips of rags often	272
served as hair curlers. Probably the most famous use of rags was in	286
the making of patchwork quilts. Rags, cut into patches of the desired	300
shapes and sizes, were fitted and stitched together to form an outer	314
cover of a quilt.	317
Another common use for rags was in the making of rugs. There	330
were hooked rugs made from short lengths of rag which were hooked into	344
canvas. There were braided rugs made from long rag strips sewn end to	358
end to form three very long pieces. These were braided together, just	372
as one would braid hair. The braid was then stitched into a coil	385
shape, forming a circular rug. Woven rugs or mats were also popular.	399
For these, lengths of rag were tied side by side across a wooden	412
frame. Other strips were then woven under and over them, and the ends	426
were bound to produce the finished mat.	434
It appears that rags have had a notable history after all – of	448
cleanliness, warmth, comfort, amusement, and beauty. That's quite an	462
achievement for something as humble as a few scraps of cloth.	475

1 | 2 | 3 | 4 | 5 | 6 | 7 | 8 | 9 | 10 | 11 | 12 | 13 | 14

Resume Planning

In your search for a job, your resume can be a highly influential	13
factor. Even if you were never to hand out one single copy, just the	27
writing and preparation of the resume is rewarding in itself. Why?	41
Because it forces you to clarify in your own mind what you have to	54
offer a future employer. The very nature of the resume requires you	68
to collect and condense a wealth of information about yourself. It	82
compels you to study your past and pull out your worthwhile experi-	96
ences and successes, and the skills you have had to use or develop as	110
a result. It is important to note here that you must not confine your	124
search to previous jobs you have held, but you should draw on social	138
and home experiences too.	143

In your search for a job, your resume can be a highly influential factor. Even if you were never to hand out one single copy, just the writing and preparation of the resume is rewarding in itself. Why? Because it forces you to clarify in your own mind what you have to offer a future employer. The very nature of the resume requires you to collect and condense a wealth of information about yourself. It compels you to study your past and pull out your worthwhile experiences and successes, and the skills you have had to use or develop as a result. It is important to note here that you must not confine your search to previous jobs you have held, but you should draw on social and home experiences too.

It will help if you can get hold of several good resumes that can serve as guides and give you some ideas. Do not, however, fall into the trap of thinking that the pattern and format of a resume are carved in stone. This is not the case. A resume is a flexible document and must be designed to set off YOUR best features, to put YOUR best foot forward. Start off your resume with your name, address, and telephone number. Remember that YOU are what this resume is all about; therefore your name is the most important thing on the page and should be the most prominent.

You may then wish to state what type of job you are seeking and perhaps what your goals are. If so, keep it brief. Many resumes today tend to omit such personal data as age and marital status; however, if you feel that this kind of information will advance your cause, for goodness' sake, put it in. For example, if a want ad mentions that a job involves travel and you are single, that fact may indicate your freedom to travel. If you think it has a bearing, include it; otherwise leave it out.

Most resumes then move on to the topic of education, followed by work experience. Feel free to reverse this order without blinking an eye. It may well be that your work experience is far more impressive than your education. If so, list it first. You want to impress the reader as soon as possible so that he or she will not lose interest and stop reading. It is also beneficial to get as many goodies as possible on the first page where it counts the most.

1 | 2 | 3 | 4 | 5 | 6 | 7 | 8 | 9 | 10 | 11 | 12 | 13 | 14

Resume Preparation

When listing time frames on your resume, just the years are quite	13
enough. If you worked somewhere from March to August of the same	26
year, just enter the year. Don't clutter the document. An employer	50
who wants more details will ask for them.	58

When listing time frames on your resume, just the years are quite enough. If you worked somewhere from March to August of the same year, just enter the year. Don't clutter the document. An employer who wants more details will ask for them.

When giving your education, you must decide which is more important and therefore should be highlighted – the schools you attended or the credits you received. The same applies to work experience. Which information is going to do the most to sell you – the positions you have held or the name of the firms for which you worked? It will all depend on your situation and the job you are after. You may also want to give a brief description of your jobs, projects you were involved in, things you were responsible for, etc. If you have been out of the work force for periods of time as a homemaker, don't hesitate to include this in your work data.

By now, you are sure to be onto the second page of your resume. Be sure to put your name, as well as the page number, at the top of the second and any subsequent pages. Otherwise, if the pages get separated, no one will know to whose resume they belong.

Often the next items covered are interests, hobbies, and/or social activities. Sometimes one of these might warrant being listed near the beginning on the first page. For instance, if you were applying for a job with a computer firm and one of your hobbies is micro computers, that information could stand you in good stead as an opener on the first page. Do not underestimate the value of social or community work you may have done. Be sure to mention any, plus any positions you may have held in clubs or groups. These show that you are willing to get involved and that you have been held in high enough esteem by your peers to be chosen to fill a higher position.

Likely the last topic in your resume will be references. Some people list them; others state they are available on request. Take your pick. If you have a good letter of reference on hand, though, attach it to the resume.

Finally, the set-up of your resume is very important. Keep in mind that often resumes are just scanned and only the most interesting ones are read completely. So keep your resume short and set up in such a way that the major information stands out clearly and is easy to follow.

1 | 2 | 3 | 4 | 5 | 6 | 7 | 8 | 9 | 10 | 11 | 12 | 13 | 14

Revolution

We learned that a rising had taken place led by rebels who prom- | 13
ised the nation a new era of freedom. The armed forces in the south | 27
refused to move against the rebels. The air force, too, refused to | 41
act, but in any case its planes were out of action for lack of fuel, | 55
for the government treasury was empty. It was clear that the presi- | 69
dent had no choice but to resign. A military cabinet was set up under | 83
General Ponce. | 86

I had never witnessed a revolution before so I, a young univer- | 100
sity student at the time, went to the town square to see what was | 113
happening. A large crowd had gathered before the palace. By the time | 127
I arrived, Ponce was haranguing the crowd in an attempt to make as | 150
much political gain for himself as he could, although with little | 163
apparent success. Then, pointing to his uniform, he offered this to | 177
his listeners as evidence of his devotion to the country. One of his | 191
supporters cried out in his favour, but was met with a stony silence. | 205

At this precise moment, a senorita standing near me had the | 218
embarrassing misfortune to discover that the elastic of her petticoat | 232
had given way. However, with great presence of mind, she marked time | 246
till her feet were free and then walked quickly away. Spotting the | 259
garment at his feet, a bystander picked it up and, hurling it into the | 273
air, yelled in Spanish, "Long live the petticoat!" Immediately the | 287
plaza echoed with an affirmative chorus. The petticoat proved to be | 301
more meaningful to them than a cartload of Ponces. His star, which | 315
gave such good promise of rising only a short time before, now plum- | 329
metted to earth. I never heard of him again. | 338

A few moments later, the crowd surged towards the mansion of the | 352
ministry. At the entrance, a guard was on duty. The guard, evidently | 366
deciding that discretion was the better part of valour, promptly took | 380
to directing the traffic flow, keeping the invading tide to the right | 394
of the entrance so as to facilitate the exit on his left of the loot- | 408
ers and their booty. | 412

The next attack was made on the residence of the president. | 425
Following the crowd, I tried to approach the house, but just as I came | 439
to the corner a shot rang out. Now a mob was surging around at the | 452
entrance and some students were pushing their way through bearing the | 466
body of one of their number who had been wounded. Having no desire to | 480
end up in a like manner, I decided to go home while the going was | 493
good. I had had enough revolution for one day. | 502

1 | 2 | 3 | 4 | 5 | 6 | 7 | 8 | 9 | 10 | 11 | 12 | 13 | 14

Robots

They're called the steel collar workers. To some people, they   13
are the stuff of which great science fiction is made. To others, they   27
are nothing more than fancy screwdrivers. For yet others, they repre-   41
sent the fearful push of technology to replace the human hand with a   55
metal claw. Robots. They don't look anything like the famous ones in   69
the movies. Few of them even have a head. Instead, they're more apt   83
to be just a mechanized arm with a metal gripper at the end that forms   97
a "hand." With that hand, robots can perform many different tasks,   111
from grasping and moving an object to feeling its contours.   123

A large number of robots are being used in industry. While the   137
robot is quite expensive to buy, it can quickly pay for itself because   151
at certain jobs it can work faster and better than a human, thus   164
boosting productivity and lowering production costs. Even as you read   178
this, robots are working away at what were once exclusively human   191
jobs: welding and painting cars, mining coal, moving hazardous sub-   205
stances, building stoves, and even washing windows and shearing sheep.   219
In some places, the steel collar brigade is working round the clock to   233
build other robots.   237

Unlike people, robots don't take coffee breaks, lunch breaks,   250
sick days, or vacations. They don't need sleep and they don't collect   264
a pay cheque. A robot can work twenty-four hours a day in unpleasant   278
surroundings and it will never threaten to quit or to go on strike.   292
In short, a robot can do the dull and sometimes dangerous work that   306
humans will not or should not do. In fact, the term robot comes from   320
a word which means forced labour.   327

Smart robots depend on computer technology to help them see and   341
feel. A robot compares what it sees and feels with information in its   355
computer memory bank to decide which pre-programmed course to follow.   369
Robots are learning to do things humans could never hope to do, such   383
as "see" infra-red light and "hear" ultrasonic sound. They cannot   397
think for themselves, though. They can only respond to things in ways   411
that have been programmed into them; and while robots can be taught to   425
program other robots, only humans can conceive and map out these   438
programs.   440

In spite of the human qualities of feeling and emotion portrayed   454
by robots on the movie screens, these are only products of the human   468
imagination. The robot has a cold, steel heart.   478

1 | 2 | 3 | 4 | 5 | 6 | 7 | 8 | 9 | 10 | 11 | 12 | 13 | 14

School Tour

Last week we received from the minister of education a letter in | 13
which we were asked whether it would be possible to arrange for a | 26
group of five or six persons to tour our school next month. The group | 40
would include three or four visitors from other countries who will be | 54
travelling our country from east to west and visiting many schools | 67
along the way to get a firsthand picture of our educational system. I | 81
propose that we arrange a tour along the following lines. | 92

First of all we will need a tour guide, and I suggest that Mrs. | 106
Chang would be an excellent choice. The tour would begin at nine in | 120
the morning in the reception area where Mrs. Chang would welcome the | 134
guests. She would give the visitors a brief history of our school, a | 148
rundown on student numbers, the types of programs we offer, the system | 162
under which we operate, etc. | 168

The group would then be taken to the electronics room where the | 182
teacher in charge would show some of our equipment and explain how the | 196
program operates. Then the tour would proceed to the typing workshop | 210
where one of the instructors on duty would describe the operation of | 224
the workshop and provide such information as textbooks in use, speed | 238
requirements, etc. A look at the practice office might also be in | 251
order, as well as an outline of when and for how long students work in | 265
the office and the kinds of duties that are performed there. | 277

The next stop would be the word processing centre for information | 291
on the setup of the course, its duration, success of our graduates, | 304
etc. A demonstration of our equipment would be given, at the end of | 318
which a cartoon picture calendar would be printed out and a copy pre- | 332
sented to each guest. The group would then carry on to the computer | 346
centre. If there are enough terminals free at the time, the visitors | 360
could try a few hands-on activities. | 367

After a brief look at our resource and audio/visual centre, the | 381
group would be conducted to the lounge where they would be served cof- | 395
fee. You and I and other personnel would meet them there. I suspect | 409
that it would be near noon before this gathering would disperse, and I | 423
suggest that you and I take our guests to the staff dining room for | 437
lunch. | 438

Does this plan meet with your approval? Please let me know as | 452
soon as possible so that I can conclude the arrangements and confirm | 466
them with the minister. | 471

1 | 2 | 3 | 4 | 5 | 6 | 7 | 8 | 9 | 10 | 11 | 12 | 13 | 14

Sheep Farming

Running a sheep farm is not an easy business. It requires know-how and hard work. Australia and New Zealand are two countries famous for sheep raising and their sheep products are exported to countries throughout the world. Most farms raise several breeds of sheep – some for wool, some for mutton, and some for breeding – and the different groups are usually kept separate.

Lambing is a busy but exciting time on a sheep farm. There may be a few hundred pregnant ewes waiting to give birth at approximately the same time. A week or so before the lambs are due, the ewes are mustered with the assistance of sheep dogs (not the big, shaggy creatures that we are familiar with) which respond with efficient obedience to their master's whistles and signals. The ewes are given shots to protect them and their newborn from disease. Also, they are clipped around the udders and tails to eliminate tags of dirty wool where the babies will nurse. In a week or two, there are soft white lambs everywhere. As with fully grown sheep, great care is taken with the lambs' nutrition and physical condition. As the lambs grow, their coats become thicker and warmer. Lambs being raised for wool will likely be in their second year before they are sheared along with the older animals.

Shearing is an important event. On a large farm, a team of shearers is usually hired to undertake the job, which often takes days. An expert shearer operates at lightning speed and is capable of shearing a sheep in less than three minutes. The main fleece is removed from the sheep's back in one piece and might weigh from three to five kilograms. The fleeces are packed very tightly into huge sacks, each weighing two to three hundred kilograms when full. They will be used not only for wool, but also for their grease which will be extracted and refined into lanolin, the base of most cosmetics and skin creams.

After each animal is shorn, it is whisked into the pen of its shearer. When each pen is full, the sheep are released one at a time so that they can be counted, for a shearer is paid according to the number of sheep shorn. Considerably lighter now, the newly shorn sheep runs from the pen, leaping into the air just as frisky as a lamb.

13
27
41
55
69
76
90
104
118
132
146
160
173
187
201
215
229
242
256
259
272
285
299
312
326
339
353
367
381
383
396
410
424
437
450
451

1 | 2 | 3 | 4 | 5 | 6 | 7 | 8 | 9 | 10 | 11 | 12 | 13 | 14

Skiing

Skiing is one of those activities which, unless mastered when   12
young, is probably best left alone. Why on earth, then, would a nor-   26
mal, rational person over thirty consider taking it up? Looking back, 40
I realize that two forces were at work which caused me to abandon my   54
better judgment and head for the slopes. Firstly, the Canadian win-   68
ter! I had been living in Canada for fourteen years and had been   81
miserable for the three months of each winter. That totalled nearly   95
four years of misery, which I finally decided was simply too much. It 109
was definitely time to do something constructive.   119

The second force at work was pressure from family and friends who   133
had been saying for years that one has to get out and enjoy the snow   147
and the invigorating temperatures. These were the same people who had 161
persuaded me to try ice skating. After skating had been painfully   174
eliminated, they began to talk of skiing. "Snow is much more forgiv-   189
ing than ice; the ski is much broader than the skate and not as high   203
off the ground," they said.   209

The trouble was they neglected to tell me that the beginner   222
slopes are mountains and the runs are almost vertical. No one men-   236
tioned that to get to the top, one uses a hoisting device which has no 250
patience with, or sympathy for, beginners. Even the clothing was a   264
challenge. In magazines and on TV one sees the beautiful people   277
schussing down, always smiling and thoroughly enjoying themselves.   290
One thing is sure: they are not wearing my boots. The designers of   304
my boots had absolutely no regard for the shape and the anatomy of the 318
human foot. My foot and ankle were held rigidly together as though   332
there were no ankle joint at all. The boot buckles bore an uncanny   346
resemblance to mousetraps and were just as hazardous to fingers.   359

I persevered. I fell down so often I lost count. I fell off the   373
lift going up. I fell getting off at the top. When I looked down the   387
hill and saw how far and how steep it was, I nearly fell over from   400
shock. For some reason, I could not make a left turn going down. I'm   414
sure I collided with every tree on my right-hand side. Getting up   427
after a fall was a ten-minute manoeuvre. I had snow down my back, in   441
my socks, inside my gloves. My glasses kept steaming up and my cap   455
kept falling off. Still I persevered. Finally the great moment came   469
when I made a complete run without a single fall. It was wonderful!   483
I began to talk about skiing vacations – the Laurentians, Vermont,   496
maybe even the Swiss Alps. I had joined the ranks of skiers.   508

1 | 2 | 3 | 4 | 5 | 6 | 7 | 8 | 9 | 10 | 11 | 12 | 13 | 14

Smith's Hotel

Mr. Smith came down to Mariposa and bought out the inside of what | 13
had been the Royal Hotel. By the inside of a hotel is meant every- | 27
thing except the four walls of it – the fittings, the furniture, the | 41
bar, Billy the desk clerk, the three dining room helpers, and above all | 55
the licence granted for the sale of intoxicating liquors. | 67

From the first, Mr. Smith was a wild success as a hotel manager. | 81
He had all the qualifications. He weighed 127 kg. He could haul two | 96
drunken men out of the bar, each by the scruff of the neck, without | 110
the faintest anger or excitement. He carried money enough in his | 123
trouser pockets to open a bank, and spent it on anything, bet it on | 137
anything, and gave it away in handfuls. He was never drunk, and, as a | 151
point of chivalry to his customers, never quite sober. | 162

Everyone was welcome at the hotel who cared to come in. Anybody | 176
who didn't like it could leave. Drinks of all kinds cost five cents, | 190
or six for a quarter. Meals and bed were practically free. For any | 204
persons foolish enough to approach the desk and pay for them, Mr. | 217
Smith charged according to the expressions on their faces. | 229

At first, the loafers and the shanty men settled on the place in | 243
a deluge, but they were not the trade Mr. Smith wanted. He knew how | 257
to discourage them. An army of char people turned into the hotel and | 271
scrubbed it from top to bottom. A vacuum cleaner, the first seen in | 285
Mariposa, hissed and screamed in the corridors. Forty fancy beds were | 299
imported from the city. A bartender with a starched jacket and waist | 313
coat was put behind the bar. The loafers were put out of business. | 327
The place had become too classy for them. | 335

To encourage the high-class trade, Mr. Smith set himself to dress | 349
the part. He wore wide-cut coats of filmy serge, light as gossamer; | 363
chequered waistcoats with a different pattern for every day in the | 376
week; fedora hats light as autumn leaves; and ties of saffron and | 389
myrtle green with a diamond pin the size of a hazelnut. On his fin- | 403
gers there were as many gems as would grace a native prince of India. | 417
Across his waistcoat lay a gold watch chain in huge square links, and | 431
in his pocket, a gold watch that weighed more than half a kilogram and | 445
marked minutes, seconds, and quarter seconds. Just to look at Josh | 459
Smith's watch brought at least ten customers to the bar every evening. | 473

1 | 2 | 3 | 4 | 5 | 6 | 7 | 8 | 9 | 10 | 11 | 12 | 13 | 14

Spring

Each year, I have been pained to notice that the approach of spring occasions a most distressing change in the conduct of many of my friends. Beside my house, I have an acquaintance who is a nature man. All through the winter he is fairly quiet and an agreeable friendly fellow, quite fit for general society. Spring, however, at once occasions in my nature friend a distressing disturbance. He seems suddenly to desire, at our every meeting, to make himself a channel of information between the animate world and me. From the moment that the snow begins to melt, he keeps me posted as to what the plants and the birds and the bees are doing. This is a class of information which I do not want and which I cannot use, but I have to bear it.

My nature friend passes me every morning with some new and bright piece of information, something he thinks so cheery that it irradiates his face. One day, he exclaims that he saw a finch; the next day, he noticed a scarlet tanager. What a tanager is I have never known; I hope I never shall. I cannot match my nature friend's information in any way. I know only two birds, the crow and the hen. I can tell them apart at once, either by their plumage or by their song. I can carry on a nature conversation up to the limit of the crow and the hen; beyond that, nothing. So for the first day or so in spring, I am able to say, "I saw a crow yesterday," or "I noticed a hen out walking this morning."

Somehow, my crow and hen grow out of date awfully quickly and I never refer to them again; but my friend keeps up his information for weeks, running through a whole gamut of animals. I am aware that I ought long ago to have spoken out openly to my nature friend; but I have, I admit, the unfortunate and weak-minded disposition that forces me to smile with hatred in my heart.

I admit that I am the kind of person who would never notice an oriole building a nest unless it came and built it in my hat. There are other people like me, too. There are signs of spring that every sensible person like us respects and recognizes. We see the oyster disappear from the club menu and know that winter is passing. We notice the asparagus appear in the local supermarket and the price of produce begin to drop, and we realize the season is advancing. These are the signs of spring that any person can appreciate.

| 12 |
| 26 |
| 40 |
| 53 |
| 67 |
| 80 |
| 93 |
| 106 |
| 120 |
| 133 |
| 147 |
| 150 |
| 164 |
| 178 |
| 192 |
| 206 |
| 220 |
| 233 |
| 247 |
| 260 |
| 274 |
| 289 |
| 292 |
| 305 |
| 318 |
| 331 |
| 345 |
| 358 |
| 368 |
| 382 |
| 396 |
| 410 |
| 424 |
| 437 |
| 451 |
| 465 |
| 478 |

1 | 2 | 3 | 4 | 5 | 6 | 7 | 8 | 9 | 10 | 11 | 12 | 13 | 14

Statues – Big and Beautiful

WORDS

Of the millions of statues which have been built through the ages	13
to the present day, only a very select few have entered the realm of	27
wonders of the world. Because thousands of statues have been beauti-	41
ful works of art, designed and built with immense care and craftsman-	55
ship, it would seem impossible for a few to be widely acclaimed as	68
surpassing all others. What made these few so outstanding? A quick	82
study shows that they had one other thing in common besides beauty:	96
size. It would appear that these statues achieved their special	109
status, not only because they were beautiful, but also because they	123
were big.	125
One of the original wonders of the world, the Greek statue of the	139
god Zeus was said to be one of the most handsome statues ever made.	153
It was also over twelve metres high. The statue was carved out of	166
wood and the flesh parts were covered with sheets of ivory, the robes	180
were plates of solid gold, and the eyes were jewels. The figure sat	194
upon a throne that was gold-plated, engraved, and inlaid with ebony	208
and gems. A statue of such beauty and dimensions would be certain to	222
create a lasting impact. The statue was destroyed by fire a long time	236
ago, but written records attest to its merits.	245
Another beautiful and big statue is the Buddha of Kamakura in	258
Japan. Thirteen metres high, this bronze figure sits in a position of	272
meditation. Its eyes are gold and there is a silver bump in the mid-	286
dle of its forehead which denotes spiritual insight. The statue was	300
housed in a temple until the building was destroyed by an earthquake	314
and tidal wave. The statue survived and is now surrounded by a lovely	328
garden. Inside the figure are stairs which visitors may climb to the	342
shoulders where there is a small window looking out the back.	354
A much more recent statue built in this century is Christ of the	368
Andes in South America. It also is lovely, but not nearly as large as	382
the Buddha. It is only eight metres tall; however, because it is	395
located in a pass that is more than sixty-one metres above sea level,	409
it is in a rather commanding position and is one of the highest	422
statues in the world. Crafted from bronze, it is a symbol of peace	436
between the two countries which border the pass in which it stands.	450
Part of its metal came from cannons that were melted down.	462

1 | 2 | 3 | 4 | 5 | 6 | 7 | 8 | 9 | 10 | 11 | 12 | 13 | 14

Statues – Old and New

One of the largest of ancient statues on record was that of	12
Apollo, the Greek god of the sun. This bronze statue was known as the	26
Colossus of Rhodes; and at thirty-two metres tall, it surely was	39
colossal. Although the statue was wrecked by an earthquake about	52
sixty years after its completion, it had already been declared one of	66
the wonders of the world. It is not known where in the city of Rhodes	80
the statue stood, but one suggestion was the harbour. Thus the popu-	94
lar picture is that of Apollo, with sun rays protruding above his	107
head, holding aloft a burning torch, and straddling the harbour so	120
that ships in full sail were able to pass between his legs and enter	134
the safety of the harbour.	139
It is highly unlikely that you would have failed to notice the	153
similarities, except for the gender and stance of the figures, between	167
the Colossus and another famous and much more recent statue which very	181
well qualifies as a wonder of the world. It is quite probable that	195
the Colossus inspired this later symbol of freedom, the Statue of	208
Liberty.	210
Facing out over the New York harbour, the Statue of Liberty is	224
the figure of a woman draped in classical robes and wearing a crown	238
from which seven spikes radiate. The broken shackles of slavery lie	252
at her feet, in her left hand is a law book, and in her right hand she	266
carries aloft a flaming torch. The figure is forty-six metres high to	280
the tip of the torch and is made of large, hammered copper plates	293
which have turned a rich shade of green from the weather.	304
The statue was a gift from the people of France. It was built	318
there, taken apart, and then shipped to New York where it was assem-	332
bled. The statue is bolted to a great stone pedestal which is twenty-	346
seven metres high. Thus the statue and base together reach a height	360
of well over seventy metres. An elevator inside takes visitors to the	374
top of the pedestal, from where they may climb a spiral staircase up	388
through the hollow statue to the crown. Here, windows provide a mar-	402
vellous view of the harbour. The statue, which is floodlit at night,	416
is in full view of all watercraft which enter the harbour day or	429
night; and for many people, it is an emotional and stirring sight.	442

1 | 2 | 3 | 4 | 5 | 6 | 7 | 8 | 9 | 10 | 11 | 12 | 13 | 14

Titanic

It was a chilly April evening, but the sea was calm and the sky   13
was full of bright shining stars. A couple of warnings about icebergs   27
in the area had come in over the wireless, but the Titanic's radio   40
operator was too busy to pay much attention. He had a raft of mes-   54
sages from his passengers to transmit to their families and friends.   68
In the crow's nest, the watch marvelled at the stillness of the night   82
when suddenly an iceberg loomed up in front of him. He rang his warn-   96
ing bell and phoned down to the bridge. The helmsman tried to change   110
the ship's course, but it was too late.   118

Most of those who felt the jolt attributed it to a variety of   131
things – almost anything but an iceberg. It was some time before the   145
extent of the damage could be ascertained and assessed. The captain   159
learned that the ship had received a long gash in her side and water   173
was pouring in. The first five watertight compartments were filling   187
up fast. It was because of her fifteen watertight compartments that   201
the Titanic was deemed unsinkable. She could float with some of her   215
compartments flooded, but not with all of the first five.   226

The captain ordered that distress signals be radioed out and   239
that rockets be fired every five minutes in an attempt to alert the   253
steamer, Californian, sixteen kilometres away. He told the crew to   267
lower the lifeboats and start loading the women and children into   280
them. Replies started coming in on the wireless. The Carpathia was a   294
hundred kilometres away and was on her way at full speed. No word was   308
heard from the steamer that could still be seen on the horizon. The   322
Californian's lone radio operator had finished his shift just ten   335
minutes before the iceberg struck.   342

It was hard at first to convince the passengers that they would   356
be safer in the lifeboats than on this big, strong ship; and many   369
women at first refused to get into the boats. Thus the first few   382
lifeboats set off with considerably less than their full complement of   396
people. When the last boat pulled away, just over 700 people out of   410
a total of over 1 500 had escaped the sinking ship. Out in the boats,   424
the occupants watched as the Titanic sank lower and lower in the   437
water. They could see people still standing at the rails, and they   451
could hear the band playing. Suddenly, the ship stood on end, then   465
started to slip, picking up speed as she went down. Then she was   478
gone.   479

1 | 2 | 3 | 4 | 5 | 6 | 7 | 8 | 9 | 10 | 11 | 12 | 13 | 14

Toolbox

People in our house have a tendency to borrow things and not	12
return them to their proper places. As a result, I could never find	26
tools when I needed them, but was certain to stumble across mislaid	40
tools when I was looking for something else. That's why I now carry	54
my tools, neatly arranged in a plastic toolbox, in the hatchback of	67
my automobile where nobody else can get at them.	77

For a while I carried just the most basic tools, like a tape 90
measure, a hammer, some nails, a few screwdrivers, and my trusty 103
pair of pointed pliers. Recently, though, I expanded this collection. 117
This was a result of helping to build an apartment in a house. 130
During the construction, I became exposed to and had to use many 143
tools with which I had not had much prior experience. 155

Some of the new tools I have acquired are a portable level, a 168
small crowbar, and an awl. A level is essential for ensuring that 181
mirrors, shelves, and the like are installed level and not on a tilt. 195
The small crowbar proves very useful for removing old baseboards, 208
lifting up old carpeting, and prying up nails and carpet staples. An 222
awl, which looks like a screwdriver except that it ends in a very 235
sharp point, is extremely handy, I discovered, for piercing holes in 249
wood or thin-gauge metal to make it easy to start screws or nails. 262

A chalk line is another tool that has been added to my toolbox. 276
Consisting of a hand-held device containing chalk powder and many 289
metres of string, it's fabulous for drawing a straight line on floors. 303
It really requires two people to operate, though. One person holds 317
the device at one marker. The other person pulls out the string keep- 331
ing it taut, positions it over the other marker, then snaps the line 345
by lifting the string and releasing it. The chalky string bounces 358
down and hits the surface, leaving a nice, straight chalk line. 371

Several times in the past, I have tried using a magnetic stud 384
finder to locate wall studs, but never with much success. Often I 397
wound up making holes in the wall and discovering there was no wood 411
stud behind it to firmly anchor the nail. Now I am the proud owner 425
of an electronic stud finder, and coloured lights tell me, quite 438
accurately, the location of studs. 445

It feels wonderful to think that my tools are now secured in 458
my car away from inconsiderate borrowers. Oh! My husband has just 471
inquired as to the whereabouts of the scissors that belong in the 484
kitchen drawer. Excuse me while I get them out of my toolbox. 497

1 | 2 | 3 | 4 | 5 | 6 | 7 | 8 | 9 | 10 | 11 | 12 | 13 | 14

Violin – First String

The violin is the best known and most widely used of all stringed   13
instruments. This queen of instruments is also known as a fiddle.   26
The violin section is the largest and most important part of an   39
orchestra, and the lead violin player is the concert master and often   53
the assistant conductor as well.   59

Violins are made with great care. The wood used in them has an   73
important influence on the tone produced and must be carefully sea-   87
soned so that no part will warp. The seventy different pieces in each   101
violin are shaped to fit together exactly. No nails, screws, or metal   115
fasteners of any kind are used. All the parts are glued together with   129
a special glue, and the finished body is carefully varnished.   141

A violin has four strings which extend almost the length of the   155
instrument from the tailpiece, which is secured to the body of the   168
violin by the end pin; over a bridge, which supports the strings above   182
the body; to the peg box, which contains the pegs, or pins, for tight-   196
ening and loosening the strings. Attached to the tailpiece is a fine   210
tuner, and this enables the violinist to achieve fine shades of tuning   224
without using the pegs. The strings were formerly all made of catgut,   238
which was most often the twisted intestines of sheep. Modern violins   252
have metal strings, although the G string, the lowest one, is often   266
catgut overwound with silver, copper, or aluminum wire.   277

The violin is played with a bow, a long curved stick with about a   291
hundred and fifty horsehairs stretched from one tip to an adjustable   305
device called a frog at the other end. The hair is allowed to rest   319
loosely when the bow is stored in the violin case. When the bow is to   333
be used, however, the hairs are tightened to the desired tension for   347
playing and are rubbed with rosin which coats the hairs and improves   361
the resonance of the tone when the bow is drawn across the strings.   375
Movement of the bow back and forth over the violin strings causes the   389
strings to vibrate and give off sound. The violinist is able to pro-   403
duce different tones or notes by depressing one or more strings with   417
the fingers of one hand while using the other hand to stroke the   430
strings with the bow.   434

Most people tend to admire the finger dexterity of the violinist   448
and do not realize that the art of the playing is in the bowing.   461

1 | 2 | 3 | 4 | 5 | 6 | 7 | 8 | 9 | 10 | 11 | 12 | 13 | 14

Violin – History and Care

The excellence of the violin as we know it today was brought about through the changes and improvements made by countless people over a long stretch of time.

In the twelfth century a fiddle called the vielle was made. It had five strings and ranked as the most important stringed instrument of the time. Another forerunner was the tenor viol which had six strings but lacked the brilliance of tone and the versatility of the fiddle. For two hundred years, Cremona, a small town in Italy, reigned as the prime centre of violin making. Here, Nicolo Amati made instruments of such sweetness and tone that for some time it was thought they could not be excelled. As it turned out, his prize pupil began making a larger and flatter model which not only equalled the master's in tenderness but which had more volume and roundness of tone.

To this day, that student, Antonio Stradivari, is considered the master of violin makers. It is believed that during his lifetime, he made a thousand or so instruments, of which some four to six hundred still survive. Needless to say, each of these is a rare item and worth a fortune. While the violins of Stradivari are justly famous, a large number of concert players prefer to use those made by Joseph Guarnerius, a member of another family of violin makers from the same town.

The care of the violin should be a prime concern of the owner. Violins, and all stringed instruments for that matter, should not be exposed to extremes or large, rapid changes in temperature. Failure to observe this rule could result in such problems as cracks, open seams, or collapse of parts of the assembly. Because the glue in a violin softens in high heat, leaving a violin in a closed place like the trunk of a car in summer for even a short time can do damage. Also, transporting a violin in a car trunk in winter poses a threat, as does the unheated baggage hold of an aircraft. In fact, a maple back can crack if it is exposed to severe cold for just half an hour.

A fiddle should be cleaned regularly and checked for cracks or open seams. Any repairs should be done by a professional. With proper care, a violin will give years and years of service and then may be handed down to children as an heirloom.

| 1 | 2 | 3 | 4 | 5 | 6 | 7 | 8 | 9 | 10 | 11 | 12 | 13 | 14 |

War

This was total war. All were in it – men, women, children, old | 13
and young alike. This war was to be fought not only in the air, at | 27
sea, and on the beaches and in the trenches of foreign lands, but on | 41
the home ground as well. The home front was where some of the most | 55
important battles were fought; if it failed, all could be lost. | 68

The enemy thought this tiny country of Great Britain was an easy | 82
mark, as had been several other countries before it; but Hitler had | 96
not reckoned with the courage, resourcefulness, and determination of | 110
his opponents. Although the odds were not in their favour, the | 123
British aim was lofty – not mere survival, but victory. | 134

On the home front, war became a fact of everyday life and every- | 148
thing was geared towards it. Close to forty million gas masks were | 162
issued in case the enemy resorted to chemical warfare. Many children | 176
were evacuated from homes in prime target areas and were sent to safer | 190
parts of the country. Food rations were imposed and nightly blackouts | 204
were enforced. Basements and cellars in many buildings were taken | 217
over for air raid shelters, and trenches for shelters were dug in | 230
parks in the large towns. Medical and hospital services, rescue | 243
teams, bomb disposal squads, and fire brigades were organized. | 256

In open fields and parks, obstacles were placed to inhibit the | 269
landing of enemy aircraft. To confuse the enemy should any of them | 283
manage to land safely, signs telling distances and the names of towns | 297
and villages were removed from roads, rail stations, and all other | 310
display places. To augment the nation's food supply, gardens were | 323
planted in golf courses, sports grounds, parks, city lots, and even in | 337
reclaimed swamps. | 341

Everyone was kept busy doing what she or he could to help the war | 355
effort. Thousands went into offices and factories to carry on the | 368
work left by those drawn into the armed forces. A number of people | 382
acted as bomb spotters, blackout wardens, or members of the fire bri- | 396
gade to put out fires started by the bombs. Many sewed and knitted | 410
garments for the troops. Others worked in the shelters or did volun- | 424
teer work where they were needed. People strove together in a cohe- | 438
sive force, united in spirit and purpose. | 446

1 | 2 | 3 | 4 | 5 | 6 | 7 | 8 | 9 | 10 | 11 | 12 | 13 | 14

War and Coping

The needs and demands of war were not always easy to cope with,	13
but in most cases the British people met them with stout hearts, broad	27
shoulders, and co-operation. The rationing of clothes brought on a	41
policy of mend and make do. Food rationing made cooking an ever more	55
difficult task and prompted the media to give out advice, hints, and	69
recipes. Those who had land, even a small plot in front of or behind	83
a house, dug victory gardens in which they grew fruits and vegetables.	97
When petrol became scarce, people took to bicycles, horses, or their	111
own feet to get about.	115
When the country fell short of war materials, it made a mass	128
appeal for anything that could be converted and used. The response	142
was phenomenal, and from then on, waste was looked upon as a mortal	156
sin. Few things were thrown away. Old blankets and bedding were	169
donated to bomb shelters. Kitchen scraps were set aside for making	183
into a brown soup, or mud pudding as it was called, to feed animals.	197
All paper and cardboard was collected for recycling. Animal bones	210
were saved to be made into glue. Scrap rubber in any form, even in	224
corsets, was given to make tires for military vehicles.	235
Any and all kinds of scrap metal were needed and salvage dumps	249
were set up for their collection. Aluminum pots and pans, old and new	263
and some still hot from the oven, were donated for the building of	276
spitfires, hurricanes, and other aircraft. Tin foil, tin cans, tire	290
rims, and even thimbles were collected. All kinds of plain and ornate	304
wrought iron fencing, freshly removed from property perimeters, were	318
piled onto the scrap metal heaps.	325
The country had developed into a big national team that was dedi-	339
cated to sacrifice and hard work. In the midst of it all, sanity was	353
kept afloat, largely through the action of a good sense of humour.	366
Songs, jokes, wisecracks, and comic strips provided a lighter side to	380
the dangers and realities of war. Needed diversions were found, too,	394
in the music halls, movie houses, and pubs.	403
The war effort on the home front was not without some strife,	416
waste, unfairness, crime, and other taints that are always present	429
under any circumstances; but by far the vast majority of people gave	443
unstintingly their share of blood, toil, tears, and sweat.	455

1 | 2 | 3 | 4 | 5 | 6 | 7 | 8 | 9 | 10 | 11 | 12 | 13 | 14

Wheat

	WORDS

The first farming settlement in the Prairies was begun by a group   13
of Scottish families who were known as the Selkirk settlers. For some   27
time, it seemed as though everything were pitted against these people.   41
The fur traders saw them as a threat, and they with some native   54
Indians made many attempts to drive them out; but each time the set-   68
tlers returned. As if that were not enough, the Scots were beset by   82
drought, floods, crop disease, and even plagues of grasshoppers.   95
Somehow, the colony survived.   101

For those early settlers, farming was hard manual labour. They   115
used simple tools: hoes for cutting the weeds, spades for turning the   129
soil, sickles and scythes for harvesting, and flails for threshing.   143
Sowing of the seeds was done by hand. With methods such as these, the   157
homesteaders could cultivate only small parcels of land in that vast   171
country, barely enough to give them a living.   180

With the advent of the plow, things took a turn for the better.   194
The settlers were able to till larger areas. Before too long, other   208
equipment became available. Seed drills replaced hand sowing, reapers   222
and binders made harvesting much easier, and threshing machines sepa-   236
rated the wheat from the straw. At first, the new machines were driv-   250
en by horses or oxen, but then the steam engine arrived to take over   264
the job. The farmers were able to plant larger and larger crops.   277

It was obvious to the farmers that the Prairies was a great place   291
for growing wheat, but the varieties they were using were not really   305
suited to short, dry summers, and they picked up diseases far too   318
readily. What was needed was a type of wheat that would ripen quickly   332
and be resistant to disease.   338

Back in Scotland, a minister happened to be strolling along the   352
dock in Glasgow when he noticed a ship unloading grain. After watch-   366
ing for a few minutes, the minister cocked his head and his hat fell   380
into the grain bin he was standing beside. He reached in and plucked   394
out his hat - plus a few grains of wheat. That night, the minister   408
wrapped up the grains and mailed them to a farming friend in Canada.   422
From these seeds, the minister's friend, David Fife, developed a   435
strain of wheat that was admirably suited to prairie conditions. In   449
time, Red Fife, as the new wheat was called, became popular in the   462
home and then the world markets; and Canada's wheat industry was   475
launched.   477

1 | 2 | 3 | 4 | 5 | 6 | 7 | 8 | 9 | 10 | 11 | 12 | 13 | 14

Why Me?

At least once a day throughout my seventy-six years, I have asked, "Why me?" Today, for instance, I came into the drawing room with my teacup in hand. As I headed for my favourite chair, I stubbed my toe on the rocking chair, spilled my tea, stumbled, and landed so heavily in my chair that one of its slender legs cracked. Why me?

As I rested in the lopsided chair wondering whether my toe was broken, I recalled the time I broke my ankle while standing on the toilet. It was a sunny spring day, and while my infant son was sleeping, I washed and ironed the bathroom curtains. When they were ready for hanging, I lifted the toilet seat and stood on the rim of the bowl to reach the curtain rod. As I stretched, my foot slipped and crashed into the bowl with such force that it stuck and I couldn't free it.

Finally, I stopped struggling and, just then, I heard the screen door open and the afternoon mail drop on the floor. I shouted loudly for help. The door re-opened and a timid voice said, "What is it, lady?" I replied that I was stuck in the toilet and needed assistance. There was a moment's silence. Then the postman informed me that he would summon my next-door neighbour. After much persuasion, I coerced him into the bathroom and I was rescued. Why me?

A cast on my foot and a new baby were trying enough, but being stuck indoors was most annoying, so one day I ventured out. Pushing the baby in the pram, I was confident I could walk the short distance to the store and back. I arrived with no trouble and left the baby sleeping outside in the carriage while I shopped. When I came out, my only thought was to reach home without dropping the milk jug. Every step was an adventure, but I arrived home without mishap. I put the milk in the refrigerator and sat down at the kitchen table – exhausted but elated at my feat. It wasn't until I noticed the baby's dish that I realized I had left my baby at the store. I was frantic. I struggled to the telephone and called the shop. Yes, the baby was there and the police had just arrived to collect the abandoned child. After lengthy negotiations, tall explanations, and desperate pleading, the policeman agreed to deliver the baby home. Was I embarassed as I watched the officer pushing my baby pram up the street! Why me?

I used to think I would outgrow my calamities, but I never did. The ringing of the telephone brought me back to reality, and I hobbled into the kitchen, banging my head on a cupboard door that was ajar. I groped for the phone and said hello. It was a wrong number. Why me?

| 12 |
| 26 |
| 40 |
| 54 |
| 67 |
| 81 |
| 94 |
| 108 |
| 122 |
| 136 |
| 150 |
| 164 |
| 178 |
| 192 |
| 205 |
| 219 |
| 232 |
| 246 |
| 258 |
| 271 |
| 285 |
| 299 |
| 313 |
| 327 |
| 341 |
| 355 |
| 369 |
| 383 |
| 397 |
| 410 |
| 424 |
| 438 |
| 451 |
| 464 |
| 478 |
| 492 |
| 506 |
| 520 |

1 | 2 | 3 | 4 | 5 | 6 | 7 | 8 | 9 | 10 | 11 | 12 | 13 | 14

Yawning

There are few of us who fail to indulge in a good old-fashioned | 13
yawn now and then. In fact, many of us spend a good portion of our | 27
day yawning. We yawn first thing in the morning. We yawn at various | 41
times through the day. We yawn at bedtime. We started yawning quite | 55
early in life. As babies, we were quite notorious yawners. Yawning | 69
feels good, especially when done in private where we can put our whole | 83
bodies into it. Sometimes we yawn at the wrong times in front of the | 97
wrong people, and that can be embarrassing. However, yawning is con- | 111
tagious and if we can get others in on the act, we can spread the | 124
embarrassment around. | 128

It's doubtful if yawning is often a topic of conversation in | 141
scientific circles where it would likely excite only yawns. Even | 154
doctors give it little thought – so little, in fact, that they haven't | 168
conjured up a fancy name for it yet. It appears that yawning is one | 182
of those natural phenomena, like blushing and sneezing, which has | 195
drawn only passing attention. | 201

Yawn is a very old word that means to be wide open or gaping, as | 215
in a yawning cavern. When used in reference to people, it means that | 229
involuntary action in which one takes a long, deep breath while gradu- | 243
ally opening the mouth to its fullest. This causes the tongue to | 256
flatten, the throat muscles to stretch, and the eyelids to droop. | 269
Often at the same time, the arms and body stretch and the eyes may | 282
water. | 283

Pretty well all vertebrates yawn. Cats, parrots, turtles, even | 297
elephants yawn. Most animals' yawning usually just means they are | 310
ready to drop off to sleep. People tend to yawn when they are tired, | 324
bored, or perhaps are sitting in a hot, stuffy room. Under such con- | 338
ditions, our breathing becomes more shallow causing our oxygen level | 352
to drop – which induces us to yawn. A nice big yawn brings added | 365
oxygen into the bloodstream, which pumps it up to the brain to perk us | 379
up. Yawning is the best method of clearing one's ears and relieving | 393
the pain or discomfort of a change in air pressure like that experi- | 407
enced on an airplane. Because so many people interpret a yawn as a | 421
sign of boredom, polite folks stifle their yawns, cover them up, or | 435
turn away; and almost always they apologize. | 444

The subject of yawning has not been ignored by humorous writers. | 458
In fact, it was defined by one wit as the act of opening one's mouth | 472
in the desperate hope that other people would clamp theirs shut. | 485

1 | 2 | 3 | 4 | 5 | 6 | 7 | 8 | 9 | 10 | 11 | 12 | 13 | 14

Typewriter History

28 GWPM

The first typewriter patent on record was issued in Great Britain in 1714 to one, Henry Mill. The earliest known typewriters were rather odd-looking machines, often incorporating features of other types of machinery. For example, at least one typewriter had a keyboard that closely resembled that of a piano. Another had a clock-like face. On yet another, the carriage was returned by use of a foot treadle, much like the treadle on an old sewing machine. Typing was done with two fingers and the typist could not see what had been typed until the paper had been removed from the machine. Most of those early typewriters were large and cumbersome and were not really practical.

14	14
28	28
42	42
56	56
70	70
83	83
97	97
111	111
125	125
138	138
140	140

32 GWPM

The first practical typewriter was built in 1867 by Christopher Sholes and two associates. Sholes continued to improve on his typewriter, and seven years later it was put on the market by E. Remington and Sons, a gun manufacturing firm. The machine did not attract much interest until Mark Twain used one to prepare a manuscript for publication. The resulting publicity spread the word and the typewriter era was launched. Oddly enough, although the shorthand writers at that time were men, it was mostly women who learned to operate the typewriter. The male stenographer would write the employer's letter in shorthand and then orally dictate the communication from his shorthand notes to the typist, who typed as he dictated. It was some time before the two functions were vested in one person.

13	153
27	167
41	181
55	195
69	209
82	222
95	235
108	248
122	262
136	276
150	290
160	300

36 GWPM

The typewriter keyboard was designed so that the most often used keys were struck by the weaker fingers. The purpose of this was to slow down the typists who, it was found, typed faster than the machines could operate, causing the machines to jam. This arrangement has become known as the "qwerty" keyboard (named after the first six keys in the second row) and is the one we still use today – not only on typewriters, but also on computers, word processors, telexes, and other communication machines. As technology developed, the speed capability of the typewriter did increase so that it reached and then surpassed the speed of the average typist. The typewriter brought about major changes in the business office. Too, it made a tremendous impact on communications and education. More than anything else, the typewriter was largely responsible for opening the doors of business to women.

13	313
27	327
40	340
54	354
68	368
82	382
96	396
109	409
123	423
136	436
150	450
164	464
178	478
180	480

1 | 2 | 3 | 4 | 5 | 6 | 7 | 8 | 9 | 10 | 11 | 12 | 13 | 14

Numismatics

40 GWPM The use of coins as a medium of exchange dates back to long 12 12
before the glorious days of Greece and Rome. It is not known when 25 25
numismatics, a fancy name for coin collecting, began, but it is now a 39 39
popular and interesting hobby which can also be financially rewarding. 53 53
Many collectors today began to collect coins when they were children 67 67
and continued their hobby into adult life. Some numismatists collect 81 81
any and all kinds of currency; others prefer to specialize in their 94 94
collections. While one collector may like commemorative coins or mint 108 108
sets, another may zero in on gold coins, while someone else may col- 122 122
lect only coins from a particular country. A typical collection of 135 135
Canadian coins might consist of large and small pennies, nickels, 148 148
dimes, quarters, half dollars, and dollars – with the coins usually 162 162
arranged in order of the year in which each was minted. It might also 176 176
include old bank and provincial tokens, old paper currency like shin 190 190
plasters, and perhaps even a few wooden nickels. 200 200

44 GWPM The popular notion has it that old is valuable. This is not 13 213
necessarily so. Many older coins can be purchased for a few dollars, 27 227
while some later ones may cost several hundred dollars or more. As 41 241
with other commodities, the value of coins is determined by supply 54 254
and demand. Usually, the scarcer the coin, the higher its value. In 68 268
addition, the price of some coins, particularly gold and silver ones, 82 282
may fluctuate according to the market value of their metal. Until a 96 296
couple of decades ago, it was common to find collectable coins among 109 309
loose change; however, with the increased number of collectors, it is 123 323
now rare to find a collectable coin in circulation. Silver coins, 137 337
too, have vanished from public change purses and tills. They began to 151 351
disappear shortly after the mints started using nickel instead of 165 365
silver. A number of investors, realizing the intrinsic value of the 179 379
metal, were astute enough to stash silver coins away. Their foresight 192 393
paid off, for when the price of silver rose to record highs, they were 207 407
in a position to sell their silver coins for handsome profits. 220 420

Most collector coins are now purchased from a dealer or, if they 434
are new issues, directly from the mint. Mint sets and commemorative 448
coins are often specially packaged to preserve their mint condition. 462
Of course, an itemized record of all coins in a collection should be 476
kept for insurance purposes. 482

1 | 2 | 3 | 4 | 5 | 6 | 7 | 8 | 9 | 10 | 11 | 12 | 13 | 14

Earthquake

48 GWPM

Of the thousands of earthquakes that occur each year, usually only about six hundred are large enough to warrant recording. Although most quakes take place under the sea or in uninhabited areas, some do occur in populated places, causing damage and some-times loss of life. Some regions in the Pacific earthquake belt, seem to be more susceptible to quakes than are other areas.

China's proneness to earthquakes caused the ancient Chinese to develop a construction design that would render a building earthquake-proof. In these buildings, the roof load was balanced on an intricate arrangement of interlocking bracket sets containing thousands of mortise and tenon joints. The free movement of these joints diverted the quake's energy as it travelled up the posts. In this way, most of the energy was dissipated before it reached the roof. It was also in China that the seismograph, an instrument that detects and records earthquakes, was invented. The seismograph was introduced there in the second century, 1 600 years before it appeared in the west. Not only did the seismograph register that an earthquake had taken place, but it also indicated from which direction the tremor had come.

52 GWPM

The seismograph looked like a large, metal urn and stood over a metre tall. Spaced equally apart on the outside were crafted eight dragons, each holding a small ball clamped in its jaws. Sitting on the ground gazing up at each dragon was a large toad with its mouth agape. Inside the urn was a heavy pendulum which hung stationary and could be triggered into motion only by a very slow vibration such as an earthquake tremor would create. When an earthquake vibrated the instrument, the pendulum swung towards the source of the tremor and lifted a lever which released the ball from the closest dragon. The mechanism then locked in position to prevent the pendulum swinging back and causing another ball to be dropped. The racket made by the bronze ball landing in the toad's mouth alerted the people in the vicinity that an earthquake had occurred. By ascertaining which ball had been released, the direction from which the tremor had originated could easily be determined.

The magnitude or destructive force of earthquakes is measured on a scale called the Richter scale. Earthquakes of magnitude 1 are hardly noticeable. Quakes of magnitude 4 or 5 could cause some dam-age. However, a quake that scores 7 or higher could be very destruct-ive and would be considered a major earthquake.

12	12
25	25
38	38
51	51
64	64
75	75
89	89
103	103
117	117
130	130
144	144
158	158
172	172
185	185
199	199
213	213
227	227
240	240
14	254
27	267
40	280
54	294
68	308
82	322
96	336
109	349
123	363
136	376
150	390
163	403
177	417
191	431
196	436
210	450
223	463
237	477
251	491
260	500

1 | 2 | 3 | 4 | 5 | 6 | 7 | 8 | 9 | 10 | 11 | 12 | 13 | 14

Knitting

56
GWPM

Needlework is an art that dates back to ancient times. It was   13   13
developed by early peoples as a means of making garments with which to   27   27
protect themselves from the weather. As time went on, new methods,   40   40
designs, colours, and materials were introduced, and a wide range of   54   54
articles ¹were made that were not only serviceable, but attractive to   68   68
look upon as well. Eventually, items that were solely for decorative   82   82
purposes became common too. Some beautiful old pieces of needlework,   96   96
such as tapestries made in the middle ages, can still be seen in muse-   110   110
ums around ² the world. Needlework was considered to be mainly women's   124   124
work. In Elizabethan and Victorian days, girls were trained in the   137   137
art from a very young age. When they became ladies, they spent a con-   151   151
siderable amount of their time at their needles. They did weaving,   164   164
sewing, tatting, mending, ³embroidery, crochet, and knitting.   176   176

Knitting is one of the earliest kinds of needlework. In knit-   189   189
ting, needles made of bone, wood, steel, or plastic are used to con-   203   203
tinuously loop or knot a long string of yarn to form a very elastic   216   216
fabric that is excellent for making warm ⁴and close-fitting wearing   229   229
apparel. Early knitting was mostly confined to the making of hose or   243   243
stockings, but now countless numbers of other useful articles are   256   256
fashioned: sweaters, socks, gloves, shawls, baby clothes, cushion   270   270
covers, etc. Even fancy lace work can be knitted. ⁵   280   280

At one time, pure wool was the primary yarn used for knitting;   294
however, with the advent of easy-care fabrics like nylon, rayon, and   308
polyester, pure wool has lost ground. Knitting is most often done on   322
two needles, but for certain types of work (for example, when round   336
knitting for socks or gloves), three, four, or even five needles may   350
be required. There are two basic stitches in knitting: purl and   363
plain. By using various combinations of these two stitches, by pass-   377
ing or slipping one or more stitches over another, and/or by using   391
different colours of thread, many variations in the design can be   404
effected. Besides creating useful articles, knitting is a pleasant   418
pastime, one that may be carried on while talking or watching tele-   432
vision. It is also an easy craft for people who are invalid. For   445
this reason, it is used in many hospitals as a convalescent activity   459
for men and women alike. As with other types of needlework, popular   473
interest peaks, wanes, and revives again in a fairly regular cycle.   487
One thing seems certain, however; knitting is here to stay.   499

1 | 2 | 3 | 4 | 5 | 6 | 7 | 8 | 9 | 10 | 11 | 12 | 13 | 14

Home Insulation

60
GWPM

Home insulation has been around Canada for ages. Sod structures	12	12
which have been excavated in Newfoundland date from early times. As a	26	26
matter of fact, sod houses were built right into the early twentieth	40	40
century by settlers on the prairies where wood was scarce. Properly	54	54
cut, five centimetres of sod[1] block are the equivalent of more than two	68	68
centimetres of fibreglass.	73	73

Home insulation has been around Canada for ages. Sod structures which have been excavated in Newfoundland date from early times. As a matter of fact, sod houses were built right into the early twentieth century by settlers on the prairies where wood was scarce. Properly cut, five centimetres of sod[1] block are the equivalent of more than two centimetres of fibreglass.

Another type of insulated dwelling was the stovewood house which was built by early colonists. It was basically little more than a woodpile with four sides – hence its name. Infilling provided insulation[2] as well as a base for holding plaster. In early Quebec, stone houses were built with walls that were a massive 75 cm or thirty inches thick. These were constructed in three layers with the exterior and interior stone surfaces insulated from each other by a middle section of very small stones mortared together. This[3] created a crude air chamber which kept the frost from being conducted to the interior.

Only in recent years have brick houses become common in the Atlantic provinces. With wood in abundant supply for both building and heating, unpainted wooden houses sheltered rural families for almost two centuries[4], while a sturdy, cast-iron stove provided endless heat. Also, each winter, planks were laid on their longitudinal edges across upright stakes so that they formed troughs along the sides of the house. The troughs were filled with sawdust which helped insulate the floor level from wind and draughts.[5]

Sawdust was also the insulation used in another type of farm house. This house was built with a space between the studs and the inner wall. The space was filled with sawdust. This led to better and more even distribution of the heat generated from the large, wood-burning kitchen stove. Brick and stone houses appeared in many variations in most larger Canadian cities, but their hollow walls provided poor insulation. However, natural gas for space heaters was cheap, and so was coal to feed central heating systems. Eventually, it became so costly to use energy in lieu of insulation that by the early 1970s, most houses had added insulation between the studs and in the roof. Caulking improved, and double glazing began to replace the old leaky storm window. The energy saving was significant.

87	87
100	100
114	114
127	127
141	141
154	154
168	168
182	182
195	195
197	197
210	210
223	223
236	236
250	250
264	264
278	278
292	292
300	300
313
327
341
355
369
383
396
409
423
437
451
462

1 | 2 | 3 | 4 | 5 | 6 | 7 | 8 | 9 | 10 | 11 | 12 | 13 | 14

Computers

64
GWPM

In the late 1930s, a math professor found all the calculations 13 13
required of him just too much, and he decided to do something about 26 26
it. What he did was to design the first electronic digital computer. 40 40

During the Second World War, there was an urgent need for a 53 53
machine that would calculate ballistic tables much more[1] quickly than 67 67
the current methods were capable of. This need provided the oppor- 80 80
tunity for the development of the first large-scale digital computer, 94 94
the ENIAC. The machine could multiply two numbers in about three 107 107
milliseconds. It weighed thirty tonnes and took up the space of a 120 120
large room. It contained thousands of[2] wires and switches, as well as 134 134
18 000 vacuum tubes for the storage of data. One of the problems was 148 148
that when a new program was required, all of the switches and wires on 162 162
the machine had to be changed. To alleviate this, the concept of a 175 175
stored program was developed. 181 181

In the early 1950s, the computer entered the business arena.[3] New 195 195
programming languages were introduced that were faster and easier to 209 209
write, and were, therefore, less prone to errors. However, the vacuum 223 223
tubes were a problem. Not only did they take up a lot of space, heat 237 237
up, use a lot of electricity, and were expensive, but they were not 250 250
all that reliable and were no[4] longer fast enough. Soon, the vacuum 264 264
tube was replaced by the transistor, thus ushering in the second gen- 278 278
eration of computers. Transistors were smaller, cooler, faster, more 292 292
reliable – and cheaper. This meant that more firms could now afford 306 306
to buy computers. The computer market expanded by leaps and bounds.[5] 320 320

The third generation of computers began in 1964 when a solid 334
logic computer was produced in which the electronic components which 348
made up the controlling circuitry were stored on small silicon chips, 362
rather than on transistors. Chips were small, fast, and reliable. 375
Because they could be mass produced, they were cheap. The chip made 389
an astounding impact on the computer industry. In fact, the industry 403
has grown into one of the four largest in the world. As new methods 417
and machines for building circuits on these small chips have been 430
devised, the capacity of the chips has increased many times over. 443
This development continues to take place, and it is estimated that 456
soon over one million circuit elements will be stored on a tiny chip 470
that is less than one centimetre square. 478

1 | 2 | 3 | 4 | 5 | 6 | 7 | 8 | 9 | 10 | 11 | 12 | 13 | 14

Conversation

68
GWPM

Regardless of our age or vocation, we all engage in the game of conversation. The game is played wherever there is social contact of two or more persons. The game may be played for pleasure or for profit. As with other games, successful players require certain basic equipment. They require a good command of words, clear diction, a[1] pleasing voice, an interest in other people and the world around them, and some interesting ideas to exchange. The ability to set other people at ease and to draw them into conversation is also an asset, and an essential one for people who are required to conduct interviews.

Skillful players in the game of conversation develop a sensitivity[2] to the needs and aspirations of others. Recognizing and responding to the rationale of others is essential if one is to acquire a most important tool of conversation – tact. Tact is the knack of knowing when to speak, what to say, and how to say it. A player who is proficient in the use of tact has elevated his/her game[3] to the level of an art.

When we stop to consider what profound effect our skill at conversation can have on our lives – personal, social, and business – it becomes apparent that conversation is a most worthy art to develop. Just as some people have a natural aptitude for music or drawing, some have a natural flair for conversation.[4] Many others are not so gifted. Where do the ungifted go for instruction and guidance in developing conversation skills? There are schools that train in music and drawing; there are schools that instruct in the art of public speaking; but there are few schools that train in the art of private speaking – the art of conversation.[5]

Developing conversation skills requires much practice; but the opportunities for practice are becoming more and more difficult to come by. Modern society and lifestyles tend to discourage conversation. Television has probably been the biggest single culprit in stifling conversation. If the art of conversation is going to survive, courses will have to be developed in the schools, and we will each have to make a conscientious effort to talk, to listen, and to share ideas and opinions – in other words, to converse.

13	13
27	27
41	41
55	55
68	68
82	82
95	95
109	109
122	122
123	123
137	137
151	151
165	165
178	178
192	192
206	206
209	209
223	223
237	237
251	251
265	265
279	279
293	293
307	307
321	321
335	335
340	340
354	
368	
382	
395	
409	
423	
437	
448	

1 | 2 | 3 | 4 | 5 | 6 | 7 | 8 | 9 | 10 | 11 | 12 | 13 | 14

72
GWPM

When the will of Charles Vance Millar, a Toronto lawyer, was read   13   13
in 1926, people thought he was either crazy or the biggest joker on   26   26
record, for Millar left shares in a race track to well-known opponents   40   40
of gambling, brewery stock to teetotallers, and money to a Roman   53   53
Catholic church to say masses for the soul of a Protestant who had   66   66
outsmarted him in a business transaction.[1] Even more astonishing, he   80   80
left the residue of his estate to the mother in Toronto who had the   93   93
greatest number of children in the ten-year period following his   106   106
death.   107   107

Although the last bequest was to have been confidential until the   121   121
decade expired, the news escaped and the marathon was on. The news-   135   135
papers kept readers posted on the latest mothers[2] who appeared to be in 149   149
the running. Mothers were interviewed, pictures were taken, jokes   162   162
were made, and baby births hit the headlines. When the finish line   175   175
was reached, the tally showed two mothers who had delivered nine   188   188
babies, three mothers who had delivered ten, and one mother who   200   200
claimed eleven babies.   204   204

Other questions now arose. Could illegitimate, still,[3] or unreg-   218   218
istered births be counted? The courts took almost two years to   231   231
decide. They ruled that neither stillborn, illegitimate, nor unregis-   245   245
tered children could be included. This disqualified two mothers,   258   258
including the mother who had declared eleven children. Both mothers   272   272
promptly threatened to appeal to a higher court. To avoid further   285   285
delay and the[4] high cost to the estate that an appeal would entail, a 299   299
settlement of $12 500 was offered and each of the women accepted. The   313   313
court ruled that the rest of the estate was to be divided equally   326   326
among the other four mothers, each of whom had produced nine eligible   340   340
babies during the baby derby decade. These mothers received the sub-   354   354
stantial sum of $250 000 each.[5]   360   360

The baby derby was acted out against the backdrop of the Great   374
Depression. It is likely that it was the cause of more laughter, was   388
the subject of more discussion, aroused more indignation, kept more   401
lawyers busy, and provided more newspaper copy than any other event of 415
those lean years. For the winning mothers, it meant the end of pover-   429
ty and the beginning of a financial security that they had never had   443
before.   445

1 | 2 | 3 | 4 | 5 | 6 | 7 | 8 | 9 | 10 | 11 | 12 | 13 | 14

Newspaper Survey

76
GWPM

We recently carried out a cross-country survey, via a written $\quad$ 12 $\quad$ 12
questionnaire, in which we asked people to tell us what daily news- $\quad$ 25 $\quad$ 25
papers mean to them. We wanted to know what they look for in a news- $\quad$ 39 $\quad$ 39
paper, how often they read and where they buy newspapers. We asked $\quad$ 53 $\quad$ 53
them to indicate and comment on the importance to them of the various $\quad$ 67 $\quad$ 67
newspaper features. We also requested that[1] they inform us of what $\quad$ 80 $\quad$ 80
things, if any, they didn't like in newspapers. $\quad$ 89 $\quad$ 89

After tallying up the results, we found that the percentage of $\quad$ 103 $\quad$ 103
homes that purchase a newspaper every day has dropped in the last ten $\quad$ 117 $\quad$ 117
years, but that those buying just once or twice a week are on the $\quad$ 130 $\quad$ 130
increase. Reasons given included the observation that newspapers have $\quad$ 144 $\quad$ 144
become too large and take too much time[2] to read. It is faster and $\quad$ 157 $\quad$ 157
easier, they say, to obtain current news from radio or from tele- $\quad$ 170 $\quad$ 170
vision. Home delivery continues to account for the majority of news- $\quad$ 184 $\quad$ 184
paper sales, but many copies are sold through stores, newsstands, and $\quad$ 198 $\quad$ 198
newspaper boxes. $\quad$ 201 $\quad$ 201

A high percentage of those surveyed said they seek a newspaper $\quad$ 215 $\quad$ 215
that contains comprehensive coverage of local news. They also[3] insist $\quad$ 229 $\quad$ 229
on being kept informed of important national and international $\quad$ 242 $\quad$ 242
affairs. Accompanying pictures were frequently mentioned as important $\quad$ 256 $\quad$ 256
news appendages. Fewer than half of those who replied read the busi- $\quad$ 270 $\quad$ 270
ness section regularly. Most of those who do, however, consult the $\quad$ 284 $\quad$ 284
stock market quotations as well. A large number of respondents, $\quad$ 297 $\quad$ 297
including a surprising number of men[4], enjoy reading articles about $\quad$ 310 $\quad$ 310
food. They like to be given recipes, especially for foods and festi- $\quad$ 324 $\quad$ 324
vals that are in season. They also appreciate cents-off food coupons $\quad$ 338 $\quad$ 338
and would like to see more of these. Many people regularly check the $\quad$ 352 $\quad$ 352
listings on the entertainment pages to find out what is going on in $\quad$ 366 $\quad$ 366
and around town – at the movies, theatres, galleries, auctions, etc.[5] $\quad$ 380 $\quad$ 380

Articles on sports and sporting events both at home and abroad $\quad$ 393
are thought to be an important part of a newspaper. A sizeable number $\quad$ 407
of people find the travel section of interest. Most people consider $\quad$ 421
the classified advertisements to be vital to a newspaper. It was $\quad$ 434
found that a surprising number of people check the classified ads $\quad$ 447
every day. Quite a few respondents said they would like to see more $\quad$ 461
features about homes and gardens. A few people complained about $\quad$ 474
worthwhile articles sometimes being lost in a maze of advertisements. $\quad$ 488

1 | 2 | 3 | 4 | 5 | 6 | 7 | 8 | 9 | 10 | 11 | 12 | 13 | 14

Office of the Future

This report attempts to present the future shape of the business   13   13
office. It is the result of personal interviews and research. The   27   27
study revealed that there will be two major goals in the move toward   41   41
the office of the future: integrated communication and speed. It was   55   55
the general concensus that if these goals are to be met, people needs   69   69
must be considered in the building, the organizing, and[1] the introduc-   83   83
tion of the technology required. The use of word processors, elec-   96   96
tronic typewriters, and computers will increase in small, medium, and   110   110
large firms. The use of electric typewriters will decline. There is   124   124
a definite swing away from large centralized word processing centres.   138   138
These will not be used because they tend to foster impersonal atti-   152   152
tudes, are unable to meet the needs of[2] all people, and make it diffi-   166   166
cult to achieve understanding between the principals and operators   179   179
when so many people are involved. Instead, there will be an increase   193   193
in small satellite centres of three to six operators.   204   204

There will be a tremendous growth in technology connected with   218   218
the telephone. Eventually, voice recognition will make much of the   232   232
present technology obsolete. Fax and other[3] electronic mail will   245   245
reduce the need for mail and courier services. Magnetic and microform   259   259
storage systems will replace paper ones. It is predicted that the   272   272
number of micro computers in offices will increase greatly as they   285   285
continue to form an integral part of the office system.   296   296

Office technology was begun at the lower end of the office cost   310   310
scale with the introduction of word processors to[4] save secretarial   323   323
time. In the future, technology will be aimed at the upper end of the   337   337
cost scale to save managerial time. As a result, we will see a grow-   351   351
ing number of terminals on managers' desks. These will be used to   364   364
analyze data, to set up financial models, to send and receive messages   376   376
and documents, to manage appointments, to write and edit reports, and   392   392
perhaps to compose correspondence.[5]   400   400

The office of the future will be in need of people who have good   414
keyboard and English skills, plus dicta and word processing. It will   428
seek people who understand the concepts of high technology and who   441
exhibit professional work habits and attitudes. Flexibility will be   455
another key requirement.   460

1 | 2 | 3 | 4 | 5 | 6 | 7 | 8 | 9 | 10 | 11 | 12 | 13 | 14

Business English Course

84
GWPM

The aim of the Business English course is to equip students to meet the English requirements of today's business office and to lay the groundwork for future language development. The course outline has been prepared on the premise that any study of English should involve the four media of communication: listening, speaking, reading, and writing. Because of the nature of the course, the application of these in business should be stressed whenever possible. No attempt has been made to set out distinct teaching packages, nor to dictate time allotments, order of teaching, or depth of study. These factors may vary widely from class to class due to the needs and interests of students, the style and methodology of the instructor, and the fact that all aspects of English are continuously and concurrently being stressed throughout the course. The course has four major areas of study: spelling and vocabulary, oral communication, reading, and writing.

The object of building spelling and vocabulary skills is twofold. The first is to enable the typist to recognize and spell words which are likely to be encountered in writing and in tape transcription. The second is to encourage the expansion of the student's own active vocabulary. Use of the dictionary, study techniques, and proofreading would, of course, be included.

The purpose of attending to oral communication is to develop the student's ability to listen and understand, to express herself or himself using correct speech and pronunciation, and, through these, to build self-confidence. Reading is a means to the end of all the other subjects outlined in this course. Too, reading can provide the student with valuable knowledge.

The writing program is meant to correct weaknesses in punctuation and grammar, to develop writing skills, and to teach students how to write the most common types of business letters. As well, all students would be required to prepare a letter of application for employment and a personal data sheet. If time permits, we may be able to add the writing of reports and minutes of meetings.

I have attached a list of the books currently in use. A list of sources of teaching materials is also attached. Most of these are available in the resource centre.

1	2	3	4	5	6	7	8	9	10	11	12	13	14

xhip

88
GWPM

One of the most important requisites of a well written report is   13
good organization. Good organization often begins with an outline   26
which lists the topics to be covered in the report. The major topics   40
should be prominently displayed, while less important points should be   54
listed below the major topics to which they relate. An outline serves   68
to put the writer's thoughts in order. It will form the basic frame-   82
work on which the report will[1] be built. It is like drawing up the   95
table of contents and then writing the report around it.   106

Good organization also requires that the outline and all material   120
in the report be arranged in some kind of logical order that will   133
render the report clear and easy for a reader to follow. There are   147
several arrangements that may be used. One of the most common is the   161
order in which events occur(red). A program, a resume, an agenda, and   175
minutes[2] of a meeting would be set out in this way. Another arrange-   189
ment is in order of importance. Topics or points may be arranged in   203
ascending or descending order of importance. For example, the offi-   217
cers of a company would likely be listed in descending order, from the   231
most to the least important. The reasons supporting a desired course   245
of action might be set out in order of ascending importance, building   259
towards a strong climax.[3]   264

Order of space is another arrangement. It is one in which infor-   278
mation may be arranged in the order of north to south, east to west,   292
top to bottom, inside to outside, or in any other spatial progression   306
that is suitable for the purpose. For example, a guide book may   319
describe the Canadian provinces from west to east.   329

Order of familiarity is often used to present new ideas to read-   343
ers. The writer starts off with ideas that are[4] familiar to the reader   357
or at least are easy to understand, and works into things that may be   371
unfamiliar or a little harder to grasp. It is an arrangement that is   385
common in textbooks and in advertising copy. Yet another arrangement   399
is the order of support. This order follows one of two paths. Either   413
it begins with a concluding statement and then provides the supporting   427
information, or it presents the data and then draws the conclusion.[5]   440

1 | 2 | 3 | 4 | 5 | 6 | 7 | 8 | 9 | 10 | 11 | 12 | 13 | 14

Word Processing History

Word processing shares with data processing the same basic cycle 13
of input, process, and output. In word processing, input is words in 27
the form of spoken or written thoughts or ideas. Process is the 40
transformation of these words into final printed output. 51

In the first business offices, the processing was done by stenog- 65
raphers who took the words dictated by their employers and transcribed 79
them into final handwritten documents. Pens were the tools by[1] which 93
the documents were prepared. In the late 1800s, a machine was intro- 107
duced into the processing system and revolutionized the word process- 121
ing industry. That machine, the typewriter, replaced the pen as the 135
primary tool by which final output was prepared. Over the next 148
several decades, the typewriter was improved and became smaller, more 162
compact, faster, and more efficient. The next major development was 176
the electric typewriter. Although its[2] main contribution at the time 190
was to further increase the speed at which words could be processed 203
into final copy, the electric typewriter was significant in that it 216
linked word processing with electronics, thus laying the groundwork 229
for all future developments. 235

In the 1960s, two new machines, the Magnetic Tape and the 248
Magnetic Card Selectric Typewriters, were put on the market. By in- 262
troducing the concept of stored documents, these machines represented[3] 276
a giant step in the development of word processing. The ability to 290
store documents meant that the operator could edit and re-use material 304
that had previously been keyboarded and stored on tapes or cards, thus 318
saving valuable retyping time. These and the other machines which 331
were developed over the next few years were blind word processors. In 345
other words, the operator could not see the changes that were made 358
until the document was printed. 364

The next important[4] advancement took place in the mid 1970s when 378
word processors with screens came onto the market. These display 391
systems were a big improvement over the blind systems. The operator 405
could now see and check the work being input and the editing changes 419
that were made before it was printed on paper. Word processing has 433
come a long way in the past hundred years, but one thing a word pro- 447
cessor has not been taught to do: it can't make coffee – yet.[5] 460

1 | 2 | 3 | 4 | 5 | 6 | 7 | 8 | 9 | 10 | 11 | 12 | 13 | 14

Time Management

96
GWPM

How often have we complained that there is not enough time to 12
accomplish everything we want to do? We each have twenty-four hours 26
available to us each day – no more, no less. Why is it, then, that 40
some people accomplish more than others? The answer is effective time 54
management. 56

Since all of our time is spent engaged in one activity or anoth- 70
er, we are dealing with two factors: time and activities. Because we 84
cannot increase or decrease our allotment of twenty-four hours[1] per 97
day, time is the constant factor. Activities, however, are a variable 111
factor; activities are something we can change. Effective time man- 124
agement means replacing the less important activities with more 137
important ones. This means deciding which activities are important. 151
Before we can do this, it is necessary to decide what our goals are. 165

Goals must be specific; for example, to write a children's story- 179
book. Goals should not conflict with one another. For example[2], it 193
would be nigh impossible to excel at a full-time job, study computer 207
programming, train for championship tennis, and write a book all at 220
the same time. Chances are that all of the goals would suffer and 233
little would be achieved. Instead, we must prioritize our goals 246
according to their importance, their ease of accomplishment, their 259
logical sequence, or whatever criteria best suit our needs. We must 273
also assign a completion date for each goal and draw up a plan of 286
action that[3] includes all the activities required for us to accomplish 300
our objectives. These are the important activities to which we should 314
devote the bulk of our time. 320

Ah, but how do we go about displacing the low priority activi- 334
ties? First, we must get organized. This is crucial to success. It is 348
the key to time management. Whether it takes several hours or 361
several days, it has to be done. We can begin by making a list of the 375
activities we currently engage in. Are there[4] any that are really not 389
necessary? Eliminate them. Are there any that someone else could do? 403
Delegate them. Could any be done more quickly and efficiently? 416
Establish new systems and procedures. When all this is done, we must 430
design a daily schedule of activities for ourselves according to our 444
own particular situations. By following it and refusing to be de- 457
toured, we will discover that we can utilize our time so that we are 471
more productive and accomplishing our goals[5]. 480

| 1 | 2 | 3 | 4 | 5 | 6 | 7 | 8 | 9 | 10 | 11 | 12 | 13 | 14 |

Diamonds

100
GWPM

Diamonds have long been known as costly, precious gems. Chemi-   13
cally speaking, however, a diamond is the same as a hunk of coal.   26
Diamonds are pieces of crystallized carbon that were formed in the   39
depths of the earth eons ago and brought up to the surface by volcanic   53
pressures. When cut into facets, the diamond is the most brilliant of   67
all gems. It is also the hardest – so hard, in fact, that it is used   81
in drills and other tools for cutting hard materials.   92

The second hardest stone, the cubic¹ zirconium, has created some   106
problems for diamond merchants. Fabricated from the metallic element,   120
zirconium, and cut into facets, it, too, is very brilliant and, to the   134
naked eye, cannot be distinguished from a diamond. Even using a   147
strong magnifying glass, some experts cannot tell the difference.   160

Diamonds are priced in accordance with their carat, cut, colour,   174
and clarity – the four Cs. Most diamonds appear to be clear and   187
white, but if held up to the light and looked at through their ²sides   201
against a white background, a touch of colour can usually be seen. A   215
few diamonds are completely coloured. The Hope diamond is blue, and   229
the Tiffany diamond is canary yellow. Diamonds contain natural flaws,   243
such as spots, fractures, etc. In the gem trade, these are called   256
inclusions. The fewer inclusions a diamond contains, the more valu-   270
able the gem. Like snowflakes and fingerprints, there are no two   283
diamonds exactly the same. This fact has made it possible for a form   297
of fingerprinting³ to be used to positively identify diamonds in case   311
of loss or theft. Diamonds are available in a number of different   324
cuts. The round cut is the most common because it is the easiest to   338
cut and is, therefore, the least expensive. Other popular cuts   351
include the oval cut, the pear-shaped cut, the emerald cut, the   364
marquise cut, and the heart-shaped cut. The size of a diamond is   378
expressed in points or carats. There are 100 points to a carat. A   392
diamond ring set with one or several diamonds⁴ is the most common sym-   406
bol of betrothal in the western world.   414

Diamonds are often set along with other gems, each enhancing the   428
other's beauty. One of the best known combination settings is the   441
engagement ring of the Princess of Wales, in which a blue sapphire is   455
surrounded by diamonds. Dealers say that from an investment point of   469
view, it is advisable to purchase a solitaire in a simple setting.   482
This way, a buyer can expect to obtain a larger and better quality   495
stone for his or her money.⁵   500

1 | 2 | 3 | 4 | 5 | 6 | 7 | 8 | 9 | 10 | 11 | 12 | 13 | 14

Accountable

Before we developed Accountable, we did a very important thing.   13
We listened. Then we took everything we heard, threw in a few sur-   27
prises, and put it all together in one incredible accounting package.   41

You said make it easy. So we did. Our automatic setup gets you   55
up and running in minutes. Accountable looks and works the way you   69
do, so you already have a good idea how it operates. Screens look   82
like your regular cheque book but are faster and easier to use, and   96
balances are calculated and entered automatically. There are no   109
accounting terms to learn, and our pull-down menu system and mouse   122
support provide quick access to all your options.   132

You said make it full featured. So we designed Accountable so   146
that it can manage your chequing, savings, and money market accounts,   160
and even transfer funds from one to another if you like. It easily   173
keeps tabs on your mortgage and other loans. It maintains a record   187
of your assets, including your home and belongings. It keeps track   200
of your investments, including stocks, bonds, and mutual funds. It   213
creates invoices, pays bills, tracks your inventory, manages your cash   127
transactions, and helps you budget. Accountable produces a variety of   241
reports, including cash flow, income and expense, and net worth.   254

You said make it flexible. So Accountable lets you track as   267
little or as much of your finances as you desire. You can track as   280
many accounts, clients, and projects as you like, and there is no   293
limit to the number of transactions you can enter. Accountable pro-   307
vides preformatted reports and prints them on laser and dot matrix   320
printers. If you prefer, you can customize and format reports to your   334
own specifications.   338

You said make it secure. So we added a password security feature   352
so that you can control who has access to your files. After all, your   366
financial affairs are your own business.   374

You said back it up. So we provide free customer support through   388
our telephone hotline, manned by our skilled staff who are devoted   401
solely to helping you. And we guarantee satisfaction. If you don't   415
absolutely love Accountable, return it with your dated receipt for a   429
full refund.   432

You see, listening to you gave us the insight to develop a finan-   446
cial management package that offers real solutions to your accounting   460
problems. It must be good because it was developed by the greatest   474
minds in the industry – yours.   480

1 | 2 | 3 | 4 | 5 | 6 | 7 | 8 | 9 | 10 | 11 | 12 | 13 | 14

Back Talk

The spinal column is a very complex structure. It houses and 12
protects the spinal cord, and supports the head, chest, and upper 25
extremities. Concurrently, it permits a considerable range of move- 39
ment so that you can turn and nod your head, touch your toes, bend 52
sideways, lean backwards, etc. 59

The price we pay for this broad range of movement is being vul- 73
nerable to joint sprain, such as locking and jamming, or possible disk 87
herniation. These can occur during seemingly innocent activities if 101
your spinal flexibility and strength are not maintained and cared for. 115

Your spine comprises twenty-four moveable bones, or vertebrae, 129
which are stacked one below the other, beginning at the base of the 142
skull and ending at your tailbone. Between each spinal bone is a 155
circular disk that acts like a water-filled, shock-absorbing cushion. 169
The spinal bones themselves resemble odd-shaped doughnuts. From the 183
base of the skull, nerve cables extend downwards from the brain, form- 197
ing the spinal cord. The spinal cord passes through the holes in each 211
spinal bone. 214

Where each pair of spinal bones clasp together, partially sepa- 228
rated by a disk, there are window openings on each side which permit 242
nerve branches to exit from the spinal cord. These nerve branches 255
relay essential information from the brain to the body tissues and 268
organs. They also relay information from the tissues and organs back 282
to the brain. Some of these nerve branches supply the nerve energy to 296
stimulate muscle contraction, secretion of stomach acids, heart rate 310
regulation, and other vital functions. These nerves also transmit 323
pain from sites of tissue injury (like a sprained ankle) back to the 337
brain. 338

The joints of the spinal column themselves are richly supplied 352
with nerve endings that are sensitive to any disturbance or alteration 366
of the spinal bones or joints. 373

Due to lack of flexibility and/or muscular strength of back 386
muscles, we commonly see spinal bones or joints that become jammed or 400
locked. In turn, this leads to irritation of sensory nerves in the 414
joints that transmit pain to your brain. When this occurs, the body 428
reacts by producing even more muscle spasm in the local area, pro- 441
ducing more pain and setting up the pain-spasm cycle. 453

That is precisely the time to visit your doctor or therapist. 466

1 | 2 | 3 | 4 | 5 | 6 | 7 | 8 | 9 | 10 | 11 | 12 | 13 | 14

Car in the Family

I learned to drive an automobile at the age of sixteen. My | 12
father taught me in our family car, an aging English model with a | 25
standard transmission. Thanks to the considerable time and effort | 38
expended by my father, the car was usually reliable except for its | 52
habit of getting stuck in reverse gear. Needless to say, we avoided | 66
using reverse gear as much as possible. | 74

One autumn day, I borrowed the family car and drove some distance | 88
outside the city to visit an acquaintance. As I was preparing to | 101
return home, I realized with sinking heart that it would be impossible | 115
to manoeuvre out of my parking spot without using reverse gear. | 128
Crossing my fingers, I gingerly eased the gearshift into reverse and | 142
backed out; but when I attempted to shift into a forward gear, the | 155
contrary car refused to comply. It was hopelessly stuck in reverse. | 169

Now I had to decide between two possible plans of action. One | 182
was backing approximately 25 km home. The other was telephoning my | 196
father and persuading him to travel the long journey on the bus to | 209
rescue me. I elected the latter. My father arrived in surprising | 222
good humour, worked his magic inside the car's gearbox, and eventually | 236
we were able to drive home – forwards. | 244

The reverse-gear problem was not this car's only drawback. It | 258
also had a faulty fuel pump which would suddenly cease working and | 271
cause the car to glide silently to a stop. My father tinkered with it | 285
but was unable to prevent its dying periodically. He did, however, | 299
come up with a foolproof way of reviving the pump. The person in the | 313
passenger seat was required to stamp furiously on the panel that | 326
separated the engine and passenger compartments. The fuel pump was | 339
attached to the opposite side of this panel, and such treatment always | 353
jolted it back into life. | 358

Since my mother usually occupied the passenger seat, she would | 371
await in dread my father's disclosure that the pump had stopped work- | 385
ing again. When the announcement came, she would immediately shrink | 399
down in her seat as she stamped vigorously on the panel, hoping that | 413
nearby pedestrians wouldn't think she was in the throes of a terrible | 427
tantrum. | 429

You can well imagine how relieved we all were, especially my | 442
mother, when my father finally conceded defeat and purchased a new | 455
fuel pump. | 457

1 | 2 | 3 | 4 | 5 | 6 | 7 | 8 | 9 | 10 | 11 | 12 | 13 | 14

Car of My Own

For about a year, I owned a tiny car with a big problem. As the engine warmed, the radiator began to leak water, causing the engine to overheat and stall. My father, unable to locate the crack he believed was in the radiator, announced that he would obtain something called isinglass to pour into the radiator where it would circulate and plug up the elusive crack.

In went the isinglass, and away went I. Everything was going perfectly until I stopped at a red light halfway up a fairly steep hill. Immediately I was surrounded by clouds of steam. I briefly glimpsed a truck driver's startled face peering down at me before the vapour swallowed me up. The isinglass was definitely not the answer.

On further examination of the radiator, my father noticed an interesting phenomenon. The rad seemed to function as a syphon. Water sputtered and steamed out around the radiator cap and didn't cease until the radiator was bone dry. My father decided to apply scientific principles. If, he reasoned, water was heating up and turning into steam, all we had to do was provide it with an opportunity to cool down and it would turn back into water. Accordingly, he rigged up a system of rubber tubing, one end of which protruded at the point where the hood hinges were.

Mobile again, I proceeded up that selfsame hill, accompanied on this occasion by a colleague. I'll never forget the expression of stark terror on her face as she flattened herself against her seat, distancing herself as far as possible from the windshield which was being sprayed lavishly with jets of rusty water from the rubber tube.

Eventually I began to wonder whether a big car might improve my luck. That was wishful thinking. The oversized automobile I acquired soon developed an unsettling habit of quite arbitrarily refusing to start. My father taught me a quick method of getting it going. I simply had someone turn the ignition while I held a screwdriver across the electrical points on the starter motor. In order to reach the starter motor, which was located way down at the bottom of the engine, I had to fling myself over the fender and almost stand on my head. My colleagues became accustomed to coming out of our building into the parking lot and seeing my feet protruding from my car's gaping maw.

Believe it or not, I continue to drive a car in spite of my growing contention that every car I purchase is genetically conditioned to wreak havoc in my life.

| 1 | 2 | 3 | 4 | 5 | 6 | 7 | 8 | 9 | 10 | 11 | 12 | 13 | 14 |

Dividend Reinvestment

If you are planning to make a long-term investment in the stock market, you should consider buying into a company that offers a dividend reinvestment plan. This type of plan, often called Drip for short, allows shareholders to have their dividends automatically reinvested in additional shares, rather than paid out in cash. Of course, shareholders don't have to join the plan, but there are major advantages to doing so.

A Drip forces you to save. With all good intentions, you may resolve to save your dividend money yourself until you have enough to reinvest, either in more shares of this company or the stock of another company. Each time your dividend cheque arrives, however, it gets diverted elsewhere. Perhaps you have an immediate bill to pay or a purchase to make, or the cheque is deposited into your bank account and gets absorbed into your regular funds. A dividend reinvestment plan automatically follows through on your decision to save and reinvest your dividends, and takes the onus off you.

With a Drip, your dividend money starts working for you immediately. Normally shares are bought in board lots of 100 shares. (Odd lots of fewer than 100 shares are usually priced higher.) If you wanted to reinvest your dividends yourself, it might be some time before you could accumulate enough dividends to buy a board lot. In a dividend reinvestment plan, your dividend purchases all of the shares it can, no matter whether that involves board lots, odd lots, or even fractions of shares. These shares are credited to your Drip account and become eligible for future dividends, which are subsequently paid and converted into more shares. This gives a compounding effect, somewhat like interest on your interest.

A Drip can save you money. If you purchase shares through a brokerage firm, you will be charged a fee for the broker's services. When shares are acquired through dividend reinvestment, however, there is usually no brokerage fee charged. Also, a number of Drips give you a discount on the price of dividend reinvestment shares. Some plans even permit you to contribute additional cash when you reinvest dividends through their plans. Although the price discount does not apply on these cash investments, you still save on brokerage fees.

Shares purchased through a dividend reinvestment plan are held for your account by the company's trustee until you either sell the shares, or withdraw and register them in your name.

13
27
40
53
66
80
85
98
112
125
139
153
167
180
193
204
218
232
245
258
272
286
300
314
328
341
349
362
376
390
404
418
432
446
458
471
485
495

| 1 | 2 | 3 | 4 | 5 | 6 | 7 | 8 | 9 | 10 | 11 | 12 | 13 | 14 |

So, you want a database search for information on Dos Bedford,   13
eh? People don't enquire much about old Dos any more, although his   26
records used to be extracted with considerably high frequency. Well,   40
organize your garbage in and garbage out in the bins beside you; then   54
settle yourselves over there on those floppy disk boxes. I'll get my   68
memory on line, download my files, and produce some fax that'll rattle   82
your windows. Sit there quietly now, and don't interrupt.   94

Old Dos was initialized by a fine family with a good background.   108
The only trouble was his parents didn't have very good financial   121
management techniques – high resolutions, you might say, but no backup.   135
They lost their whole operating system. Dos couldn't support them,   148
and he certainly wasn't going to tag along after them. So he left to   162
reset his path and reconfigure his own environment.   172

Dos elected to become a printer. After scanning the tutorial and   186
serving an extended apprenticeship, he installed himself on a little   200
tugboat in the bay. He hung up his mailbox and before you could say   214
one, two, three, his printing business was up and running. Dos went   228
into turbo mode and no programmer nor analyst could stop him. Why   241
his run time for exporting a batch of documents registered in the   254
megahertz.   256

Business was booming and eventually the footprint of the tugboat   270
was no longer big enough for Dos's operations. Dos decided to cache   284
in a few chips and expand and reformat his tugboat's platform. With   298
an interface device, he drew up a menu of ideas. From the menu, he   311
selected the most desirable items for his expansion program.   323

Two rows of seven columns would support an upper deck and permit   337
the addition of four workstations. A fancy gateway at the gangplank   351
entrance would provide random access for customers. A lifelike ram's   365
head, configured by a renowned graphic artist, would project from the   379
prow. At the high end of the mainmast would flutter a crimson flag   392
with the initials DB in scaleable script.   400

Now Dos Bedford believed in hands on. Why, he monitored all of   414
that renovation himself, even to supervising the placement of the   427
battery operated clock over his desktop. When all was completed,   440
hundreds of people from the surrounding countryside stood in a queue   454
for hours waiting to inspect the results. Dos handed out cards and   468
free light pens, just to show his appreciation. Everyone declared it   482
was a fine ship and the architecture was true state of the art.   495

1 | 2 | 3 | 4 | 5 | 6 | 7 | 8 | 9 | 10 | 11 | 12 | 13 | 14

One day a fellow named Unix came to see Dos. Unix wanted to   12
co-process with Dos, run a parallel port, so to speak. He would pay   26
handsomely for access to Dos's database, spreadsheet, and root direc- 40
tory. Dos wouldn't byte because he knew Unix wasn't compatible with   54
his operating system. In a matter of nanoseconds, he booted Unix out. 68

Now Unix was one smart mouse. He applied a paintbrush to Dos's   82
notebook. He programmed a virus that wiped out Dos's entire network. 96
Then he unplugged Dos's motherboard and squirted ink jets over all his   110
keyboards. As if that weren't enough, he created so much static he   123
initiated a horrendous power surge that brought the hard disk failure   137
message to every video screen in the country. The final blow was   150
stealing all Dos's cache.   155

Dos's business was ruined. His equipment could not be debugged.   169
His interlaced network had come apart at the seams. The chances of   183
recovering his cache were slim. All that remained of his thriving   196
business empire was his lowly tugboat.   204

Dos endeavoured to catch fiche to sell at the market. Not a   217
nibble! Disgusted, he threw his whole ethernet overboard and became   231
a pirate. After consulting a bit map, he plotted his course. He   244
pirated software, hardware, and peripheral devices. He loaded them   257
into his 32-bit bus, then logged them onto his boat. He sold his   270
stolen merchandise to third-party vendors in numerous serial ports.   283

Eventually the law became aware of Dos's activities. Dos set up   297
a filter, but the law outsmarted him. Undercover agents installed a   311
bug in his workstation. The digital connector provided them with   324
enough records and files to convict him. Instead of being auto-   337
executed, Dos was sent to a prison with lots of bars and codes. Dos   351
was not an adapter, and finally he couldn't hack it any more. So he   365
attempted an escape. As Dos microsoftly whispered the password at   379
the last security gate, the guard triggered a dip switch. Dos bolted —   393
but he didn't make it, of course.   400

Dos is buried in yonder field where the pathways merge towards   413
the lotus pond. On his headstone are inscribed these perfect words: 427
Wysiwyg — What you see is what you get. The old tugboat lies rotting   441
away at the waterfront. You'll notice its location indicated on the   455
signboard on the directory tree farther along the highway.   467

Well, my internal prompt is reminding me to hang up, exit, and   481
power down immediately after this final postscript: Dots all, folks! 495

1 | 2 | 3 | 4 | 5 | 6 | 7 | 8 | 9 | 10 | 11 | 12 | 13 | 14

Insurance Video

Let's assume the worst. During your absence one day, someone	12
drives a truck to your front door and carries off everything but the	26
kitchen sink. Unless you've been meticulous in obtaining and storing	40
receipts, your chances of collecting for all your stolen property are	54
slim. One way to ensure you do receive full compensation is to have a	68
visual record of your possessions. Here's how.	78

Beg or borrow a video camera. The camera should have an auto-focus feature and a built-in microphone. Have enough tape for about a half hour of recording. Have a partner who can move things around while you operate the camera. Have a flashlight ready for lighting darker corners and closets.

Before taping, go through every room, closet, nook, cranny, and corner of your home, making note of where every possession of any value is located. Gather all your receipts, deeds, and other vital documents, and lay them out all in one place.

Stand with your partner in front of your home, turn on the camera, and start walking. Tour the exterior, keeping a running commentary on what improvements were made and at what cost, and where any hidden features might be. Move and talk quickly. If something must be inspected closely for insurance purposes, the tape can be frozen, but be careful about maintaining sharp focus. Don't forget the garage. Rifle through any old clothes being stored there. Open up boxes or other containers for a quick inspection.

Inside the house, head immediately for the receipts, deeds, and other documents. Have your partner turn each one over as quickly as possible. As long as they are visible on the tape for a split second in sharp focus, they'll be readable. Endeavour to fill the viewer with each document so the print appears larger and easier to read.

Begin in the basement, and quickly scan every item you can find, including inside chests and boxes. Keep talking. Mention every piece of information that might affect the value of the item being taped. Move up through your home, taking care to be as thorough as you can. Don't forget furnishings, carpeting, and fixtures.

Review the finished tape on the camera's monitor screen. Make note of anything you forgot or mistook. When the tape is over, photograph the missing items and any retakes. File the completed tape well away from your home, perhaps in a safety deposit box. Don't risk losing your record in the same disaster that destroys your home.

1 | 2 | 3 | 4 | 5 | 6 | 7 | 8 | 9 | 10 | 11 | 12 | 13 | 14

Investing in Stocks

Trading stocks can be exciting and fun. The stock market offers   13
many opportunities for tremendous, and often rapid, returns. It can   27
also result in substantial, and equally quick, losses. There are five   41
steps you should follow to make your portfolio pay off in the long   54
term.   55

The first step is to start with a plan. Long-term investment   68
success is more likely if you begin by deciding what your particular   82
objectives are. Are you seeking income, growth, safety of capital, or   96
a combination of these? Build a portfolio of stocks that meet your   109
objectives. Buy mostly high-quality stocks. Investing in value   122
reduces your risk and offers you a better chance of success in the   135
long run.   137

The second step is to diversify your portfolio. This means not   151
putting all your eggs in one basket. Then if one basket falls, you   164
will not lose all of your eggs. No matter how carefully you plan, not   178
all of your choices will work out as you expect. Wise investors   191
diversify their holdings over the five major industry sectors: bank-   205
ing and finance, utilities, consumer products, manufacturing, and   218
resources. Resources includes mines, oil and gas, and forest   231
products.   233

The third step is to monitor your investments. Wouldn't it be   246
nice if you could simply set up a portfolio, then rely on it to ful-   260
fill your investment goals while you turn your attention elsewhere?   274
Unfortunately, investing rarely works that way. You must constantly   288
track your investments to make sure they continue to perform the way   302
you want. Shrewd investors check the business press and other sources   316
of information regularly so that they can make informed investment   329
decisions.   331

The fourth step is to review your objectives periodically.   344
Remember that your needs are apt to change over time. For example,   357
when you are young, you might decide to concentrate on growth. When   371
you grow older, you might want to switch to preserving the safety of   385
your capital. As you near retirement you might be more interested in   399
generating income.   403

The fifth step is sometimes a difficult one. Be patient. It   417
takes time for quality investing to work. Remember your objectives   431
and don't get sidetracked.   436

1 | 2 | 3 | 4 | 5 | 6 | 7 | 8 | 9 | 10 | 11 | 12 | 13 | 14

Landscaping

Thoughtful and creative landscaping can transform a rather	13
ordinary country home into a picture of serene beauty. It can change a	26
house perched on a lot into a home with an integrated and well bal-	39
anced landscape. It can blend buildings with nature so that they are	53
no longer confined within their walls but extend into, and become part	67
of, the warmth and beauty of the surrounding terrain.	78

Thoughtful and creative landscaping can transform a rather ordinary country home into a picture of serene beauty. It can change a house perched on a lot into a home with an integrated and well balanced landscape. It can blend buildings with nature so that they are no longer confined within their walls but extend into, and become part of, the warmth and beauty of the surrounding terrain.

The ideas and aspirations of the owners are the key factors in any landscape design, but many people are not quite sure how to identify their exact needs. They should discuss with a landscape expert the mood they wish to create and the intended uses of the property. The landscape expert can then assist them in exploring the various options open to them and in drawing up a design plan. Owners usually find guidelines helpful in building a mental picture of their dream landscape.

The entrance to your property is your first hello to visitors. The scene that greets them creates an impression of what to expect from you. Spacious country driveways are both practical and in keeping with the surroundings. A curve in the driveway can add intrigue and depth. Of course, the design for the driveway and all the property should take into account factors such as snow drifts and other maintenance features.

Although each area will have its own unique features, most well planned country landscapes have an atmosphere of warmth, hospitality, and informality. Lawns blend into a nearby grove with underplantings of shrubs and ground covers. This technique allows trim lawns to melt into the natural surroundings.

Some of the most attractive landscapes are the easiest to maintain. Mass plantings of shrubs on slopes can mature into a weed-free ground cover with year-round beauty. Lawns can be laid out to express creativity, but also to minimize cutting time and other care.

Vibrant flower beds can add seasonal colour to the total picture. Perennials can be selected to give a steady flow of colours throughout the spring, summer, and fall. Beds of annuals can become outstanding focal points, but the time available for their maintenance must be the guide to their size and number.

Country homes are surrounded by nature. Defying the guidelines that nature dictates for each landscape can lead to disappointments, increased maintenance, and a landscape that never really fits.

1 | 2 | 3 | 4 | 5 | 6 | 7 | 8 | 9 | 10 | 11 | 12 | 13 | 14

Maglor

There was once a time when only one being existed. He led a | 12
lonely life, and so he decided to make a universe filled with hap- | 25
piness. This being spent the next eight thousand years preparing | 38
planets filled with spectacular scenery. Finally he had done enough | 52
and he decided to make a man on his first planet. He created Maglor. | 66
Over the next several hundred years, the first being taught Maglor | 79
many different things. He showed Maglor things that our imaginations | 93
couldn't begin to comprehend. They were happy. | 102

There was one problem, however. Maglor had never seen his cre- | 116
ator. His Originator lived in an entirely different realm. So one day | 130
while conversing with the Originator, who had given him life, Maglor | 143
begged to be allowed to go and reside with him on his planet and | 156
help him fulfil his great purpose. | 164

The Originator was pleased with this request, and in an instant, | 178
Maglor was brought to live with him. Together they created eighty- | 191
three races of people. The years passed, and during that time the | 204
Originator and Maglor had revealed themselves to only one man, Rhone. | 218
To him had been assigned the duty of teaching everyone about the | 231
Originator. | 233

In time, Rhone proved to be a very devious individual. He even- | 247
tually came across the secret of what kept the Originator alive: | 260
everyone's belief in him. If nobody believed in him, then he would | 274
simply not exist. Belief hadn't mattered when he was alone since | 287
there was no one to not believe. | 294

From the time of his discovery onward, Rhone neglected his job. | 308
He didn't tell another soul about the Originator's existence, and | 321
eventually everyone but Maglor forgot about the Originator. This | 334
caused the Originator to become very ill and Maglor began to believe | 348
that he might die. When talking one day, the Originator confirmed the | 362
truth of Maglor's fears and gave Maglor a key. "You must return to | 375
the planet from which you came and journey to the centre of that world | 389
where Rhone lives. Once there, you must put this key into the lock of | 403
truth. The lock must be opened and the truth must be revealed." | 416

Before Maglor had a chance to ask any questions, the Originator | 430
disappeared. Instantly the key began to glow. The echo of the | 443
Originator's final words burnt into Maglor's heart and he knew that | 456
from then on, the entire fate of existence itself depended on him. He | 470
must find the lock and open it. | 476

1 | 2 | 3 | 4 | 5 | 6 | 7 | 8 | 9 | 10 | 11 | 12 | 13 | 14

Metamorphosis

WORDS

I slowly awaken from a deep, almost drugged sleep. I feel
refreshed, but different somehow. Thank goodness that heavy sluggish-
ness seems to have departed. Now there's something unbelievable
happening. A tiny, irresistible spark has been ignited inside me.
Curled up in the soft darkness, I feel a strange vibration filling me
with wild anticipation of some impending event. The time is approaching. I am so excited I can barely restrain myself, but my instinct
says to wait a little while longer. Somehow I know I must be patient
and my life will unfold according to the great laws of nature.

Snuggled up in the darkness, I reminisce about the past that now
appears so distant. My world then was enormous, filled with colours
and rich smells, the singing and buzzing of a million tiny voices.
Shafts of sunlight mingled with cool purple shadows, everything danc-
ing together over the never-ending waves of green foliage that com-
prised my home.

With my numerous legs and sinuous, segmented body covered with
black, velvety hair, I was a skillful climber. My many brothers and
sisters and I spent endless days climbing over vegetation, clinging to
and sometimes dangling from delicate leaves while we sucked the sweet
moisture that hung beneath them and then devoured the leaves themselves. We had to beware of humans, however, for they considered us
ugly and harmful.

After many days of climbing, chewing, and sunning ourselves, I
remember suddenly beginning to feel very heavy and extremely tired. I
wandered away to be alone, seeking a private retreat that was deep in
shadow. An unusual inspiration prompted me to construct a tent and I
remember fashioning it out of soft white fibres. I crawled in and
must have fallen asleep because that's all I can remember.

The spark is burning deeper inside me, and violent tremors are
making me gasp. This is it. The anticipated moment has arrived. I
begin to thrash about, my body twisting and convulsing in a desperate
frenzy to unfold itself, to escape from the clinging white fibres. I
struggle for release with every particle of my being, choking and
pushing until, with a final wrench, the shredded cocoon falls away and
I step out, shivering, into the bright sunlight. As I stretch to
capture the warming rays, a pair of brightly coloured wings unfold.
Why, I am no longer a creepy caterpillar, but a beautiful butterfly.
With a happy heart, I flutter my delicate wings and fly away.

12
26
39
52
66
80
93
107
119
133
147
160
174
188
191
205
219
233
247
260
274
278
291
305
319
333
346
358
372
386
400
414
427
441
454
467
481
493

1 | 2 | 3 | 4 | 5 | 6 | 7 | 8 | 9 | 10 | 11 | 12 | 13 | 14

Royal Encounter

My first encounter with a member of the royal family had been too | 14
fleeting to make me feel I had really rubbed shoulders with royalty. | 28
Always the optimist, I was certain that another opportunity would | 41
arise. Sure enough, another opportunity did come my way. | 53

I was at the ripe old age of 22 and living and working in London, | 67
England. One morning in autumn, I read in the newspaper that the | 80
Queen would be attending war memorial services in the city. This was | 94
the opportunity I had been praying for. I would be present at those | 108
memorial services, too, I determined. | 116

It was a chilly, bleak, drizzly, and altogether unpleasant day, a | 130
perfect day for curling up in front of a blazing fire with a mystery | 144
novel. Still, if it was good enough for the Queen, it was good enough | 158
for me. I departed for the services in plenty of time with the idea | 172
of securing a position that would afford an unobstructed view of Her | 186
Majesty. To my consternation when I arrived, however, it was obvious | 200
that the entire city of London had had the same idea. There were men, | 214
women, children, and umbrellas everywhere. The Queen did make a | 227
gracious appearance – or so I read in the newspaper the following day. | 241

It was seven weeks later and my stay in London was almost over. | 255
I was walking home to my apartment one evening after enjoying a fare- | 269
well dinner with several friends. On the way, I noticed a handful | 282
of people gathered outside a rather imposing building. Curious, I | 295
stopped and enquired what was going on. I was informed that the Queen | 309
and Prince Philip were attending the mayor's banquet in this building, | 323
and they would be leaving very shortly. Needless to say, I eagerly | 336
joined the waiting group. | 341

In about fifteen minutes, the ornate wooden doors opened and out | 355
came the royal pair. I was close enough to touch them. I heard them | 369
compliment their host on the delightful entertainment and his wonder- | 383
ful hospitality. I marvelled at the Queen's slender, petite frame, | 396
splendidly clad in a golden gown. A brilliant tiara adorned her head. | 410
I admired Prince Philip's tall good looks. | 419

Along with the other onlookers, I waited until the royal couple | 433
had made their way to their waiting limousine and climbed in. The | 446
doors closed, the engine purred, and the automobile glided away. Then | 460
I wandered home in a daze. The outing with intimate friends and the | 474
unexpected encounter with royalty had made the evening the crowning | 487
event of my entire stay in London. | 494

1 | 2 | 3 | 4 | 5 | 6 | 7 | 8 | 9 | 10 | 11 | 12 | 13 | 14

Tenacious

If there's one single word that describes our golden-haired, elder son Scott, it has to be tenacious.

The dictionary defines tenacious as resolute, determined. At fourteen, Scott acquired a new, ten-speed bicycle, and in the summer resolved to test his expertise and endurance by biking to another city two hundred kilometres away. Determined to go in spite of the inclement weather, Scott left at eight o'clock one summer morning. After twelve hours of riding through sweltering heat, rain, a freak blizzard, and a tornado, he arrived, tattered and exhausted, at his Nana's. News of his triumphant journey was leaked to the press, and Scott's photograph and story appeared in our newspapers under this headline: "Teenage boy cycles 200 km to visit his grandmother." Scott's classmates kidded him for weeks.

Tenacious is also defined as persistent. At fifteen, Scott decided he needed employment, money, and an automobile, in that order. Scott applied for a dishwashing position at a restaurant near his school. Not accepted right away, he persisted. He visited the manager every day until she finally gave in and hired him. That job supplied the money he needed to buy his first car, and insure and maintain the car until he finished school.

The next winter, Scott expressed his determination to play drums. Supposing his enthusiasm would gradually fizzle out, my husband and I bought him a starter set. It wasn't long before he had upgraded the set, and his band had commandeered our recreation room. Over the next six years, we exhausted several sets of earplugs, and were constantly straightening pictures on the walls and picking up the remains of breakables that had been vibrated off their shelves.

Another definition of tenacious is not readily relinquishing things like property, rights, principles, etc. From his teenage years onward, Scott always maintained that he would never, ever leave home. We thought this was a passing teenage phase, but when he was 25 and still living at home, we realized he was serious.

Tenacious also means sticky or adhesive. Three years later, Scott announced he was moving out. He had resolved to adhere to a certain young lady. Now that the wedding is over, my husband and I are enjoying our peace and quiet, straight pictures, stationary knick-nacks, and our recreation room. We know, however, that we would gladly surrender it all for another tenacious, golden-haired child.

| 12 |
| 20 |
| 33 |
| 47 |
| 61 |
| 75 |
| 89 |
| 102 |
| 115 |
| 129 |
| 142 |
| 155 |
| 163 |
| 176 |
| 190 |
| 203 |
| 216 |
| 230 |
| 243 |
| 252 |
| 266 |
| 280 |
| 294 |
| 308 |
| 322 |
| 335 |
| 345 |
| 358 |
| 372 |
| 386 |
| 400 |
| 410 |
| 423 |
| 436 |
| 450 |
| 463 |
| 477 |
| 491 |

1 | 2 | 3 | 4 | 5 | 6 | 7 | 8 | 9 | 10 | 11 | 12 | 13 | 14

WORDS

Advance planning can help you create a will that will last well | 13
into the future, eliminating the need to rewrite your will too often. | 26
Here are several areas to consider while planning your will. | 38

You may have thought of naming a trust company to act as your | 51
executor, and in some cases this may be necessary. Remember, however, | 65
that an executor is entitled to compensation from the estate. A | 78
friend or family member may waive the fee out of concern for the bene- | 92
ficiaries, but a trust company won't have such sentiments. | 104

Avoid naming an executor who lives outside the country. In most | 118
cases, the probate court will compel a foreign executor to post a bond | 132
before allowing him or her to administer the estate. Avoid naming an | 146
executor who may have a conflict of interest; for example, a business | 160
partner. You should check with your proposed executor and alternate | 174
executor in advance to be sure they are willing to act for you. When | 188
consents have been received and your will has been finalized, remember | 202
to tell your executors where your original will is being kept. | 214

Try to estimate the value of your assets and liabilities, and | 227
determine which of your assets have appreciated in value. Also, make | 241
sure you know how your assets are being held. Is the house in one | 254
name or is it jointly owned? Have you nominated beneficiaries for | 267
your registered retirement savings plan? What about your insurance | 280
policies? Will the proceeds be paid to a named beneficiary, or be | 293
paid to your estate? If you are uncertain about these things, take | 306
your deed, insurance policies, and similar documents to the lawyer's | 320
office. If you are separated or divorced and are paying support, take | 334
the applicable legal papers along with you. | 343

If any of your proposed beneficiaries are under the age of | 356
majority, funds left to them will have to be held in trust. Consider | 370
whether you want your trustee to be able to use the investment income | 384
and possibly the capital for them, say for medical expenses, tuition | 398
fees, and the like. Would you want to defer young children's inheri- | 412
tances until they reach some greater age, such as 25? | 423

Make sure you know the full legal names of everyone who will be | 437
mentioned in your will, and how to spell them. If you are known by | 450
something other than your real name, tell your lawyer. | 461

If you follow these suggestions, your trip to the lawyer's office | 475
will be brief and productive, and will likely result in a highly | 488
satisfactory and reasonably priced will. | 496

1 | 2 | 3 | 4 | 5 | 6 | 7 | 8 | 9 | 10 | 11 | 12 | 13 | 14

GWPM = no. of words keyed ÷ no. of minutes
NWPM = GWPM − 2 for each error

Name _____

Keyboard Speed Record

Date	GWPM	Errors	NWPM	✓ by	Date	GWPM	Errors	NWPM	✓ by	Date	GWPM	Errors	NWPM	✓ by
		x					x					x		
		x					x					x		
		x					x					x		
		x					x					x		
		x					x					x		
		x					x					x		
		x					x					x		
		x					x					x		
		x					x					x		
		x					x					x		
		x					x					x		
		x					x					x		
		x					x					x		
		x					x					x		
		x					x					x		
		x					x					x		
		x					x					x		
		x					x					x		
		x					x					x		
		x					x					x		
		x					x					x		
		x					x					x		
		x					x					x		
		x					x					x		
		x					x					x		
		x					x					x		
		x					x					x		
		x					x					x		
		x					x					x		
		x					x					x		
		x					x					x		
		x					x					x		
		x					x					x		
		x					x					x		
		x					x					x		

Net Speed Achievements

Date Achieved	NWPM		20		25		30		35		40
	45		50		55		60		65		70
	75		80		85		90		95		100